Committed:

A Memoir of the Artist's Road

Patrick Ross

First printing

The author has tried to recreate events, locales and conversations from their memories. In order to maintain anonymity in some instances, the author may have changed the names of individuals and places. The author may have changed some identifying characteristics and details such as physical properties, occupations and places of residence.

ISBN: 978-1-61296-429-4

PUBLISHED BY BLACK ROSE WRITING

www.blackrosewriting.com

Printed in the United States of America

Suggested retail price $16.95

Committed: A Memoir of the Artist's Road is printed in Adobe Caslon Pro

Author Photo courtesy of Marisa Ross

AUTHOR'S NOTE

"To read about yourself in somebody else's work is like failing a test you didn't know you were taking."— Stephen Elliott, editor of *TheRumpus.net*

"Writers are always selling someone out."— Joan Didion, author of *The Year of Magical Thinking*

In many respects this is a work of journalism. In chronicling my cross-country U.S. road trip, I benefited from a great deal of primary material: hundreds of hours of video, a multitude of photos, and audio recordings in a daily journal, to name a few. And yet this is also a work of memory. As Tobias Wolff writes in the preface of his memoir *A Boy's Life*, "memory has its own story to tell."And the story my memory tells must differ from that of others.

I wrote the first draft of this travel memoir in a Masters in Fine Arts program I enrolled in shortly after I concluded this trip. For two years I drove my instructors up the wall as I resisted putting my story on the page. While I found it difficult to write about myself, the greater challenge was writing about others, in particular members of my family. Yet what I learned from often painfully direct reader feedback is that my story is incomplete without depicting those who made me what I am.

And so in this memoir I, like Wolff writes in that preface, "have done my best to make it tell a truthful story."I have also sought to emulate guidance William Zinsser shares in *Inventing the Truth: The Art and Craft of Memoir*. The greatest memoirs are great, he wrote, because "they were written with love. They elevate the pain of the past with forgiveness, arriving at a larger truth about families in various stages of brokenness. There's no self-pity, no whining, no hunger for revenge; the writers are as honest about their own young selves as they are about the sins of their elders. We are not victims, they want us to know. We come from a tribe of fallible people, prisoners of our own destructiveness, and we have endured to tell the story without judgment and to get on with our lives."

Thank you for choosing to read my story.

Committed:

A Memoir of the Artist's Road

INTRODUCTION

You could argue my cross-country trip began when I entered the Knoxville Crowne Plaza Hotel just before midnight with two frightened children. I feared an adult male traveling in darkness with a pajama-clad fourteen-year-old girl and ten-year-old boy would arouse suspicion. Would I be arrested as a suspected sex offender? I decided that was a fate preferable to returning to my parents' home.

I chose the Crowne Plaza because, from my view of downtown while driving east on I-40, it appeared the most upscale that Knoxville, Tennessee, had to offer. Pedophiles, I suspected, frequented run-down motels on the edge of town. When I approached the desk clerk, a pale-faced man sporting a tight maroon vest and an even tighter smile, I spoke with confidence. This is a special vacation for me and my kids, I said, but traffic has been terrible. We're all exhausted so I decided to stop for the night, but to ease the pain I'd like your finest suite.

The clerk, by my guess only a few years older than my daughter Marisa, looked at me, then at her. He couldn't get a good look at my son Parker, as the counter was too tall. Then he glanced at a computer screen in front of him, informed me that the Presidential Suite was booked, but offered me a room with two queen beds on the 3rd floor. That will do, I said. Once in the room I deposited the kids on the bed nearest the TV and headed back to the car to get our bags. I knew that the kids would surely have questions, so I ran my mind through the evening's events, locking in place every detail.

It started at dinner, I realized. My mother and father equate love with the amount of money one spends, so I had taken the five of us to one of the priciest restaurants in the Knoxville suburbs. My wife, Laura, was back home in northern Virginia, as we had an understanding that spouses need not accompany their partner on every family trip. My mother never clamored for her presence anyway. From arrival to departure the five of us were at the restaurant about two hours, enough time for me to lose track of how many glasses of red wine my mother consumed. She loved a captive audience, and the bestselling novelist treated us to one story after another, none of them new to me. But I couldn't fault my mother for that. Telling the same stories over and over is a crime I routinely inflict on my children. And my mother is a fantastic storyteller. I enjoyed hearing her adventures anew, each with the creative twists and reinventions she inevitably adds to her recollections. For the first time on the trip I felt secure.

Up to that point I had largely avoided the presence of my mother for the three days I had been under her roof. The goal was preventing a conflict similar to one three months earlier, when my parents had visited us in suburban Washington, D.C. It had appeared we would make it through that weekend without any blow-ups. I believed that was because any time I was near my mother I arranged not to be alone; Laura and the kids were always by my side. My mother's self-control had for some years been in decline, but she always managed to present a happy face around the three of them. It wasn't until I was driving her and my father to the airport, without Laura and the kids, that she was free to strike. Within minutes of departing the house my mother informed me that I was a horrible, evil person. As I stopped in Reagan National Airport's drop-off lane, she huffed that she would never visit me again and flew out of the front passenger seat. My father leaned over from the back seat, put his left hand on my right shoulder, and assured me she didn't mean it, that of course I knew how she could be and needed to let it go. I stayed in the car as he stepped out, remotely unlocking the trunk so they could remove their suitcases. My father proved to be right, as he usually was in such cases. Two weeks later my mother called me, eager to fill me in on her progress with her latest novel. As always, we pretended she had not said what she had so clearly said. But I had not forgotten it. In my forty-two years I had still not learned how to forget.

Braving a trip to Knoxville three months later, I believed my children were talismans, wards against the dark spirit that dwelled in my mother. I kept them near me as much as possible. If they were otherwise occupied I locked myself away in the bedroom my parents

8

had put me in, citing work for the lobbying coalition I ran. But I was a fool to think my mother could go an entire visit without releasing her toxins.

Manic energy bubbled in her that August night on the drive back from the restaurant. Her speech grew more rapid. But I felt enthusiasm projecting from her, which put me at ease. The moment we pulled into the driveway she insisted we all join her in the family room. "I've got a treat for you on the TV. I've been saving the recording for months."

Once inside I sent the kids upstairs to change into their pajamas. My mother took her spot on the sofa directly in front of their large-screen television, my dad in the wing chair to my mother's left. I took the chair on the far side of the room.

The children returned, Marisa taking the cushion next to my mother, Parker the end of the couch near me. My mother pulled her legs up and tucked them under herself, an action I used to imitate when I was young. I watched Marisa adopt the same pose. Then my mother fired up the digital video recorder and started one of those dance-competition shows. "You'll love this," she said. As she fast-forwarded, dancers in bright costumes flew across the screen like dinner mints spilled from a bowl. Then she stopped. "Here we go! I know you've never seen anything like this. He's amazing. You'll be wowed."It was a young man wearing nothing but black spandex pants. His chest and abs appeared chiseled from dark-brown marble. To say he gyrated would be an understatement. It's impossible for me to fully describe his motion, other than to say it appeared he imagined himself surrounded by a bevy of invisible women and was attempting to make love to each of them in turn, tight pants be damned.

I looked over at Marisa, wondering if she would be offended or embarrassed. She was neither. I knew that face, the one where she would desperately try to hold in a sarcastic teenage riposte. My mother had consumed a lot of wine, but I had put back a couple of glasses myself. I blame that for my inability to mirror Marisa's restraint. I laughed before letting escape the words "Oh my God he's ridiculous."

If I could go back in time I would praise that dancer on the TV. I would tell my mother that he was magical, and thank her profusely for sharing him with us. And perhaps we would have continued our own dance uninterrupted, giving my children a little more time living a childhood my parents had denied me, one in which their grandparents were not estranged.

I didn't see my mother's reaction, or hear it. Not at first. I felt it. It was a sensation I experienced once during an ill-advised attempt at home repair, the unsettling buzz from a live wire. That early warning forced me to look at her. My mother's eyes glared from a flushed red face. She ground her jaw. The fingers of her left hand, where she gripped the TV remote, twitched ghostly white.

"Hateful."

The word hissed out of her clenched teeth like air from a crushed balloon. The tingling was gone but its message wasn't. I had finally given her an opening, and she was ready for release, even with my children in the room.

"Hateful. Hateful son, hateful family."

My mother stood, looking not at me or her grandchildren, but at some distant fantasy realm far beyond anyone else's vision. Then she hurled the TV remote. It crashed in the real world, smashing into the brick hearth. Two AA batteries flew out, narrowly missing my father, dead still in his recliner. Then she stormed from the room, her rapid steps pounding against the thin floorboards of the stairs. I heard her slam the door of her office above the garage.

My father sighed, rising to follow her. "You know, Patrick, this visit had been going pretty well until you had to go fuck it up. I'll try to calm her down, but you're going to have to fix this."

The first thing I had to do, I knew, was exit my children from this drama. I looked at Marisa, and saw her eyes had grown as large as the anime characters she liked to draw. Parker appeared to be disappearing into the sofa cushions.

"Come on, kids. Don't worry about Gramma, it's nothing. Your dad will take care of it." I took their hands and led them upstairs. They didn't resist, no "Dad, we're too big to hold hands." We walked past the door of my mother's office—her sanctuary—and slipped into the room my parents had placed them in, which adjoined one for me via a connecting bathroom.

My father was right. I would have to fix it, just like he would always fix it if he were the trigger. His ability to appease my mother had improved during the last twenty years, ever since he was diagnosed with bipolar disorder and put on lithium. His first day on the medication, he liked to say, made him a different man. Just like that. In his more reflective moments, he would claim a life-long dark cloud had been lifted, a metaphor I've since read regularly in literature on the condition. He hadn't actually been aware of the cloud, he said, but once it parted he wondered how he had functioned so long under its shadow, denied the light and warmth of a normal existence.

I know that cloud, having inherited his disorder. For me the cloud resembled the violent monsoons I experienced each August during my childhood in the suburbs of Phoenix, when the high blue dome of the southwestern sky would collapse under the weight of blackened storms carried from the Gulf of Mexico. The saguaros longed for those rains, storing the vital liquid so as to survive the dry months to follow. But for me, once my bipolar disorder manifested as a teenager, it was always monsoon season, darkness and fierce winds enveloping me.

My father was diagnosed when I was in my early twenties. He encouraged me to seek out a psychiatrist, and once diagnosed and treated, I too found lithium cleared some of my clouds. The small white pill gave me just enough control over my mood swings to increase my guilt when I lost control, but I learned through therapy to better mask my struggles. Lithium provided stability, but all gifts come at a cost. The sky was no longer black, but the resulting sun now illuminated a flat plane, a field lacking peaks waiting to be climbed. Years passed. My psychiatrist shrugged each time I said I felt "flat." Then, a year before that night in Knoxville, that doctor informed me she intended to wean me off lithium. She had a new medication, lamotrigine. In a few patients, she warned, it triggered a fatal skin condition. But if the pill didn't kill me, it held the promise of containing my mania and staving off depression without flattening my horizon. To Laura's great relief I did not die of a drug-induced leprosy. And the sun slowly began to illuminate a landscape of inviting peaks, seemingly easy to climb and safe to descend.

The new medication also triggered something in my mind I can only describe as creativity, that spark I saw in the artists I championed as a lobbyist on Capitol Hill. Shortly after taking my last lithium pill, I conceived of an adventure that would be all my own, a life-defining event I imagined might in some small way approach my mother's accomplishment as a *New York Times* bestselling novelist. I envisioned a cross-country road trip, winding through more than thirty states, in which I would produce video interviews of artists of all types discussing their creative process. I wanted to learn their secrets less for reasons related to any plans for personal creative activity—fear of mental instability had often led me to avoid strenuous creative pursuits —but more out of a deep-seated curiosity, a need to confirm my hope that my mother's hyper-manic approach to artistic generation was not in fact the only path.

My father had visited that psychiatrist more than two decades earlier at the insistence of my mother. She had tired of holes in her drywall left by his fists, of a husband disappearing for hours to engage in unknown activities in unmentioned places. And she got her wish. But my mother hadn't consulted a psychiatrist since I was in middle school, when she had been told she was a hysterical woman who should take Valium so as not to be such a pain in the ass to her poor husband. From that time on my mother insisted that my father undergo constant psychiatric attention while maintaining that she would not seek treatment because psychiatrists were witch doctors. So with no medicine to temper my mother's mood, that role had fallen on my father and me. He was right that night in Knoxville. I would have to fix it.

"I know you must be surprised," I said to my children after I closed the door to their room. Parker sat down on the floor in a pile of Lincoln Logs. He had for the most part outgrown the toys, but they were some of the ones my parents had bought years earlier in anticipation of such visits, and when we had arrived three days earlier Parker had pulled them out of the closet for want of something better to do. He rolled a log bearing three hard-angled cutouts, back and forth, over the hardwood floor. Marisa sat down next to him, close enough for one of her knees to touch his.

The room was strewn with toys and clothing. I started picking up the latter, not bothering to distinguish between clean and dirty. "Kids,

Gramma gets like this sometimes. But she'll be fine."

Marisa's words came out in a whisper: "She doesn't seem fine."

"Well, I know. We just need to give her a little time to cool down. But just in case she needs more than a little time, I want the two of you to help me pack up your stuff."While they packed, I entered my room through the adjoining bathroom and packed my things. It only took a moment. Normally when I travel I settle immediately into my new location, even if I'm only staying for a night. I don't like feeling out of sync with my environment. I hang shirts in the closet, tuck away underwear in a dresser drawer. But on this trip I had been living out of my suitcase, remaining in my mind connected with my home back in Alexandria, Virginia.

A few minutes later I returned to the children and helped them finish packing. Then I heard a knock. "Patrick Christopher Ross?" my father said. "I know you're in there. You can't hide any longer. She's waiting."

I gathered the kids in my arms and gave them a big hug. "I'll be back shortly. Whatever you do, stay in this room. I mean it."

My father was no longer there when I opened the door. I walked the length of the hallway to my mother's office and knocked. "Come in," my father said.

I wasn't surprised my mother hadn't sequestered herself in her bedroom, where she would sleep for three to four hours after her nightly manic writing sessions, but in her office. It was the room where she performed remarkable magic, cranking out novel after novel, more than a hundred in all. That magic paid for this five-bedroom house, complete with the two-bedroom suite currently serving as the hiding place for my children. That writing did not, however, pay for our visit. I had learned to pay every penny of travel expenses on trips to Knoxville, even though my mother always wanted to demonstrate her love by paying herself. Allowing my mother to assume an expense inevitably bought a lifetime of debt that couldn't be repaid in any amount of cash.

I saw my mother stiff-spined in the far end of the room, seated behind her Victorian desk. My father sat dutifully at her side in a chair normally covered with books and magazines. I found a place not covered in research material to stand in judgment and felt another

13

buzz. The electrical charge that had triggered my mother's blown fuse earlier had not in fact dissipated.

"You hate me."

She projected her words with force. I answered almost in a whisper. "No, Mom, I don't. You know I love you."

That exchange held promise. We were following the usual script. This would end with my profuse apologies for all alleged sins, and then we would all move on. Perhaps we'd enjoy a slice of that German chocolate cake my mother had baked earlier that day, with a side of my father's favorite vanilla bean ice cream.

"You've always hated me. I've done so much for you, tried to be the perfect mother. But what can I do? My son has an evil heart." It always hurt to hear that. But over time the words had lost their sharpness. My scar tissue was sufficiently thick that she did not draw blood. Seeing that, my mother changed blades. "You only want me for my money," she said, her voice rising. "I bailed you out of debt after your divorce."

I acknowledged her contributions during my financial spiral a decade earlier and thanked her yet again. Then she threw out a dollar figure twice the total incurred debt, and five times what she had actually given me. The board of directors of the lobbying shop I ran paid me well, and I knew I had more than her exaggerated total parked in a savings account. Perhaps at this moment it would have been best to stay quiet, or simply thank her again for her generosity. But I pushed back slightly. I pointed out her math error, then added, "How about I write you a check for the amount you claim, right now?" I reached for my wallet.

"It's not about you paying me back," she snapped. She leaned forward over the desk, eyes narrowing. "It's that you're so ungrateful for everything I've done for you, all of the sacrifices I've made for you."

Now I tasted my own blood. My mother had indeed made many sacrifices for me. I likely had been insufficiently effusive in expressing gratitude. I understood now, as a father of two, that personal sacrifices by parents can go unacknowledged by children. No amount of repayment would reverse time and allow her to spend her first royalty checks on that mountain cabin she desired instead of my college tuition. No check I could write now would reimburse her for the three years she raised me as a single mother after my father walked out on us, struggling in a low-paying job while still managing to pay a child psychologist to treat a troubling mental condition that manifested in me after my father left.

"Mom, you're right. I've been thoroughly ungrateful. Selfish. Greedy. I've been all of those things you say. Hateful. Evil."

A full confession would end this, I thought. It always did.

"You've never been the same since you knocked that girl up and made her abort your child," she continued. "Your evil heart surfaced that day, and you've been hateful ever since."

As always, that slice pierced flesh. But also as usual her characterization was inaccurate. I had briefly considered the possibility of raising the child, even though I was sixteen and could no longer stand being around the would-be mother, the girl to whom I had lost my virginity. But the ex-girlfriend had slammed shut any possibility of carrying the child to term. She had informed me, in our only conversation after our break-up, that she would be undergoing an abortion. She did permit me to pay for it. Upon learning of her decision I felt pain at the loss, but my mother was thrilled. She said she wouldn't have tolerated her son's bright future being ruined by some slut who couldn't keep her legs closed. And I didn't argue. As I always did when reminded of that loss, I ran the numbers: My child at that very moment would have been twenty-six, ten years older than the idiot who fathered that life and then paid to terminate it.

My mother's observation about my "evil heart" surfacing that year had some merit. My psychiatrist long ago guessed that my bipolar disorder had manifested when I was sixteen. Did the trauma of the abortion trigger the shift? Or did the onset of my illness prompt my risky sexual behavior? My doctor has never been interested in the answer to that question. Her focus isn't on cause and effect, it's on treatment. But for my mother, cause-and-effect is everything.

Standing in front of my mother on that magazine-free spot of carpet in her office, I had hoped her critique of my sixteen-year-old self was her grand finale. It hurt, but it wasn't new. But then she surprised me with something I had never heard from her before.

"Your children are evil as well."

15

For the first time in the conversation, my voice was as loud as hers. "What?"

"You heard me."

I had, but my brain kept rejecting the signal.

"Mom, you don't mean that. You don't. Let's pretend you never said that. The problem isn't them, it's me. I'm the bad one."

"No, I can see it in them," she said, her voice now a full shout. "Evil. They don't love me. They don't respect me. They just want my money. They're just like you, waiting for me to hurry up and die."

I knew the kids were at the other end of a long hall, presumably far out of earshot. But my parents' McMansion had been built by a contractor who put all of the focus on intimidating exteriors. The interior walls were tissue-thin. Hoping it would lead my mother to lower her volume, I whispered my reply. "That is not true. They love you."

"They hate me!"

I turned to my father. He hadn't said a word during the entire exchange, and I had almost forgotten he was there. "Dad, we both know she doesn't mean it. Please, help me here."

"Leave your poor father out of this. He's not the one who raised such ungrateful little demons."

My father looked down at a *Romantic Times* newsletter lying at his feet. "Listen to your mother."

"They're hateful," my mother said, her voice now a scream. "Just like you. I never want to see you or them again."

My father had fetched me too soon. I couldn't fix this, not right now. I would leave the room. I would go back to the kids and make sure they hadn't heard anything. And then I would figure out what to do next. Maybe my mother would sleep it off, and we could all pretend things were fine tomorrow morning. My father would make French toast and bacon, my mother would tell me about the latest scene she was working on, and I would tell her it sounded like it would be her best novel yet. I turned and opened her office door. And there they were, Marisa and Parker, in their pajamas, white as the wall. They had been listening at the door, for how long I did not know.

I stepped into the hallway and they rushed me, my son grabbing

16

my leg, my daughter my waist. The next few moments went by in a blur. My father crossed the room and said I should come back, that my mother wasn't done. Then he saw his grandchildren and fell silent. My mother soon was behind him.

"Marisa! Parker!"my mother sang. "So good to see you, darlings! Please, come in."

Parker's grip on my leg tightened. Marisa, still clinging to my waist, turned herself so I was completely between her and her grandmother. Without breaking their connection I took them down the hall.

"Kids, don't you dare walk away from me!"my mother yelled. "Come in this room now. Your father is disturbed, he's crazy and dangerous!"

With that I picked up the pace, guiding Parker with my left arm and Marisa with my right. As I arrived at the kids' bedroom I heard my father, the words cracking in his throat.

"Patrick, please. Come back to your mother's office. We can still fix this."

I kept moving. Once in their bedroom I saw that Parker had cleaned up all of the Lincoln Logs. Our suitcases were lined up in a neat row just inside the room. I wanted to turn, to face my imploring father and my shouting mother. But I couldn't. I could only see ahead of me, and what I saw was Marisa, Parker and our baggage. I bent down, gave my children a hug, and whispered that we would all be taking our things down to our car. My father followed us downstairs.

"Please," he half-whispered behind me on the bottom step. "Don't leave. I'm begging you. You know that if you do this, it can't be fixed."

He was right. I paused at the bottom of the stairs while my children went into the garage. But then I saw my mother at the top of the stairs. She hadn't stopped yelling since I had left her office, and I stopped to listen.

"Kids, come back here right now! If you leave with him he'll hurt you. Don't choose a crazy person over the grandmother who loves you and will keep you safe. Your father is clinically insane. He needs to be committed!"

For the first time since leaving my mother's office I made eye contact with my father. We were close enough to embrace. I looked hard at him, offering a wordless question for him to answer. And he did answer, giving the only rational one for a man who had nothing else in his daily life other than his spouse. He sighed, then turned to go up the stairs and join his wife. And I left.

I failed that night in Knoxville. My father told me to fix it, and I had done anything but. A little less than a year later I began my cross-country trip with the rift unrepaired. It was unclear to me if my mother and father even knew of my trip, although my media consultant had announced it in a press release. My funders, mostly Hollywood studios, were thrilled with my plans to post online artist interview videos from the road, with a different state going live each day. Each state had two senators and a varying number of House members, all of whom they were lobbying to gain support for secret legislation still in the drafting stage. If passed into law, those major corporations would gain significant assistance in enforcing their copyrights online. The artists I would interview could not be told of the yet-to-be-introduced legislation. But I knew the bill as drafted would do little to help independent artists. This knowledge troubled me. Yet it wasn't enough to deter me from the trip.

I would not be completely separated from Laura and the children during my travels, a five-week journey in which I would spend my first night in Portland, Maine, and my last in Portland, Oregon. I crafted the trip to allow some time with those I most loved. I would start by spending just a few days in New England before returning home. Interviews in the Mid-Atlantic would be day trips, with the exception of New Jersey. There I would conduct my interview with my family in tow, turning the trip into a vacation on the South Jersey shore. But during the rest of the cross-country journey—through the Southeast, the Deep South, the Midwest, the Great Plains, the Mountain West, and the Pacific Northwest—I would be alone. Well, that wasn't quite true. Marisa would accompany me from Virginia to Georgia, so I could take the aspiring artist on a tour of the Savannah College of Art and Design. The prospect of her first visit to an art college excited her. She appeared less enthralled at the cost of the visit, namely several days stuck in a car with her father. Since our return from Knoxville a year earlier everything about her had changed. She had replaced her bohemian skirts and blouses with black t-shirts, skull pendants, and vinyl knee-high lace-up boots. And she had nearly failed half of her classes in her first year in high school. If her poor academic performance continued, there would be no need to worry about college. But I knew she had lost more than a grandmother that night we fled to the Knoxville Crowne Plaza. Marisa had lost her creative muse, the woman to whom she genetically attributed her own artistic talent. And she had to be wondering if she was destined to develop the same loose grip on reality as her grandmother. I didn't know for sure if that was a fear of hers, because she had largely refused to talk about my mother during the following year.

Parker seemed to be holding up better, but he was always hard to read. My son was too much like me, inclined to withdraw into himself, sharing frustratingly little of his deepest thoughts. My reticence to share was what led me into a career first in journalism and then advocacy, telling others' stories rather than my own. And Parker's inclination to keep his thoughts to himself was evident the morning after we left my parents' house. Parker, Marisa and I sat in the Crowne Plaza dining room before a breakfast of pancakes, eggs and bacon. I loaded up on carbs and protein in silence. Marisa glared at her plate, too angry to eat. Parker looked around the room at the tacky attempts at opulence—red curtains, faux-gold leaf trim, white tablecloths—and said, "This is a really fancy place. I like it here." Marisa stared at me in disbelief. I shrugged. To be honest, I envied Parker's ability to focus on the now.

I had spent nearly a year doing my best to put aside the trauma with my parents when, at the end of a particularly warm July, I flew to Massachusetts to begin my road trip. I said goodbye to Laura, the soulmate I had married five years earlier after a lengthy period as a divorced father, and to my children, who shrugged because to them this was no different than any other of their father's business trips. On that note they would prove to be quite mistaken.

PART ONE: NEW ENGLAND

JULY 30: MASSACHUSETTS, NEW HAMPSHIRE, AND MAINE

I refuse to tell my story.

The man with a matted gray beard, tattered Army-issue jacket, and carved-wood cane presents no such resistance. While killing time in this Haverhill, Massachusetts, park before my first interview, I stand with him before a memorial to local residents lost in the Korean War. Like many of its ilk, the memorial eschews subtlety. A statue atop a ten-foot block of granite depicts an oversized soldier. His pose suggests motion as he leans forward, bayoneted rifle leading the way. But he is frozen, frustratingly unmoving. The only motion comes from the flags, flapping in the light morning breeze, tethered on the eight poles that encircle the soldier.

The grizzled stranger points out that, along with a U.S. and Korean flag, there are others representing the various U.S. armed forces. They are supposed to fly clockwise in the order of their founding, he says, but the Coast Guard flag is out of order. As a veteran, he says the misplacement troubles him. He's complained to the groundskeeper to no avail. His voice resembles a truck's tires spinning on gravel, and his face reflects the grooves the spins would produce.

Having long been paid to listen to people, I let him continue. His name is Bob. He's been in town a month, staying at the homeless shelter because all of the ones in southern New Hampshire are full. The economy, he says with a shrug. If he hadn't had to go into the hospital for three months with heart complications, he would have earned enough from random construction and maintenance work to keep up on his rent. But he'll find work and get back on his feet.

"What are you doing in Haverhill?" he asks.

I focus my attention on the Coast Guard flag. "Just passing

20

through," I say. I offer him a $20 bill, but he waves his callused right hand in refusal.

"I can get back on my feet on my own. I don't need handouts."

I admire his New England pride, but in this case a better term might be ill-advised stubbornness. Perhaps his refusal stems from a reflection of how he sees himself, not as a homeless man, but instead a man temporarily without a home.

A clanking noise echoes across the small park. I identify the source as the bell tower attached to the Haverhill Public Library. When it stops chiming after ten eardrum-assaults, I know it's time for me to part ways with Bob. I thank him for sharing his story, then head to the library to meet novelist Brenna Lyons. I walk across the short grass, tempted to turn right toward the devilish odor arising down the street from the Heavenly Donuts retailer. To my left the tall spire of a white-sided church thrusts its way toward Heaven while passing judgment on me. I continue on a straight path toward the library's wide steps.

Brenna is like every other artist I'll be interviewing on this trip, in that I've never met her in person. Along with being a prolific novelist of books combining romance and suspense, she's a passionate advocate for the rights of artists, which should please my funders. I tried to read one of Brenna's novels, intrigued by the warning on its cover of sexual domination and anal play. I didn't make it to any such scene, however. The plot confused me, something about a forbidden love between an alien man and an illegally bred half-human, half-alien woman. But this trip isn't necessarily about interviewing artists of whom I am a fan.

My mother resists being categorized as a genre writer, but for the first ten years of her publishing career she wrote Harlequin romances. For the last fifteen years her books have reached bookstores as standalone works from a major New York publisher, but they remain, at their core, love stories. When giving media interviews my mother likes to tell of her first-ever creative writing, a love story she wrote in grade school of two Mallard ducks inspired by her learning that the species mates for life. I know from our pre-interview conversation that Brenna is aware of who my mother is. I'm hoping the topic doesn't come up.

I don't know what a woman who writes about alien sex should look like, but I wouldn't have guessed who I would find waiting for me just inside the library. Brenna's soft round face is made more prominent by her long black hair tied back in a ponytail. Plastic-rimmed glasses reflect the overhead fluorescent lights. She appears to be a bit younger than me. It is only because she greets me by name that I know she is not one of the librarians. Flashing a toothy smile, she introduces herself, then guides me back to the room she's reserved for our film shoot. The space has an antiseptic flavor to it, with yellow walls and a floor covered by squares of industrial rust-orange carpeting.

"I can't believe you chose me for your first road trip interview," Brenna says while I set up the camera tripod. "How many are you doing?"

I tell her it will be about forty artists in thirty-three states over about five weeks.

"Goodness. Well, I'm thrilled to be a part of this."

After conducting a sound check, I turn on the camera and suggest we begin by discussing the novels that separate us across the table. They're the books she's had published in print, she says. Most are only offered in digital form. She says she has had eighty published in the last decade.

That would seem an impossible task, but I know it's not. My mother has published at nearly that rate, more than a hundred novels over the last quarter-century. I suspect that had my mother and I been talking while I planned this trip, she would have sought to forbid me from interviewing a romance novelist who is mostly published in e-book format. My mother feels digital technology has allowed hacks and no-talents to compete with her more polished prose. The only individuals she holds in more disdain than e-book authors are her blood relatives, the parents and sisters whom she cut out of her life when I was two years old.

To please my funders, I shift Brenna from discussing the publication of her books to the rights she has as an author. I learn none of her novels to her knowledge have been copied and shared without her authorization. Her focus instead is on ensuring authors are treated right in publishing contract negotiations, and is active in a nonprofit that has written a model contract for e-book authors. In other words, her focus is on protecting authors from middlemen like my funders. I'm familiar with her organization. It was founded in part because the romance author organization my mother is active in wouldn't allow e-book authors to join. Then Brenna shifts to discussing her passion for creative writing.

"You know, I've stocked shelves," she says. "I've worked as a special-ed teacher, having to physically restrain adult-sized students. And I can honestly say, after I've pushed myself to meet a deadline and I pour myself into bed after four days of cutting myself short of sleep, that I'm in worse shape than having been bruised up by a student who has gone into a rage."

Her passion will leap out to viewers. I seek to capitalize on her excitement by asking her about her creative process.

"I am a character-driven writer," she says. "I may have an idea that the book is headed a certain way, but the protagonist will tell me it's going a different direction. It's like I've already written the entire book up here somewhere and I'm pulling it out piecemeal." She pantomimes pulling something out of her ear, like a magician does with a string of handkerchiefs. "Still, I spend a lot of time arguing with my characters, but in the end I let them do what they want. Sounds nutty, right?"

I'm not the best person to assess one's sanity, but Brenna need not know that. I also understand what Brenna is talking about. My mother always refers to the characters in whatever novel she is writing at the time as if they are real. "But you don't think of the characters as made-up, right?" I ask. "You bring the characters to life in your book, so they're alive to you while you write."

"Yes!" Brenna exclaims, slapping the table. "You know, no one ever seems to understand that. My husband doesn't, not really, but he's wonderful about letting me be me. When he finds me in some kind of zombie-like state, working things out in my mind, he just pats me on the head and leaves me to it."

"You said earlier that you have multiple books in progress simultaneously," I say. "Don't you find it hard to keep track of all of those characters?"

"No, it's usually pretty easy."

"Oh, I'm sorry, Brenna, I should have mentioned this," I say. "I'd like you to incorporate my question into your answer, such as 'I don't find it hard at all to keep track of different novels in progress at the same time.' You see, I'm editing myself out of these videos. All we'll see is you, so I can't use footage where you need to hear the question to understand the answer."

"Okay, then. So you won't be heard at all, not even off-camera?"

"Nope. This trip isn't about telling my story. It's about the artists." A consistency throughout my professional career—as a journalist and a lobbyist—has been voicing the stories of others, not myself. There are many things about my mother worth emulating, but a focus on the self is not one of them.

Brenna repeats my newly formed sentence almost verbatim, and then discusses how when she gets stuck on one project she'll shift to another. The key, she says, is knowing when a novel is complete. "When my muse tells me a book is finished, I fire it off to a publisher. That's probably the most important lesson I tell aspiring writers. If you write something, don't let it sit around. Do everything you can to get it published."

What Brenna couldn't know is that six years ago I completed a suspense novel I wrote in stolen pre-dawn hours over the course of two years. It was a terrifying experience, constantly awaiting the onset of mania I so often witnessed in my mother when she wrote. But I completed the novel without incident. My mother congratulated me on the accomplishment and told me to send it to a partner of her literary agent, one who represented suspense writers. A few weeks later he mailed back the manuscript. Scrawled on the cover page was a short note saying he was rejecting the novel because he disliked the narrator's voice. I took his rejection to mean the manuscript had no future. My mother agreed, and said I should strongly consider putting aside my dream of publishing a book. Not everyone has what it takes, she said, but there is no shame in that. Not knowing what else to do with a box filled with three hundred pages of useless paper, I tucked it away behind some cleaning supplies in my laundry cabinet, and returned my focus to my family and my employer.

Brenna begins to describe one of her latest works, which features a bloodthirsty vampire as the hero. "You know, I've been writing about vampires long before books like the *Twilight* series appeared. But my readership isn't teenage girls."

"Those girls seem to love how sensitive the vampire protagonist is in those books," I say, thinking of the phase Marisa went through when she was addicted to Stephanie Meyer's series. Now she is a *Twilight* hater, instead trying to be the most counter-mainstream fifteen-year-old the world has ever seen. "Do your vampires express their feelings?"

Brenna's brow furrows and her shoulders scrunch in. "My vampires express their feelings," she finally replies. "They express their feelings by killing people."

We've made it pretty far without Brenna asking about my mother, so I decide to end the interview on a line I love. I then film some B-roll, footage I'll include with Brenna's voice superimposed over it. Her speech becomes more rapid, almost manic. I'm ready to leave. I've seen this behavior before, when the process of being interviewed creates an excited state in the subject. For me, I've had enough life experience with mania.

I head back to my rental car and detect once again that alluring distraction, a scintillating scent of sugar and sin. Moments later I'm driving away from the Heavenly Donuts with an apple fritter in my lap while summarizing my day so far on a digital voice recorder. I pass a depressing strip mall anchored by a Tae Kwon Do studio, but as I leave town on Main Street the scenery improves. The road follows the bank of the Merrimack River, flanked on the opposite side by inviting homes with wraparound porches and winking dormer windows. I suspect these may have once been summer cottages for the Boston elite, a getaway escape north of town. I would welcome this trip being an escape for me. My job exists because of the generosity of my board of directors, and this year they have pressed to get full return on their investment. I'm in no position to complain, but I have made clear to them that while on the road I will be spending most of my time conducting interviews, editing and uploading video, and of course driving. I very much desire to be offline, avoiding the legislative drafting process being done in conjunction with the staff of a powerful U.S. senator. I have a lifetime's worth of experience at self-delusion, and my fantasy for this trip is that I am free.

. . .

New Hampshire greets me with a large sign: LIQUOR AND LOTTERY TICKETS FIRST EXIT. It appears the "Live Free or Die"state seeks to profit from the vices of its downstate neighbors. I already indulged a vice at the Heavenly Donuts so I drive past the exit, but the state wins my coin anyway as I hit a toll booth. After a half-hour or so I exit the interstate onto a state highway, then onto a narrow, winding road called Portsmouth Avenue. I'm under a thick tree canopy, sunlight penetrating at odd moments with a strobe effect. I see no cars, just leaves and shadows.

My schedule on this trip is such that I will be forced to spend most of my time on interstates rather than "blue highways," the name for routes off the beaten path referred to by William Least Heat-Moon in his road-trip book of the same name. But I will have some off-interstate adventures as well. I read *Blue Highways* again a few weeks ago, inspired by his journey of self-discovery. His trip was spontaneous, a reaction to losing his job and his life partner. Mine is meticulously planned for an express purpose of satisfying my funders, not necessarily as a vehicle for personal growth. His companion was his trusty van, Ghost Dancer, which doubled as his home at night. I am also traveling solo, but in a rented sedan, and I'm staying in motels. But much of his book features conversations he had with those he met on the road. I will be conversing each day with artists, but I dread the amount of time I will be forced to spend alone with my thoughts.

I cross a narrow stream and slice through some more trees before the green curtains part. I am on yet another Main Street, entering Newmarket, New Hampshire. The downtown appears to exist solely along this short stretch of road, but it's a lovely stretch. Small shops and taverns wrap along the bank of the Lamprey River, a body of water that, like Newmarket itself, appears to have abandoned any pretense of urgency.

I find the Beatnik-style coffee shop where I will be meeting singer/songwriter Ernest Whaley and purchase a cup of joe from a pierced and purple-haired young woman. She is not much older than Marisa, who also has been experimenting the last year with unnatural hair color. I take a seat on a stool worn smooth in front of the coffee shop's window. An acoustic rock song with string guitar and an ethereal female vocalist finds me through a nearby wall-mounted speaker, but what I hear is Brenna, insisting that creative writers submit their completed works. That time a few years ago when I wrote the suspense novel was not my first imagining of myself as a novelist. I think back to a conversation I had with my mother shortly before the first time she cut me out of her life. I was in my early twenties and newly married to my first wife. I told my mother on the phone that I aspired to be a novelist like her. She greeted me first with silence. Then she said that I needed to understand something. If I ever were to cross her, it would only take her a few phone calls to have me blacklisted throughout the publishing industry. Even though those words were mere sound waves translated across a copper phone line, they hit me with sufficient force to cause my legs to fail. I lay flat on my back on the bedroom carpet of my Capitol Hill townhouse and wished once again I could map my mother's moods sufficiently to avoid being on the receiving end of one of her rages.

Ernest arrives. I recognize him from his publicity photos, but also because he is the only African-American man I have seen so far in New England. As he walks toward me, hand extended, I am struck by the way he carries himself. It's not self-confidence, or arrogance. I would call it self-comfort. His relaxed manner matches his casual but sharp attire. White pants and a white shirt contrast with his black sunglasses and a salt-and-pepper goatee and mustache. A gray cap rests atop short silver hair.

"Let's head down to the river," Ernest says. "Maybe we'll get to meet the girls." Was that a wink? I grab my coffee and follow, anticipating young sun worshippers in bikinis, the sworn enemies of the purple-haired girl behind the counter. Instead, the "girls" Ernest introduces me to by the river are three non-migratory geese. They honk in delight at seeing Ernest and appear to tolerate my presence. I find myself thinking of those mallard ducks that launched my mother's writing career.

I begin the interview with an expression of gratitude. "Ernest, you picked a fantastic spot." It is so superior to what Brenna produced in Haverhill. I'm glad to see sunlight passing in and out of frame due to wispy clouds. That constant changing of natural light will convince a viewer this wasn't filmed in front of a green screen image that resembles a painted backdrop stolen from a Sears portrait studio.

"I spend a fair amount of time down here," Ernest says. "It's peaceful, and the girls are loyal friends." Ernest tells me about a song he wrote for his two children called "Fare Thee Well," about the loss of nature to housing developments and strip malls. "I had a life like this," he says, sweeping his hand around him. "I had a river, a lake, forest, marshes. My kids grew up in a subdivision with their mother. So when I would have them in the summer I'd take them to a nature preserve and force them to walk through it with me, fording streams and looking for frogs. I wanted them to know the best parts of my childhood."

Ernest, like me, has lived the life of a single father. My first wife and I divorced when Marisa was four and Parker not yet a year old. Six years passed before I remarried. I've never written a song for my children, but I understand his desire to provide a window on his past. That was a gift I did not receive from my parents, who left behind permanently their family in Oregon when I was two years old to make a new life for themselves in Phoenix. I took my children to Arizona five years ago, an exploration of my childhood roots two months before their lives were due to change with my marriage to Laura. The Sonoran Desert had been my sanctuary as a child, the place where for brief moments I could distract myself from the troubles present both in my home and in my mind. I returned from that trip with a small vial of desert soil. At the modest outdoor wedding ceremony that fall, I poured my soil into a glass carafe, Laura poured in sand from the New

Jersey barrier island of her youth, and Marisa and Parker added dirt from the grounds of the hospital where they were born in Washington, D.C. Each contribution had its own color and consistency, and the end result was a layered effect that combined while allowing delineation.

As Ernest describes his idyllic childhood, he breaks eye contact with me and his spine straightens. Perhaps he doesn't like talking about being a single father. It would be hypocritical of me to press on a subject I would rather not discuss myself, so I ask him when he first took up music. He smiles, and I know he's back. He explains that he has no formal musical training. He taught himself the guitar as a teenager and then spent years playing in cover bands, mostly in Los Angeles. But his songwriting—tunes combining folk, blues and rock in a mix Ernest calls "gumbo"—came much later in life.

"It didn't really start materializing until after I had gotten divorced and was, you know, basically living in an apartment again. I bought a guitar and began picking away at it. I had a lot of time on my hands and a lot of anguish. Songs started coming out. A friend asked me to perform one at an open-mike event. I was drenched in sweat, like I had just run a marathon. The songs were so personal, and I couldn't imagine anyone would want to hear what I had to say, what I felt inside."

"That's what we music listeners want most, Ernest. We want you in those notes."

He nods. "I understand that now. But it was hard. And it still is. You're a writer and filmmaker. I imagine it's the same for you."

"These films are about you and the other artists. I'm not even going to be in them."

"Sure you will be. You'll be everywhere in them. You're picking the interview subjects, the locations, the questions. You're choosing what stays in and what gets edited out. You're making artistic decisions throughout the process, and creating unique works of art."

"Let's get back to you," I say. I understand his point that any story is unique to its teller. But I'm following a professional code I know well. A good journalist combines information while staying out of the story. I'm bringing that same approach to my advocacy films. Inserting me in the narrative could trigger self-examination, and I might not like what I find.

Ernest takes my deflection as a lack of self-confidence. "Let me tell you, Patrick, you don't want to be stifled by insecurity. That has probably been my biggest obstacle in life. Take this singer-songwriter series I've organized. I'm surrounded by people who are technically so much better than me that I tell myself I can't play with them, but I do, and it's great. I've come to accept that it's okay to play like me."

"Ernest, I've listened to your songs online. You've obviously developed skills through four decades of simply doing it." I say this as a former musician. I spent ten years training to be a classical singer as I looked for a creative path separate from that of my mother. I abandoned singing when I felt I was no longer improving. But perhaps the primary reason I walked away was that I failed to make the transition Ernest has. Like Ernest when he began his musical career, I was a cover artist, but singing works by Bach and Mozart and Duruflé. I had been raised by a creative writer, and it seemed within my reach to write my own songs. But the art of songwriting eluded me. I could emulate the Masters, interweaving overlapping lines of melody and harmony. But the music itself had no life. Ernest says his songs seem to work because he learned audiences want to see himself in his music. I failed to find a way to connect with an audience without taking that step.

I steer the conversation to copyright, but learn Ernest has never made much money from sound recordings. He instead tells me a few amusing stories about his adventures in various cover bands. I then suggest we wrap up. After I pack up my camera, the three geese waddle up out of the shallows of the water. They look at me expectantly, as if it is now time for me to feed them. Ernest laughs.

"Sorry, girls, no treats today."

The geese turn in unison and stroll back to the river.

I sling my camera bag over my shoulder. "So you grew up here?" I ask.

"Not far," he says, pointing downriver. "My father lived out in the country, and I would spend summers with him."

"That sounds like the life your children had."

"Yes, my folks separated when I was really little. I lived most of the year with my mom, in a public housing project. Before I was old enough for school I was left alone at home. My mother had to work, you see. I'd lay on the hard floor, all the windows open. You could hear the guys out there, people up to no good, doing drugs, getting in fights. Sometimes I'd hear a bang. Not a gun, although I heard those too. No, someone would start banging on a trash can, you know, in rhythm, then someone else would join in, smacking a fire escape or some such thing. It would turn into a chorus, then a full concert, all of these lost people coming together for a few minutes of art."

I'm disappointed he's telling this story now that the camera is off, but I suspect it is because I have stopped filming that he's willing to share this.

"And when you were old enough to go to school?"

"Oh, I was a pretty awful student. Difficult. Rebellious. I flunked fourth grade, and then I flunked freshman year of high school because I refused to diagram a sentence. I didn't see the point, and I just wouldn't, damn the consequences. Then I lost my eligibility for sports, so I did the minimum to keep playing football and basketball. That wasn't enough, though. Eventually I dropped out and joined the Air Force, the day after Christmas of 1964."

"That was during Vietnam."

"It was. I didn't care. I had no future to worry about losing. But the Air Force didn't send me to 'Nam. They kept me here, and over time they taught me a cool job skill, using software for industrial design. Working out the hulls of ships, that kind of thing. I teach that software now. The Air Force gave me a future."

"That's a remarkable story, Ernest."

He nods. "You know, I had a good feeling about you from our first phone conversation. And the girls seem to like you. We're both on a journey." He pauses. "A creative journey of discovery."

"I don't know if I'd go so far as to say I'm on a 'creative journey of discovery.'"

Ernest laughs. "Call it what you will, but you barely asked me one word about copyright. You kept coming back to my creativity, to why I write songs, why I perform, what music means to me. What being creative means to me. And I'm looking at a guy who at about the same age that I started writing music has decided to become a filmmaker. I'm honored to be interviewed on your first day of this trip. I can only imagine the person you'll be at the end of it."

A wall has been broken, the sacred barrier between interviewer and interviewee. I'm grateful to Ernest for the way he sees me, and I'll admit to being envious of Brenna and Ernest for their embrace of their art. But he has my journey all wrong. I have already abandoned the artist's road. I now get my creative fix from admiring Marisa's passion for the visual arts and by working on behalf of artists in Washington. By being around creative individuals I can pick up a bit of third-party buzz, the way an alcoholic still tastes tequila when a friend of his enjoys a Margarita. That hint of flavor has to do. When people ask me how I came to do what I do, I say, "I am a failed creative. Those who can, create. Those who can't, advocate."

. . .

It takes a little more than an hour to reach Portland, Maine. I arrive fueled by a jumbo Diet Coke, Raspberry Zingers, and a fierce determination to wrap up a long day. Driving isn't a problem, it is a source of joy. Being behind the wheel affords me complete control of both my present and my immediate future, the power of hundreds of horses and thousands of pounds of steel bending to my will. But I have little strength left today to continue maintaining a journalistic distance with my interview subjects.

Quaint, three-story, federal-style buildings of Portland's Commercial Street greet me, each decked in matching red brick. Retail establishments occupy the first floor, and what I assume are residences sit atop. A jewelry store is followed by an art gallery, next to a wine bar. A sandwich board outside poses a query for me: "Do You Have Maine on the Brain?" But the harbor-town charm glides off of me, an impressionistic blur.

Equally out of focus is my visit to Brian Fitzgerald at his photography studio on the third floor of a weathered brick warehouse. I realize once I am in his studio that there's much to like about Brian. He's engaging, helpful—he arranges his studio lights and reflectors to improve the video shoot—and quick to share. We have a lot in common. We're both husbands and fathers. We both grew up in Arizona. We both spent most of our careers in journalism. He has a lot to say about running his own commercial photo business so he can free up time for personal photography of a more creative nature.

I have lived that life. My first job after college was for a U.S. senator, a back-bencher who in later years would go on to become the body's Majority Leader. I was not yet being treated for bipolar disorder, and I repeatedly failed to project sanity to my co-workers. So I left the job after two years to work from home as a freelance writer and editor. That kept me physically separated from my clients, allowing me to better feign mental health by phone and fax. Not too long after that transition I was diagnosed and started on lithium, and a short while after that my mother cut me out of her life, upset in part at me having married. She hadn't gotten over her frustration that I had refused the generous amount of cash she had offered me the day before the wedding to call the whole thing off. The absence of my mother's critical eye and the cleared mind medication provided me combined with the flexible nature of my workday to encourage me to pursue creative writing. It was during this period that I first began to write a novel, the aspiration I had mentioned to my mother in that phone call. Yet I remained cognizant of the risk of creative pursuit, of a possible descent into behavior oscillating from expressed hostility to a refusal to leave bed. That was my mother's creative pattern but also the means in which my diagnosis would manifest. I have found over the years that the best way to reduce the risk of such extreme behavior is to channel and control my creativity. I abandoned creative writing in my early twenties after three years, when I called my mother to reconcile because my then-wife was pregnant with Marisa. I control my creative impulses now by channeling them into fulfilling the agenda of my board of directors.

I see so much of myself in Brian. But perhaps that is why I find myself wanting to leave. Once I have sufficient footage I move on, declining his invitation to join him and his wife for dinner. The path to my motel means I need to cross the Fore River, but the drawbridge spanning Casco Bay is up. In front of me an elderly man in an aging sedan honks. I'm not sure what he's hoping to accomplish. None of us can move, not until that drawbridge is lowered. Surely he sees the flashing light to our right informing us of this fact. It's possible he can't see the drawbridge itself, though. I can't. There are too many cars, and too much development. I feel restrained, held back, as motionless as the Korean War statue I saw this morning in Haverhill. I run my usual self-diagnostic, looking for racing thoughts, checking to see if I have growing rage that is not proportional to my situation. I don't believe I'm becoming manic. Perhaps I see more today what is wrong with my life and how I also lack any insight on how to improve it. And so I sit, waiting for that unseen drawbridge to move. I am staring ahead at an obstruction I know is there, and yet it remains frustratingly beyond my line of sight.

JULY 31: VERMONT AND CONNECTICUT

As I drive west I search for positives from last night's motel experience. It was challenging to find sufficient power outlets to charge my numerous electronic devices. I also know now to request rooms far from the pool, as it turns out some parents allow their children to swim and play Marco Polo at eleven o'clock at night. I attempted to begin edits on Brenna's video but was thwarted by repeated shouting of the name of a long-dead Italian explorer.

My route to today's first interview has me backtracking across southern New Hampshire. Printmaker Sabra Field's postal address is South Royalton, Vermont, but on the phone last week she said she actually lives in a community of a handful of homes called East Barnard. I've never heard of either location, but to reach her I must traverse New Hampshire along Route 11 and pay more tolls to the Live Free or Die state.

In her sixties now, Sabra is rare among my interview subjects in that she fully supports herself with her art. My favorite part of her bio is that a few years ago one of her prints was chosen to be the state of Vermont's bicentennial stamp. The print features a foreground of golden crops to the left of a red barn. Rolling green hills dotted with trees form a backdrop, and behind them we see a sloping deep-blue mountain. Three wispy clouds emerge into an otherwise clear sky from the mountain's highest point. But as I cross the state line into Vermont I don't see any fields. I am enclosed instead by an impenetrable phalanx of trees.

My phone rings. It's Sabra, telling me in a firm voice that I must follow specific directions she is about to impart. I won't be able to call her back from my phone for more guidance, she says, because as I get closer I will lose cell coverage. I half-listen. After all, I have a hand-drawn color map to her home that she sent me. Then I realize I have already passed the exit she told me to take. I choose to take a different exit, which should be fine because it is also on Sabra's map, marked with Crayola Blue Gray. I pass over a Burnt Sienna bridge extending over a lazy Cerulean stream onto a road of Indian Red. That road turns out to be a rutted monstrosity of mud and gravel. Stones ping the undercarriage of my rental car, and my GPS displays only an unmarked brown line piercing a sea of green. As the road winds and bends through the trees I realize the map lacks both orientation and scale. I press forward. Then I see rays of light piercing the tree canopy. A clearing appears, amber-green like one of Sabra's prints. At the far end of the field sits a charming yellow house, a larger version of the one at the center of Sabra's crayon map.

"You're late," Sabra says as she opens her door. Her voice is stern yet polite. She's fairly short, with a Katherine Hepburn frame topped with silver hair spun into a crisp bun. Rectangular glasses with lines as precise as the delineations on her prints rest on her nose. The look is softened by her coral T-shirt and thin smile. Looking down at the weathered planks of her hardwood floor, I confess to her that I didn't follow her directions and feared I was lost.

Sabra stands on the balls of her feet, arms folded behind her. "Here's a bit of trivia. I live the furthest from a paved road of anyone in Vermont." I hear the same pride she conveyed when informing me she had no cell phone service.

Her large workshop is lined with original prints of every size. I position her on one of her work stools in front of a large set of prints depicting the beaches and mountains of Bali, a way to demonstrate that Sabra depicts more than just pastoral New England. She sits spine-straight like the former schoolteacher she is. I start recording. "My daughter Marisa would really enjoy being here," I say, explaining how she is an aspiring visual artist and will accompany me on a portion of my trip.

Sabra fiddles with the lavaliere microphone attached to her shirt and says only "That's nice." Then she discusses her recent trip with her granddaughter in Greece. "It was special," she says. "Normally a holiday for me involves painting and drawing, but I played tourist this time. It's good to be back, though. We Vermonters travel so when we come home we remember how lucky we are." Then she turns away, her face out of frame. I wait, and then hear soft sobs. "I'm sorry," she says.

"There is a tender part of me that we won't go to."The words come from deep in her throat and almost don't escape her lips. "It was my first trip in decades without my husband. He died in April."

"Sabra. I'm so sorry."

Sabra wipes her eyes with a tissue.

"How long were you married?"

"Thirty-nine years." She breathes in deeply, her hand on her chest. "I never know when I'm going to do this, so I'm doing it now before we begin filming."

I look away, not knowing what to say or do. I have lost relatives, but not loved ones. Three of my four grandparents died before I was an adult, but their losses were abstractions to me, since my parents had banned them from our lives. I did have some idea of what it was like to lose a family member, when my father left us. I saw him only rarely during the three years before he returned to my mother, and thus also to me.

Shortly after he left I found myself once a week enveloped in a chocolate-brown bean bag chair in the office of a child psychologist. My mother had noticed that I often wasn't listening to her. I was, but I wasn't hearing what she was saying. I was instead taking her words, projecting them as text in my mind, and then parsing the letters into multiples of two, three, four and five. I longed—I craved—to find a paragraph that would hit on at least three of those multiples. But I couldn't be expected to perform this comforting mental task while also processing the meaning of those words. My psychologist found no comparable example of my obsession in the published psychiatric literature, so he christened a name for it: pyramiding. He had my mother post a sheet of paper on our refrigerator breaking the week into one-hour increments. Every hour I managed to avoid pyramiding I put an X in the box. When I returned to the doctor's office, I was given a penny for every X but could only "spend"the pennies in his office. My first week there I filled up on gumballs. But then I discovered his Pachinko machine, a Japanese gambling device in which the player bounces shining metal balls down a wall of small nails. If the ball lands in a prettily painted trap, more balls pour out of the bottom for further play. I earned a single ball for each X. Each week I spent fifty-five minutes assuring the psychologist that I knew it wasn't my fault that my father left, and five minutes enjoying the unpredictable slide of smooth silver while I silently took back my words.

Sabra's breathing had grown heavy, but now it is returning to normal. Composure regains her face. Rigidity again owns her posture. She is restored, like a shaken Etch-a-Sketch. "I'm ready."

I don't know how to express how impressed I am with her recovery, so I launch into the interview. I ask when she first knew she wanted to be an artist. "Oh, Patrick, that is a question I don't even think about anymore. Ever since I wrote in my autograph book at the age of eight 'I'm going to be an artist.'" She earned a teaching degree at Wesleyan in Connecticut, but later moved to Vermont. "I needed to be where it was quiet, and where a home occupation was valued."She's been making prints in this same Vermont house on the same massive wooden press, she says, for forty-two years. "Once I put my press in I couldn't move."It was around that time that she pursued her printmaking career full time, with her husband as a business manager. "It's a case of fools rush in where angels fear to tread," she says. "I had the confidence that I was set to go. I had the determination."That is exactly the model followed, with equal success, by my mother.

A key to Sabra's financial security, she says, is her willingness to work on commission, something she notes Rembrandt also did. "I never thought that was beneath me. You work with the client. When I did the stamp for the state of Vermont during the Bicentennial, I was assigned an art director. That print ended up being heavily art-directed, if you know what I mean. But I needed a jolt of publicity so I was willing to be amenable."

Her words suggest flexibility, but her tight posture and modulated voice tell me she still harbors frustration from the experience. My videos are commissioned works, but I am fortunate in that my funders have no desire to play the role of director.

I admit to her that I didn't really know much about printmaking until my daughter made one in middle school. Her print won an award in a local art competition. Sabra explains the process to me, how she starts with a set of drawings, then puts those drawings on a series of blocks, then carves them and prints them in a precise order. "I'm a planner," she says, "I'm too Scottish."It comes to me now, what it is that speaks to me about her art. Not her Scottish heritage. I have Scottish blood in me too, but other than pleasure at the fact that my last name is shared by a character in *Macbeth* I've never focused too much on that. No, what I value is her use of both her left brain and her right brain in her creativity. My circles of friends have always been filled with artists. I feel at ease around creative people, and enjoy a sense of creativity by osmosis when with them. But I also find myself pretending a bit. I am a planner. I obsessively embrace organization, with this trip—broken down to the hour—the latest example. Most artists I've met celebrate spontaneity and the mystery of the unknown. But planning and organization is intrinsic to Sabra's art.

A knock at the door breaks our flow. Sabra apologizes. Her gardener has arrived, she says, and on the wrong day, she adds with more than a hint of annoyance. She takes off her microphone and I turn off the camera. I walk over to a far wall filled with prints from her *Cosmic Geometry* collection, sixteen prints depicting various iterations of mathematics in nature. My eyes follow the precisely delineated lines of a nautilus shell curving in on itself, finally reaching an unseen center. The progression speaks to me, an organic path leading to a safe center.

When Sabra returns we film a bit more, but the spell has been broken. I ask to see her press. She smiles broadly, and we head down a short set of steps to a room at the end of the house that appears to be an addition. The press dominates the space. On various tables are portions of a print she is working on. One cutout is of a foreground of grass. Another features a line of trees. Still another one will form the sky. I particularly like the cutout in the shape of three cows.

"This is a real place," she says of the landscape. "Well, in a way. It's a view of a pasture you used to be able to see from a hill not far from here. Unfortunately, the state has adopted a policy of letting trees grow unchecked, so nowadays you can't actually see that field."

I tell her about my frustration in driving here, flanked by walls of tall trees. I was disappointed I couldn't see the Vermont she depicted in her Bicentennial stamp. "Well, speaking for Vermonters," she says, "we're sorry to hear you say that. But you're absolutely right."

I fear intruding on her any further, and I am scheduled to meet another artist in Middlebury in a few hours. But one item remains unresolved. "Sabra, what advice would you give my daughter as she pursues the visual arts?"

She gives me the smile I offer my kids when I deny their request for dessert. "When you first mentioned her, I thought you were in your own sweet way asking for some advice on her behalf."

I nod.

"There isn't any advice I can give an aspiring artist," she continues. "Well, except that if you are driven to do it, you will figure out how. You might find you are much happier not doing it. There are other ways of being, ways that are less arduous, with fewer disappointments, where you'll end up in a place that's more suited to your personality."

Sabra has given me a precise answer to a vague question. It is not what I wanted to hear, but I feel I must listen. There is so much to admire in her. Sabra has reminded me that the art-committed path is not an easy one. It is a journey of long nights and short rejections. It is Sabra's gravel road, one that shows no markings on a GPS screen, no foreshadowing of what lies around the next turn. It can't be mapped. It's no surprise that most of us stay on the interstate.

· · ·

The car's odometer tells me I've already driven more than two hundred miles today. I will drive another three hundred before my day is done. I am again off the interstate, wandering blue highways through mountainous terrain. Trees are many, people are few. I arrive in Middlebury for my next interview but I am only there in physical form. In my mind I am in Knoxville, walking my children into a hotel lobby in the middle of the night.

Adam Glazer finds me at the coffee shop and I try to focus on the task at hand, an interview with an illustrator who doesn't look much older than my daughter. Marisa loves to sketch, and I had showed her Adam's illustrations, which often feature fantastical beasts you'd find in a late-night science-fiction movie. Marisa was impressed. I was drawn to the images because they reminded me of my passion for antique maps, which often feature sea monsters in stretches of open ocean and terrifying beasts in patches of uncharted land. Had I lived four hundred years ago that is a visual arts passion I might have pursued, illustrating maps I had charted myself as an explorer.

Adam and I say hello, and he reminds me that because he is deaf I will need to keep my lips visible. This makes it impossible for us to talk while I drive him to our filming location, a classic Vermont background of fields and mountains just like Sabra's bicentennial stamp. He has a lot to say as we drive, however. Watch for that guy on a bicycle! Look out, that woman wants to walk across the street! Do you see those kids up ahead? None of these so-called hazards are anywhere near me. He's revealing to me what life is like when you're a pedestrian who can't hear.

The interview is a bit of a blur. I look at Adam's young face and black, almost gothic attire, and I see Marisa. I'm focused enough to keep Adam talking, and I realize he's giving me some interesting material about how often deaf artists are taken advantage of by middlemen. Of course many of my funders are middlemen, but I didn't know about this problem and while it's not a pure copyright matter, I decide it's serious enough to include it in the video. My funders will have to live with my choice. After the interview I drive Adam back into town, thank him for his time, and head south. I'm tempted to return to Sabra's house, and ask to be comforted by the woman who in many ways models the seasoned and wise artist my daughter saw in my mother. But that is a ridiculous thought and I press on toward Connecticut. Tree after tree flies by as I leave Vermont and traverse Massachusetts. I depart the interstate for a local highway in Connecticut and the trees no longer keep to the side of the road. A thick canopy envelopes me. A road sign tells me I should use headlights at all times. And then the trees are gone and the harbor of Groton, Connecticut, shines ahead. I have reached the sea. I pull into the first parking lot I see, one of a decaying motel, in desperate need to abandon the car and embrace the day's remaining sunlight.

A round woman in a red housedress holds a large black trash bag in one hand while unlocking a Dumpster padlock with the other. I ask her for a place to have dinner favored by locals. The trash bag moves to her left. I see a line of people outside a waterfront pizza joint. None of them are in housedresses. The pizza proves worth the wait. I wash down the ham-and-pineapple special with a goldfish bowl of the house red, and enjoy the chatty waitress, who transforms from ogre to angel after returning from a dockside smoke break.

I've longed over the last year, since returning from Knoxville, for something that would provide me a quick path to tranquility. I've experimented plenty with both of the items on tonight's menu, junk food and alcohol. But I know there is no easy way to reconcile yourself to a life apart from your parents. This isn't the first time they've cut me out of their lives. But while I am not free from thoughts of my mother and my mental health legacy on this trip, I have been temporarily liberated from my funders and the coming war in which they wish me to be a front-line infantry soldier. Here on the road it is proving to be just me, the artists, and my thoughts. Perhaps I am already experiencing the equivalent of that waitress' cigarette, the freedom of a cross-country trip that is my creation. For the next several weeks I am the sole navigator, the captain of my own voyage. I will chart my own map.

AUGUST 1: CONNECTICUT AND RHODE ISLAND

I am warmed by Surya Iacono's smile, the former flight attendant's perfect teeth greeting me in welcome. How many weary travelers were lifted by that smile when boarding an international flight, I wonder. Then I see the rest of her, olive skin and jet-black hair that nearly reaches her waist. I hear the wise voice of Albus Dumbledore coming from a Harry Potter movie playing on the television. A young boy sits transfixed on a futon, aware only of the magical world of Hogwarts and not of a stranger standing behind him.

"That's my son. He's five years old and smart as a whip."

I didn't know Surya was a mother. There is much I don't know about Surya. What I do know I learned in a pre-interview by phone, that she is a Florida native who after about ten years traveling through the skies sought a new career as a documentary filmmaker. Her home now is in Las Vegas, but she's renting this duplex overlooking Groton Harbor for the summer to concentrate on final edits of her first film. She leads me into her kitchen and offers orange slices and cantaloupe cubes, then proceeds to provide random facts of her life, such as how much she loved growing up in Florida, the pleasure she found in dining in a different foreign capital each night, how she's pressed on after her boy's father left shortly after the birth. And interspersed with her information nuggets she interviews me, rapid-fire questions I answer monosyllabically. Do I have children? Do I eat meat? What's my zodiac sign? She is the intended interview subject, not me, so I suggest we start filming. I have a second interview in Rhode Island today, I say. You know how tight filming schedules can be.

She nods vigorously, kisses her son on the back of the head, tells him she'll be right across the street along the harbor, and we head out. Her chosen location to film puts the morning light directly in Surya's eyes. I wait for the filmmaker to tell me that won't work but she says nothing, so I set up the camera and begin.

"How does one go from being a flight attendant to a documentary

43

filmmaker?"

"I realized pretty early on in my personal journey that I wanted to make a difference," she says. "I was going to have to become a filmmaker to convey my message."

Her message is that our country isn't safe.

Surya had just returned to the U.S. from Tokyo on the night of September 10th, 2001, and was overnighting in Florida with plans to return to her home base of New York City the next day. She was awakened by a ringing phone. Moments later Surya, like tens of millions around the world, was glued to a television news channel. Her phone continued to ring, friends and family wanting to confirm she was alive.

"As I'm talking to you right now I'm getting goose bumps again," Surya says, but after a deep breath she continues. The newscasters didn't have any details on the planes, so she called her employer and learned that two of her airlines' planes were missing, and the four pilots were part of her New York-based team.

The poised flight attendant who had greeted me at her door slips away. Surya's shoulders slump, tears form in her eyes. She wipes them away, clears her throat, and pushes herself straight in her chair.

"I'm sorry," she says.

"I understand, take your time."

Surya clears her throat, then continues. "I couldn't believe that people of unknown origin would come into this country and destroy dear colleagues. Friends." A swallow. "I want to make sure that their memories are never, ever forgotten. They were the first people murdered on 9/11. They got the brunt of the terrorists' anger, their misplaced anger."

Surya had already provided me a rough-cut version of her documentary, "Green Cards for Al Qaeda," and I watched it last night in my motel room. She interviewed border patrol agents, former high-level government officials, a member of the congressional commission that had investigated the attacks. The conclusion was that our leaders had done little or nothing to make us safer after the tragedy that took so many lives on that fateful day.

"But why make a film?" I ask.

"We are visual creatures. We believe what we see."

That is the philosophy behind my short films. I write a fair amount about artists and their rights, but I felt I could make a stronger impact by allowing viewers to see a few minutes of someone who could be a friend or neighbor telling her own story. But I'm not taking much of a risk here. My expenses are being covered by my organization. Surya quit her job and enrolled in filmmaking school. I'm driving about six thousand miles in five weeks. Surya says she hired a film crew out of her own pocket and then spent about the same amount of time traveling to film her interviews, but covered sixteen thousand miles. And somehow, during all of this life transition, she became a mother. I admire her bravery, and envy it as well.

"So the film is just about done. What now? Will you now reinvent yourself again?"

She tells me there is still much to do. She's submitting it to festivals, seeking distribution deals and funding. But it won't be her last film, she says. "Life brings new projects. I'm going to keep making difference-making films. I'd really like to keep knocking on that door of creativity."

I ask her the same question I asked Sabra Field, the question I'm asking for my daughter, what advice she would offer someone just starting out on the path of an art-committed life.

Now Surya laughs. "I'd start by saying there's a lot of bad advice out there. Our society is so gung-ho about being success-driven. Always smile, keep moving forward, and keep having great days. Every day has to be a great day, we're told, but in reality, for human beings, that's not how life works."

Surya is starting to sound a lot like Sabra.

"You know what?" Surya says. "You'll feel like giving up. You'll feel like throwing in the towel. And it's okay to have those days. I think a lot of those motivational speakers out there are setting people up for failure because they're telling people 'Every day is a new day and you're going to be successful and don't grieve and don't cry,' but that's just not how life works. You just have to set yourself up in the long run to create something that is truly worth your time, and truly what you sought to make."

Keep moving forward. That's what I'm hearing Surya say, and it's what I do as I thank her for her time and start driving to Providence, Rhode Island. Surya was talking about moving forward with her art, but I suspect she meant far more than that. She was talking about the path of recovery after a loss. When you keep moving, you have a destination to which you can apply your focus, rather than that point of pain to which you are so tempted to look back. That word—*loss*—has been taunting me the past year. I felt its weight last night just down the street from here at the pizza parlor as I reflected on my parents. But they are still alive. We grieve when someone dies, yet I may once again have my parents in my life. They walked away from me once before, shortly after my first marriage. But I convinced them to return when Marisa was born. Of course it is more complicated now. But the lack of finality keeps me frozen in a not-quite-grief state. I can't shake it out like Sabra's Etch-a-Sketch transformation. And as I no longer engage in creative writing, I can't process it through art like Surya.

As I leave Groton, I pass a thirty-foot-tall dinosaur wearing shades and holding a massive soda. The advertisement for a children's museum fails to distract me from Surya's loss, and mine. I shift my focus to the odometer, counting the miles to Providence. As I approach the city, the interstate brings me back to the water. With some time to kill before meeting film director Eileen Boarman. I first choose to stroll a waterfront park. I am the only individual who is neither holding hands with a lover nor capturing with a camera the sun glinting off the harbor. Hungry, I head into downtown and leave the car on the second floor of an eerily vacant parking garage. Nearly every spot on the ground floor is vacant, yet I am unnerved by the emptiness and feel the need to stash my car out of view of what few pedestrians I see. Most of the storefronts on this Sunday afternoon are closed, but I find a pizza-by-the-slice shop open for business. The stiff crust is as barren of sauce and cheese as the garage was of vehicles. When I'm finished, the sullen man behind the counter refuses use of the restroom, saying it's for employees only. Full of morning coffee and lunchtime soda, I need to go, but I find no other shops open. I return to the garage, walk up to the second floor, and to my shame relieve myself on the concrete. The slow flow of urine informs me the structure isn't level. This isn't what I imagined when I conceived of this trip—public urination in a tired New England commercial district —but as I've learned in my current job, sometimes in life you have to do what is distasteful.

I rinse my hands from the water bottle in my car and head off to find Eileen. She has invited me to attend a public service announcement she is directing. I am chagrined to find it is only a block away, in a bar with a working restroom. I push past a black drape hung to block sunlight from the front door and enter the shoot, which Eileen is doing as part of a filmmaking class. She told me when setting up the interview that she is currently "underemployed." It seems there is not much demand for film directors in Providence, not since a TV show she worked on that was filmed in town, *Brotherhood*, ceased production. This shoot is part of a competition for a TV spot denouncing drinking and driving. The idea Eileen came up with features a man who finds himself in an alternate universe where consuming candy gives you an alcoholic buzz but also leads to sneezing fits. This leads to car accidents when an addict's eyes close mid-sneeze.

My skepticism of the concept is confirmed when I take in the scene, a cross between Mardi Gras and a gay pride parade. A statuesque redhead decked out in an orange ball gown talks with a dark-skinned young man wearing a tattered clown suit next to a pudgy silver-haired man in thick glasses wearing a lime green Slinky like a beauty contestant's sash. A bank of silver-lined umbrella lights light the wooden bar, bringing to life a strip of glass block embedded behind the bar. All of the characters at the bar are sneezing, some rather violently. There is one exception to the sneeze fest, a gangly young man holding a large red jawbreaker in front of his mouth. Patrons chant rhythmically, urging him to bite a large jawbreaker. He does so, and their sneeze-interrupted urgings are replaced by cheers.

"Cut!" a woman yells. It's Eileen. She appears to be about my age, with auburn hair, a few hints of freckles, and determined eyes.

"You've got to really show that confusion when you walk up to the bar," she says to the man with the jawbreaker in his mouth. Turning to the Slinky wearer, she says "you need to be more vocal when chanting."

I whip out my camera. Once filming, a calmness envelopes me, making me realize I had until that moment been anxious. Still fairly new to filmmaking, I have much to learn about lighting and sound, but the role of invisible storyteller is a comfortable one. My career in journalism has provided a professional excuse to detach from moments in life that would otherwise induce stress, such as scenes depicting mentally aberrant behavior.

"It's something, isn't it," a woman next to me says. She introduces herself as Linda, the film shoot's makeup artist. I welcome her sane attire of white t-shirt and casual jeans. She tells me that until recently she managed an upscale cosmetics store, but the creative bug led her to launch her own makeup business. "The pay is a lot less, but I'm happy. It's the best thing I've ever done. No regrets."

I keep my income level to myself, but it's surprisingly good. Working journalists don't expect much in the way of salary, but my board is paying me lobbyist dollars. When I started the job I bought my first-ever luxury car, and since then Laura and I have upgraded from a modest-sized townhouse to a roomy stand-alone home with a two-car garage. I may have sold myself to my board of directors, but I didn't come cheap.

Eileen interrupts us. "Sorry for not greeting you right away," she says. "I've put us on break. Let's get out of here and find a better place to chat."

I excuse myself from Linda, and Eileen and I set up an outdoor shot outside a local theatre. Eileen is full of energy, like Brenna was after our interview. In a quick staccato she describes the rush she feels when collaborating with enthusiastic and talented individuals. She began her career as a stage actress before moving into the director's chair. As she talks, I realize how different she is from most of the other artists I've interviewed, who produce their work in isolation. I prefer solo work. My films—if in fact they are creative works as Ernest said yesterday—are largely products of my own creation. I identify the artists, I conduct the interviews, and I edit the film. I don't take direction well, a truth my funders may be starting to suspect.

My model of creative living is my mother, who works very much alone. She disappears into her office for hours on end, sometimes so long that my enabling father brings her breakfast, lunch and dinner. She works in a manic frenzy of writing, day and night, until the next book is finished. From conception to publication, my mother's novels are her own. That is especially true of her characters, sometimes recognizable from stories she would tell of her childhood. My grandmother makes frequent appearances, although my mother's stepfather also has inserted his way into a few books. My mother often spoke with pride of her choice to break with her family. She claimed that severing had helped her heal from the wounds they had inflicted upon her. But when she needed to produce another novel, she wasn't shy about pulling back the scabs.

I continue the interview with Eileen but find I am not listening closely. The camera separates me from the scene, but doesn't shield me from racing thoughts of my parents, my life choices, and my aborted creative path. I wish I could sneeze and have my closed eyes wipe my mind free, shake the Etch-a-Sketch and wipe out everything I know about manic bursts of creativity and the inevitable pain suffered by loved ones in proximity. Fortunately, Eileen talks without prompting, providing more than enough footage to produce a short film. After some time passes I thank her for the interview and pack up. The first leg of my road trip is done, at least as far as the interviews are concerned.

This trip is proving to be far different than what I had so carefully planned. I have maintained my itinerary, but I had not anticipated forced reflections on my own creative past, or the roots of said creativity. But what is clear is that, just as my mother's demons followed her from Oregon to Arizona, I am, on this trip, transporting uninvited—and unwelcome—travel companions. Over the next five weeks I will spend a great deal of time with people I admire sufficiently to capture on film. I will focus on engaging with them, real people leading real lives. They will tell me their stories. And I will listen, and try to learn.

PART TWO: THE MID-ATLANTIC

AUGUST 3: DELAWARE

The single-engine plane barrels toward the front of my car, its fuselage perhaps only twenty feet above the ground. I quickly check my dashboard to learn my speed, suspecting I have just been caught by a traffic-control plane. I discover my error as the plane banks to my right and a mist sprays out from below the tail. I don't think I've ever seen a crop duster before. Its toxins spread widely across the five-foot-tall corn stalks, raining death on whatever pests are seeking to feast on the farmer's bounty. The crops stretch as far as I can see in every direction, level farmland with nothing breaking the horizon. If there is such a thing as reverse claustrophobia, I'm experiencing it.

The crop duster lifts upward, moving from right to left, and then banks for another pass behind me. I continue driving on the narrow, empty road, following Glenn Palmer Howard's directions to his home in Camden. He lives far from the Delaware I know, the commercial hub of Wilmington and the hip beach town of Rehoboth. Two hours ago, I was answering emails in my D.C. office, but two days ago I was free, driving across New England. It is good to be back on the road, even if it's only a day trip to interview a self-described over-the-hill rocker.

But I am not alone. Voices emerge from the phone resting in the center console cup holder. A member of the board of directors of my non-profit—a longtime lobbyist for a Hollywood studio—invites everyone on the call to introduce themselves. Nearly thirty people do so, including other lobbyist funders of mine from the entertainment industry. It's a power network of copyright interests, highly paid experts in the arcana of the legislative process. When the line falls silent I state my name and affiliation, even though everyone on the call knows who I am. Their dues pay my salary.

The legislation these lobbyists have drafted, the board member says, will be introduced in the Senate in mid-September. That, I know, is just after I return from the last leg of my road trip. The senator authoring the bill, a committee chairman, has instructed those on the call to line up other senators as co-sponsors. One by one, voices identify which senators each will lobby. I remain silent. Then the board member running the call turns his focus to my video project.

"As many of you on the call know," he says, "the chairman will make his first public appearance on the bill at Patrick's big event in the Senate Russell Caucus Room on Capitol Hill. Patrick's going to have on display video interviews with artists. The chairman's very excited about this, everyday artists providing air cover for his bill. You just got back from Vermont, isn't that right, Patrick?"

"That's right. I filmed seven artists in New England, including two in Vermont." I know my board member singled out that state because it is where the chairman is from. "I'm actually in the car right now," I add, "driving to an interview in Delaware." I don't need to remind anyone on the call that Delaware is the home state of the Vice President of the United States, whose support is also being actively sought. The plane has returned, flying directly overhead. I speak up a bit to be heard over the engine growl. "I should point out, however, that since we're still keeping the bill and its pending introduction a secret, I'm not getting explicit endorsements in these films. The conversations are more general, artists talking about why their rights matter to them."

What I don't say is how grateful I am that I am busy conducting these interviews, because it gives me an easy excuse not to be spending my time on the Hill pushing members of Congress to endorse the bill. I actually am rarely asked to do that type of work. They appreciate the writing I do for them, mostly editorials and blog posts and research papers on the importance of copyright to individual artists. But they know I have no training as an actual lobbyist, a term some say came into use when early practitioners of the craft would wait in the White House lobby for President Ulysses S. Grant to pop out for a cigar.

As others chime in with their plans to win support for the bill, the former investigative reporter in me listens with fascination, thinking how much easier that job would have been had I been able to eavesdrop on calls like this. But I feel unclean, as if the crop duster has sprayed me through an open sunroof. I just want to find Glenn.

Shortly after the call ends I come across a welcome sign for Camden, beyond which sits a gas station, a drug store, and a fast-food joint. Glenn's split-level home is behind that strip mall, accessed by a road that curves off from behind the pharmacy's trash bins. Glenn greets me dressed not as a bad-ass rocker but as a Margaritaville retiree in a dark-blue Hawaiian shirt tenting over a generous paunch and most of his too-short white shorts. His home transports me back to my 1970's childhood, with a fleur-de-lis gold couch, chocolate brown shag carpeting, and avocado green wing-back chair frozen in time. His "little studio" upstairs is crammed with a large synthesizer, mixing board and computer on one wall and an olive love seat with saggy cushions and a faded arm rest against the other. The "atmospheric, new-agey" composition he plays for me does not provide sufficient relaxation in a space in which I am now feeling real claustrophobia, so we migrate to the living room, where he slouches into a wing-back chair. I learn he has tasted success in his forty-year career, having opened for REO Speedwagon; Kansas; and Emerson, Lake and Palmer. But he keeps returning to years' old traumas in which he was done wrong by rock legends who likely have forgotten who he is. Seeking a success story to share, I ask him about his first record deal, which he signed at seventeen.

"It was awful. I was too young. The labels are always looking to take advantage of you. That album is still sold around the world, and I don't see a dime. They own the copyright."

That story will not help us woo the Vice President. I push for a positive anecdote. But instead I hear about the many times record producers faulted him for not writing a smash hit, and how his latest deal in Florida blew up in his face, bringing him back home to Camden. He's landed a job as a special-ed instructor at his old grade school, but they won't let him teach music. There is so much he wants to do. Continue to pursue new-age music, which he says our stressed-out world needs. And finish his symphony, which I learn he has been working on since he was in his teens. But he says he gives all of his creativity to his teaching job. At the end of the day he has nothing left in his creative tank for his music.

I hope Glenn has one more fight left in him. I long for him to find a way to stop dwelling on those who have wronged him and instead focus on finding the time and energy to do something he believes is right. And I say that with some level of empathy. I had never really thought about creativity as fuel in a tank, which can be drained and refilled. But the analogy works for me. My job leaves my creative needle at empty. I am reminded of the songwriter I interviewed Friday in New Hampshire, Ernest Whaley. He said my videos are a form of creative expression. He told me I am on a creative journey of discovery. If he's right, that doesn't feel like my journey today. Rather, it's as if I've sold my creativity to Hollywood lobbyists.

AUGUST 10: NEW JERSEY

The four of us walk past boutiques and restaurants, together but apart. Parker plays to perfection the role of an eleven-year-old boy finally liberated from what to him was a too-long car ride. He bounces left and right across the narrow pedestrian mall, reading shop signs in an attempt to fulfill the quest I have assigned him: finding Cape May, New Jersey's Soma Gallery. Laura walks beside me while being somewhere else. Perhaps she is channeling better times from her childhood on a barrier island just north of here. Marisa takes up the rear, sun striking the back of her head while the phone she is attacking with her thumbs illuminates her face in a ghostly pallor.

This excursion to Cape May is a chance for us to spend some time together on this week-long vacation. We're in our third day, renting a three-bedroom apartment blocks from the beach in Ocean City, New Jersey. Every other year, we rent a home along the South Jersey coast, a week of swimming, sand castles, miniature golf, waffle houses, and boardwalk amusement rides. We had reserved the house long before I conceived of my road trip. Three months ago, as I started setting up interviews, I saw this vacation as a last chance to spend time with my family before beginning my cross-country leg. But while the three of them have hit the beach and the boardwalk each day, I've worked at the rental's dining room table, frantically editing videos.

In six days these videos begin to go live online, and to please the sponsor of the forthcoming legislation, I'm starting with Vermont. Our press release commits me to a new state each day, all the way until the last videos from the Pacific Northwest go live in mid-September. The end of the series will coincide with the introduction of the bill. It seemed like a great plan when I announced it a few weeks ago, but I have grossly underestimated the time involved in video editing. At the start of this vacation, Laura drove to South Jersey while I edited footage on my laptop. Parker remarked that he couldn't remember a time in his life when his father, a self-confessed lover of driving, had sat in the passenger seat.

"Here it is!"Parker shouts. The gallery is in one of those miniature malls I've seen in many beach towns, where an interior passage connects vendors. Laura, Marisa and I follow Parker into the mall and find the gallery at the end of a short hallway. It's an intimate space, two modest rooms with high ceilings and white walls. I'm guessing every painting I see is a Victor Grasso original; his hyper-realist style, like photography mixed with surrealism, is in every work. I'm struck by a large painting depicting a life-size bikini-clad woman with her arm around a swordfish, hitchhiking next to the iconic Garden State Parkway Exit 0 sign that is just outside of Cape May. Parker scampers over to what at first glance appears to be a typical beach scene, but the driftwood in the foreground becomes, upon examination, a triceratops. Marisa drops her phone into her shoulder bag decorated with skulls and drifts toward a painting easily five feet wide and three feet high. It depicts the head and torso of a naked woman, upside down, with splayed hair morphing into an octopus. One tentacle forms a curve around the nipple of the woman's exposed left breast.

"You must be Patrick."

I turn. Victor Grasso extends his well-tanned hand to me and I shake it. He's bronzed and fit, but shorter than I expected. I also guess that he's a bit younger than me. What strikes me, however, is his handshake, as firm as his ownership of this room: He commands the space as boldly as his paintings redefine reality. I try to imagine what it would be like, to stand in a gallery housing nothing but my work. Would I feel proud? Self-conscious? Victor seems more inclined to the former.

"It's great to meet you, Victor. My family is here as well."I introduce Laura. Marisa and Parker drift back from the paintings they were studying to meet the artist.

"And this is my wife, Alicia," Victor says.

She had been hanging back a bit, and I hadn't associated her with Victor. Thick black hair frames a fair complexion. Alicia is strikingly familiar to me. Then I realize she is Octopus Woman. I had tried to put myself in Victor's place, surrounded by his own creative output, but now I imagine myself as Alicia, flanked by displays of me in various states of undress. I shudder.

We talk, the four adults, about art, life, work. Victor and Laura swap stories about growing up on the Jersey Shore. Parker returns to the triceratops. Marisa hangs on the periphery, pretending not to listen. I learn the show opened three days ago, and Victor has already sold most of the paintings. The Exit 0 hitchhiker went to a local art collector for $10,000. I know that fine paintings, unlike those advertised on late-night cable channels, are not sold by the square foot. But I look around and do some quick math based on stickers and painting size. Victor, like Sabra Field, fully supports himself with his art.

Victor and I agree that we'll film down the street in Congress Hall, a grand hotel that was a summer retreat for U.S. President Benjamin Harrison. We part with Alicia, and then I leave Laura and the kids in a first-floor hotel lounge while Victor and I head down to the Boiler Room, a stone-lined basement bar that won't be open for business for a few hours.

I position him on a chocolate couch lining one of the walls. The lighting is terrible, and there will be challenges with sound. I discovered when testing my equipment an hour ago that the battery in the lavaliere microphone is dead. I didn't know until today, amateur videographer that I am, that it was battery-powered. So I'll be recording Victor with the camera's built-in microphone. A few feet away from me, three young women of Eastern European origin, the summer labor force in South Jersey, sit at a table, folding napkins and giggling. They'll have to be ambience, creating the impression I am interviewing Victor in a hopping bar.

I start the interview by asking him to define his style of painting.

"I'm a realist. My paintings are meant to be like photos but with a twist, adding things that could never happen." I think of the octopus entwining his nude wife. "With this show, I've really started embracing the shore where I grew up. You know, showing a classic beach scene, but then making a hunk of driftwood into a monolithic, iconic figure."

"The triceratops."

"That's right." He says he loves how Andrew Wyeth converted a seemingly mundane river region of Pennsylvania country into something magical. "But I paint women more than he did; I can't not paint them. My wife is my main model. She has an acting background, is very comfortable in front of a camera. But she's also always around."

"Didn't I read Wyeth painted his mistress?"

"Well, I think that's just marketing spin put out by his widow. It certainly was effective. It landed Wyeth on the cover of *Time* magazine."

Victor tells me he had always loved to draw but never picked up a paintbrush until at seventeen he got a summer job in Atlantic City painting casino murals. "From that moment I was hooked on painting," he says, but he also hated supervision. The mural gig turned into a full-time job, and by the time he was twenty-one he owned his own mural-painting company. "I knew then that I could never work for another person, and I haven't since." He's self-taught, he says, and has come to peace with never having attended art school. "I learn by going to museums. I get up close to the paintings and stare at them, and get yelled at by security. Because I don't have somebody's list of rules of how painting is supposed to be done I'm learning every time I paint."

Victor is an easy interview, quick to share, generous with self-reflection, and best of all, he never turns the conversation back on me. I learn about his time in L.A. and how he grew tired of its phoniness. As someone who travels there several times a year to meet with studio executives, I can attest to his assessment but keep that to myself. He tells me how he's happy with the income flow from his gallery shows but remains open to a casino mural job if the terms are right. After all, he says, he will soon have another mouth to feed. Alicia, I learn, is expecting. He's excited to see how being a parent will change his art. Alicia has set down one rule, however: He's not allowed to paint the birth.

"Nothing beats being a father," I say.

Victor nods. "So my father tells me. I like that you brought your kids today. I imagine sometimes having my child at my side as I work."

"Well, I think they'd rather be at the beach right now, but it was clear to me that they liked your paintings. And Marisa is an aspiring artist as well."

"You know, I could tell that. I saw her examining one of my

paintings up close while we were talking in the gallery. We artists look at art differently, you know."

"Well then," I say, "I'm glad she wasn't chased away by a security guard."

I could spend all day with Victor in this basement bar, perhaps the only place in Cape May where the summer sun isn't allowed to join in the festivities. But my own family is waiting for me. I wrap up by asking Victor to share some advice for aspiring artists like Marisa. He begins by talking about painting what you're passionate about. But then he reconsiders. "The more I think about it, the main thing is to have support from people in your life. I have Alicia, of course, but I come from a long line of artists who nurtured the next generation. My grandfather on my mom's side was a carver and sculptor, my other grandfather was a painter, my grandfather's brother was a painter, my mother painted and sculpted. My grandfather, the sculptor, filled his garage with beautiful works of art but never showed them to anyone. It was tragic. He didn't have that support from his parents. It's an easy thing to create something, but it's really hard to show it to the world, to risk criticism and rejection. Having that love and support gives you the strength to do it."

I thank Victor and turn off the camera. Victor said he didn't pick up a brush until he was seventeen, but he was drawing his entire childhood. He, like me, had an artist mother to inspire him. I never got a chance to see if any of my grandparents were artistic. But there is no question that my mother inspired me to write. She modeled the life of a writer, and praised me when I wrote something she felt merited attention. But I'm coming to realize she simultaneously sought, consciously or not, to prevent me from actually allowing others to see that creative work. In that sense I am more like Victor's sculptor grandfather, except my creative writing—the novel my mother suggested I abandon—is hidden away not in a garage but in a laundry-room cabinet.

The three giggling girls behind us have been joined by two teenage boys. The girls' squeals escalate in volume and pitch. Victor watches them as I pack up my equipment, and then we head upstairs to say our goodbyes. After Victor returns to the gallery I turn to my family.

"Since we're here," I say, pointing out the window at the surf, "why don't we walk down to the beach?"

None of us are dressed for such a trip. I had insisted that we dress appropriately for an art gallery—pressed shirts and blouses, long pants and skirts—not really processing that the people who visit a beach town gallery are, in general, casually attired. But I hear no objections, so we walk out of the back of Congress Hall toward the sound of crashing surf. As we leave the hotel I grab Parker by the waist and swing him around me. He squeals as I flip him like a bandleader spins a baton. We stop at the sidewalk separating the hotel from the beach. Marisa begins snapping photos of those strolling the path, which include a young mother pushing a stroller and a male rollerblader twirling in neon-yellow spandex shorts. Parker eyes an Adirondack-style white wooden chair on Congress Hall's grass lawn, and scampers up its back like a monkey. Laura gazes across the beach. The afternoon sun behind us alights her auburn hair, accenting the gentle curls that come to rest on her neck. I never grow tired of seeing her take in the ocean; it's as if she's looking back on the past, not just as someone who grew up on its shore, but almost as if she is reconnecting with humanity's origins. I imagine Laura lying naked and try to picture what resident of the sea would emerge from her hair. I don't conjure an image of organic material. Instead I see the waves themselves, unfolding from her head into a warm embrace, providing the comfort she gives me.

The hotel has set up a cluster of oversized yellow-and-white striped umbrellas on the sand in the distance. I can just make out a handful of couples reclining in the shade. It reminds me of a Renoir painting, Nineteenth Century well-to-do enjoying a summer constitutional.

"Maybe you should change your schedule for this road trip," Laura says, still watching the waves. I almost don't hear her over the surf and the laughing seagulls.

"You mean shorten it? I've already booked most of the interviews."

"I mean the posting schedule, when you've promised to upload the videos. I know your press release said you'd put up a state a day starting next week, but so what if you don't? Plans change. And go ahead and skip some states if you want. Don't go to Mississippi. Drive straight through Ohio without stopping."

Laura has mentioned two states that do not yet have interviews scheduled. The artists I contact are nearly always amenable to being interviewed, but aren't always available in the narrow windows in which I will be passing through their state. There are other holes in my itinerary. Nebraska. Wyoming. Oregon. And I leave in a week.

"It's not that simple," I tell her. "I've made a promise to the Board." But perhaps she has a point. I conceived of this trip, not my board of directors. I saw a chance to drive across the country on someone else's dime, but west this time, unlike the trip twenty-one years ago when I drove from from my college in L.A. to start over in the nation's capital. The resistance I faced from my funders was that I would be out of town as the finishing touches were put on the bill being introduced in September. Still, I'm determined to stick to posting a video a day, and to hit all of the states I've scheduled. I've made a public commitment. The truth is that as busy as this trip has made me, it is not the true cause of my anxiety. I created this trip. I control every aspect of the project. It is proving more ambitious than I thought, but it is still mine. What stresses me is how much in my life is absent my control.

Laura turns to look at me, her gentle hazel eyes hidden in a squint as she faces the sun. "I'm just worried, is all," she says. "You're popping lorazepam like they're Tums."

"Dr. Lewis told me it's okay to take them during the day when I feel stressed."

"I thought it was a sleeping pill."

"She first prescribed it to help me sleep, but it's actually an anti-anxiety medication," I say. "It just, I don't know, takes the edge off at night, gets the thoughts out of my head. It allows me to sleep."

"But you still wake up about three hours later."

"The thoughts come back. But I take another one and I'm good."

"Thoughts," Laura says. "You mean racing thoughts. You've told me that's a sign that your bipolar disorder is flaring up. Is that what happened this morning?" She slips out of her dress sandals, picks them up, and walks away from me, onto the sand.

I was up before dawn this morning to do some editing. The short cord that connects my laptop to the hard drive containing my raw video had gone missing. I looked all over the rental apartment's main room, a combination living room/dining/room/kitchen, and found nothing. It was excruciating, seeing that little black rectangle of video sitting right next to the larger white rectangle of laptop, the two born to mate but unable to connect. I couldn't imagine where, at 5 a.m. on a South Jersey barrier island, I could find another cord. I flipped out and stormed into the master bedroom. Louder than necessary I ripped drawers out of cabinets that I hadn't even bothered to fill with clothes. I looked under the bed and my pillow, even though I had not attempted any video editing in this room. Laura awoke, as I knew she would. She rose, groggily, to help. It only took her a few minutes to locate the cord. It was in my camera bag, where it belonged. She stood before me in the rental's main room, directly under the peak of its cathedral ceiling. Soft orange light tickled its way through the wall of windows behind her. We had just missed an ocean sunrise. I thanked her but she said nothing. She simply shook her head, grabbed our one house key, and walked out. She was gone about an hour. When I asked upon her return where she'd been, she said she had walked along the beach. But when I tried to continue the conversation with an apology she cut me off. No more, Patrick, was all she said. No more.

I kick off my loafers, strip off my socks, and follow her. The sand is hot, and after a few steps I'm regretting being barefoot. But I continue walking, keeping pace with Laura. How many times have I done this, walked with her on a Jersey beach? This is where she is most herself, and where I find myself falling in love with her all over again. And now I've infected her sanctuary with the toxin that is my professional life.

Laura stops when she reaches the waterline. A cluster of sandpipers rush in her direction, the birds' tiny feet scampering away from the incoming tide. The water stops about a yard from Laura's toes. As it retreats, the sandpipers chase after it, pecking in the moist sand for whatever it is they're trying to eat.

"Be patient with me," I say when I catch up. "I know I'm a wreck. But let me get through this trip, as scheduled. Then they'll introduce the bill and I can take a breath. I won't need the extra drugs. It will be like it was before this job, before things got crazy."

"The bill's introduction is just the beginning," she says. "You've told me that. Things will only get worse. It's going to be hugely controversial. You'll be attacked, maybe even by some of the artists you're trying to help."

A sandpiper shimmies near my left foot. I swing my leg out, and the bird spins away in a blur, scampering back to its friends. Laura is right. She is right because I tell her, and only her, everything that is happening with my life.

"You don't have to stay in this job," she says. "There is other work you can get. We'll figure it out."

I walk past her, toward the approaching surf. A wave's crest hits a divot in the sand and splashes on the cuffs of my khaki slacks. I keep walking, letting the water swirl over my feet, feeling my toes sink into the moist sand. Victor gave me the gift of his time, and his name to associate with my cause. Can I then walk away from the cause I asked him to support?

Parker flies past me, rushing into the water. He's rolled up his pants such that they are clumped above his knees. I watch as he mimics the sandpipers, running with the tide to keep the water at calf height. He's in that place where he goes so easily, where nothing exists but the now. There is no future, there is no past. It's a place I found myself in during brief moments a few days ago on stretches of highway in New England. I have failed to capture that place on this vacation, and Laura is suffering as a result. I would like nothing more than to find that place again once I return to the road. I will, of course, be trapped alone with my racing thoughts. But perhaps if I am forced to listen to them instead of chasing them away with drug-induced sleep, I'll be able to find a way to meet Laura's challenge this morning. No more.

AUGUST 16: PENNSYLVANIA

I'm curious to see the home of science fiction and fantasy novelist Michael Swanwick. I know he's a successful novelist. He's won several prominent awards in his field, including a Hugo and five Nebulas, the type of awards I'd see on the dust jackets of the books I often read as a teenager. First I pass Philadelphia's Fairmount Park lined with stand-alone mansions expressing wealth without ostentation. They give way to brick ranchers, then aging rowhouses built right up to the sidewalk, repeating patterns of bar-covered windows united by beige brick. I cross an aging bridge and park on a steep, narrow road lined with cars. As I stand before Michael's door, I feel I am back on Washington, D.C.'s, Capitol Hill, in the home my ex-wife and I bought when I was twenty-three and she was thirty-two. I was six blocks from the capitol but one block from a take-out ribs joint. I see Michael is ten houses down from a similar storefront, this one selling cheesesteaks.

It is close to noon. The sun has cleared the rooftops and is directly in my eyes. I barely see Michael when he opens the door. He invites me in and I adjust to the dark living room, blocked from sunlight by heavy curtains. Then I see the clearest feature of the room—books. Stacks of them, ten to twelve in each pile, at least a dozen such towers rising precariously from every available surface. Paperbacks, hardcovers, all variety of sizes. The only thing they appear to have in common is wear.

Michael sports a thick gray beard that extends at least three inches from his face. He reminds me of a wizard from J.R.R. Tolkien's *Lord of the Rings* trilogy, one series of fantasy books I devoured as a child. I would often study the map of Middle Earth printed at the start of the book, imagining making my way through hazardous woods and mountains to the evil land of Mordor. The drive here today was a bit less challenging.

With Michael's permission, I move the lamp next to the one piece of furniture not covered in books, a red-cushioned chair with wide wooden armrests. As I set up the camera with Michael in the chair, I see there will be two stacks of books in view over his left shoulder, and several piles of magazines leaning precariously to his right.

I haven't read any of Michael's books, although I had intended to before I became buried in video editing. I ask Michael to explain his fiction as much for my benefit as for the video's viewers. He says he writes all types of fantasy and science fiction. He'd make more money if he stuck to one genre, but then again, he says, he'd make more money as an accountant. He likes being a full-time writer, which gives him the freedom to write whatever he wants. Doing so means he doesn't always choose the most lucrative publication path. "It is, however, the most satisfying way to spend your life."

Michael says he began writing fantasy and science fiction at sixteen when he started reading Tolkien's *The Fellowship of the Ring* at 11 o'clock one night, and finished it the next morning just before the school bell rang. He lost a night of sleep but gained a life passion. "Tolkien just picked me up and rang me like a bell," Michael says. He committed himself to writing fiction, he says, and eleven years later finally finished his first story.

"That took a while," I say.

"Well, I wrote out all of the bad stuff you have to write in order to learn how to tell a story the way a story should sound. I don't have a lot of early embarrassing work out there."

"I hadn't thought of it that way, how not being published could be a good thing."

"Well, it's still nice to be published. I sold my first story at twenty-nine, which was just in time. I was coming up on thirty, when it stops being cute to be an unpublished writer."

I'm now forty-three. Were I to renew my efforts at creative writing now, by Michael's standard, that would not be cute.

He tells me about the book he's just finished, which features a dystopian future involving a genetically engineered dog who walks on two legs, once burned London to the ground, and is on his way to Moscow to seek his fortune. I also learn of a book in which a girl is kidnapped by elves and forced to work in a factory making fairy dust. Michael says the opening is "very Dickensian." I perk up when he mentions he has just written a biography. As much as I love fiction, I am obsessed with reading true stories well told. I ask who the subject is, and he mentions a fantasy novelist I've never heard of, Hope Mirrlees.

"She wrote one poem, an amazing work in 1926 called 'Lud-in-the-Mist.' The twenty or so of us who have actually read it are convinced it was an inspiration for T.S. Eliot."Michael comes alive as he tells me how his obsession with her grew into a hobby, in which he began compiling facts and details about her life. Soon, he says, he was becoming one of the world's foremost experts on this overlooked writer. This seems a logical step from fantasy writing relying on readers following characters on a map. Michael sought to map the influences of a favorite poet.

"You had a passion for this subject, and kept learning more."

"That's right. But I was careful not to use any of my real writing time on it."

"Yet you ended up writing a book."

"Not with any hope of making any money off of it, that's for sure. But yes, that's what I tend to do with anything in my life. I say 'Okay, how can I make a book out of that?'"

The novel that I wrote a few years ago and quickly shelved after my mother's literary agency rejected it had a subplot that grew out of a personal obsession of mine: antique maps. As a child my bedroom walls were covered with free maps that came in occasional issues of *National Geographic.* I spent a lot of time alone in my room, and like Victor Grasso studying paintings, I would gaze upon each map's every detail, learning how the cartographer marked the rising altitudes of Japan's Hokkaido Island or rotated colors to distinguish the overlapping borders of central Africa. By the time I was a teenager I had moved on to the artistic visions of Sixteenth and Seventeenth Century mapmakers. The Golden Age of Discovery is rich with tales of both adventure and tragedy, explorers discovering new lands and peoples profiting and suffering as a result. Cartographers captured all of this on paper, combining fact and fable with a few simple lines carved into copper plates. Yet while many authors have written about the explorers and their royal funders, few have focused on the mapmakers. I have over the years devoured just about every English-language work on the great European cartographers, enough that I consider myself to be a lay expert on some of the more obscure ones. But rather than attempt to write a biography, I chose to fold in a fictional cartographer's story as a historical backdrop for the novel. It was a forced marriage, I see now. The book was most truly alive when I was describing the mapmaker, not the fictional modern-day investigative journalist modeled after me. By attempting a novel, I was treading the path well worn by my mother. But she has never attempted a book-length nonfiction work. There is no family legacy in that genre with which I would be competing.

Michael says he is thrilled with how the book came out, even if it wasn't greeted with the kind of praise he has received as a novelist. He says he'd do it again, however. "It's a funny thing being a writer. You have to think writing is the most important thing you could possibly be doing. But you're going to feel a little sensitive about it. You're going to yearn for praise, and wince at rejection."

That is true for all artists, I think. My mind goes to the Delaware living room of Glenn Palmer Howard as he relived a lifetime of slights. "So your recommendation to writers would be to move on from rejection and keep writing."

"It would. But let me tell you something else about the importance of writing something that really matters to you. My first novel was published as a paperback original. At the same time a totally unknown writer named William Gibson came out with his first novel, *Neuromancer*. Now, my ambition was to write and get published a science fiction novel. William Gibson's intention was to rewrite the syntax of science fiction, so you'd never be able to write a novel the old way again. He failed and I succeeded." Michael raises his right hand. "But because I'd only aimed so high," he says, putting his hand flat in front of him, "and because he'd aimed so much higher"—now the hand goes up above Michael's head—"his book is considered to be a classic, and my first novel is justifiably forgotten. It's very hard when you're unpublished to aim that high, but that's the best thing you can do for yourself. The greater your ambition, the better your failure."

I know I've got a keeper for the video, and I want to stop while we're ahead. So I wrap up, thank him for his time, and return to the street, where the sun is now behind the rowhouses on the other side. I realize I missed lunch, so I swing into the corner shop and buy a cheesesteak sandwich. The woman with a worn face and stained T-shirt asks me what I want on it, and I tell her to surprise me. I can't focus on toppings right now. I'm somewhere else, imagining grand ambitions and spectacular failures.

I take the sandwich to Fairmount Park, where I sit alone on a stretch of grass near two stone Roman-style gates with bronze sculptures of soldiers and horses. I bite into the cheesesteak and realize about half of its volume is fried onions, a vegetable of which I'm not particularly partial. But I eat them all, focused on envisioning possible futures.

Both Michael and my mother support themselves by writing fiction. Michael and his wife live modestly in a suburban Philadelphia brick rowhouse. My mother has embraced the trappings of her income with a five-bedroom faux-mansion in a wealthy neighborhood in Knoxville, a city she and my father moved to from Arizona after Marisa was born. When they chose to live in Tennessee, my mother said they liked the state's lack of an income tax, but also appreciated being only a day's drive from their grandchild. The move occurred soon after we began speaking again after years of silence triggered in part by my decision to marry my first wife over my mother's objections. I had restored our connection by informing my mother of Marisa's impending arrival. Her desire to have a granddaughter overrode her determination to maintain a disconnection with her son. After moving to eastern Tennessee, however, my mother and father rarely made that drive to D.C. It was almost always incumbent upon me to bring the grandchildren to them. At least they had plenty of room for us. I was glad I had driven rather than flown last summer, as it gave my children and me a vehicle for escape.

While in Knoxville last year before our abrupt departure, Marisa overheard my mother tell my father she could no longer stand Tennessee. She wanted to return to the Pacific Northwest. I suspected Marisa must have heard wrong, as that was the part of the country she would never allow me to visit as a child. It was the place full of memories so painful she couldn't share them with me, a region that housed relatives I would never meet. But from hints of conversation at our two-hour dinner the night of the incident, I heard enough to realize Marisa was correct. They were looking to move west. My mother could tell herself I had severed our relationship by leaving her home that night. Thus, I realized, she could now feel free to move thousands of miles from her grandchildren without guilt.

In less than forty-eight hours Marisa and I will hit the road, and my mother has no knowledge that we're about to share this adventure. Marisa will fly back to D.C. after four days, but I will press on, three straight weeks of open highway and free-flowing conversations on creativity. A world of possibility awaits me. This is my Golden Age of Discovery. I hope to be like the explorers of old once they reached the open sea, cut off from communications with their funders. I'm ready to set sail. Like those cartographers from the Age of Discovery, the map before me is a virgin sheet of copper plate, and I am the engraver.

PART THREE: THE SOUTHEAST

AUGUST 18: VIRGINIA

The empty country road fronted with large expanses of farmland suggests Marisa and I are the only two people for miles. Our location is remote, and so is my teenage daughter. "Watch for a white mailbox, Marisa. That's how we find the road to Colleen's house." Marisa doesn't bother to acknowledge my request. Her ears are tethered to her music player, her eyes adhered to her phone's small screen, her thumbs mated with the device's keyboard.

We've been driving far too long on this narrow road of gentle curves and canopies of maples and oak. According to Colleen Doran's directions, we should have seen the mailbox by now, which has me wondering if this is even the right road. I make a U-turn, and with a screech a thorny branch introduces itself to the rental sedan's front passenger-side door, a coupling unnoticed by my fifteen-year-old daughter. I stop watching for a mailbox. Instead I open myself to the possibility of a hidden turnoff. After about a mile I see it, marked by a squat tin box shrouded in a lanky witch hazel. Sometimes you find what you're looking for by not looking for it.

A windy gravel path leads to a cream-sided rancher nestled in the shade of trees that I suspect have seen more years than the two of us combined. The end of the car's motion attracts Marisa's attention. She removes the ear buds, thus preventing them from grafting to her flesh. We are greeted by a friendly wave from the porch.

"Glad you found the place, I'm pretty tucked away," Colleen calls as I step out of the car. Her smile is warm. Thin wire glasses circle her eyes. A white cotton button-down shirt and well-worn jeans amplify her casualness.

Colleen is my ideal vision of Marisa in twenty years. They both are fair-skinned with long blonde hair. But Colleen isn't dressed like a goth or an emo or whatever it is that antisocial teens wearing black and studs call themselves. I also imagine Marisa becoming the accomplished artist Colleen is now. Few artists I will interview on this trip are as successful in their fields as Colleen is in hers, being perhaps the most accomplished woman in the comic-book industry. She's drawn for series such as Spider-Man and my daughter's favorite, Sandman, but also has authored her own graphic novels. My daughter is an illustrator and a storyteller. I try not to put "aspiring"in front of those nouns, because Marisa already draws and already writes stories. But she does aspire to improve, and to be published. I hope the same for her.

After a quick handshake with me, Colleen embraces Marisa. My daughter appears to hug her back. The three of us step inside, and as my eyes adjust to dim light an intoxicating aroma washes over me, a scent of comfort and reassurance. "Pasta sauce," Colleen says. "Smells good, doesn't it? I'm cooking up a batch with tomatoes and herbs from my garden. After you leave I'm making cucumber dill bread from scratch, with my own herbs, my own cucumbers. I tell you, it just tastes better."

We're in the front room of a cozy country home populated with walnut furniture – a sofa draped in a knitted blanket, a table topped with a large tree's cross-section, a lamp with illuminated oak leaves pressed into the shade. There is little sign of living in this living room – no open magazines, no half-consumed iced teas. I'm guessing Colleen doesn't get many visitors so she may have straightened up for us, but given how much art she produces I suspect she spends little time away from her drawing desk.

After Colleen returns from the kitchen she leads us to her office. This room is lived-in, each surface covered by books, paper or pencil, often all three. A large drafting table sits at the far end of the room, flanked on both sides with flat-drawer cabinets five feet high, maybe ten drawers per cabinet. Marisa heads straight to an easel on our left, holding a large painting of a surreal, multi-colored fantasy scene that includes an androgynous white-haired male rising from a pedestal of crystals, two acolytes gazing at him in awe, and a golden boy hovering overhead via some sort of Da Vinci-type flying device. "Oh Lord,

Marisa, don't look at that. I painted it years and years ago, I can't believe how flat-out crappy a painter I was then. That was the cover art for my first *Distant Soil* graphic novel."

"I recognize it," Marisa says.

"Oh goodie! Well, I'm re-releasing the book but I won't do it until I've painted a much better cover."

Colleen says she prefers working with pencil. She and Marisa discuss the nuanced differences of artistic utensils while I set up the shoot. Then I convince the women to end their pow-wow, and Colleen takes a seat at her drafting table. Marisa stands off to the side, black sketchbook clutched in her left hand, eyes begging a question. This is the first time I've had somebody with me when shooting a video, and I realize I don't know what to do with my daughter. "I'm sure you can sit there if you want," I say, pointing to my left at an office chair. She opts to sit cross-legged on the Oriental rug.

Colleen gives me an unsolicited overview of her work space, sparing no detail. She is a talker. Perhaps she's just starved for an audience. I tell her how grateful we are that she's met us here today in such a lovely part of Virginia.

"It doesn't get more secluded than this," she says. "It's pretty inspiring as an artist, being here in the country, but you'd better enjoy your own company. It's so peaceful, and so low stress, that now when I go into a city I'm kind of like, 'God, look at all these people, and they're all barking at each other, and why is that man honking his horn?'"

"In D.C.," I say, "every licensed driver is legally required to honk at least once every hour."

"In New York I think it's every ten minutes. There are other challenges to living out here. Last night some skunk let fly right outside the house. I don't know if you all have that problem." I shake my head. "They like to come up near the house because we have yellow jacket nests and they love to eat them. But something scared that dude at 4:30 a.m. and that stink filled the house and I'm like, 'Man!'"

I turn to see if Marisa is as delighted by Colleen as I am. My daughter is laser-focused, her pencil in flight across a sketchbook page. I can't remember a time when Marisa wasn't drawing.

"Colleen, when did you know you wanted to be an artist?"

"When I was five years old I entered this contest to draw a Valentine's Day card for Mickey Mouse, and I won and I said, 'Well, that was easy.'" She was living in the Tidewater region of Virginia at the time. When she was about twelve, she read a friend's comic book collection and was hooked. "I started going to sci-fi conventions, comic book conventions and art shows," she says, and landed her first drawing job through an editor she met at a show when she was fifteen, the same age Marisa is now.

"My first comic, one I wrote myself, wasn't published until I was nineteen," she says, pointing at the painting. "That was *A Distant Soil.*" Colleen struggled with her publisher over the rights to her own work, a conflict that dragged through the courts for years until Colleen finally prevailed. This is, of course, a story my funders do not want me to tell. The new threat to her livelihood, she says, is people stealing and selling her book's images online. That is exactly the type of predatory behavior the legislation being introduced next month is intended to target. This could be the video that will justify this trip to my board of directors. As Colleen describes her vigorous pursuit of her infringers, she brings to that task the same tireless dedication that led her to become a published author while still a teenager. I tell her how impressed I am with her commitment to everything she does, from drawing to growing food to going after bad guys online.

"I don't know where that comes from," she says. "But those folks who steal my stuff don't understand all the work that goes into that. I don't remember the last time I met somebody who had a day job who was working until three in the morning, or who sat at their desk so long that when they tried to get up their legs wouldn't work and they had to crawl to the bathroom. But I've done that, and I've done it more than once. I know about hard work. I live on a farm. You can see I live on a farm. Look at all the farminess! I grow my own food, I plow my own fields, I do my own cultivating, blah, blah, blah. If I have one more person come up to me and give me any BS about how real work is doing labor, I'm going to smack them silly."

I had planned to ask Colleen the question I've been asking on Marisa's behalf—the one about advice for young artists—but Marisa's already hearing everything she could need to know. Then Colleen catches me off guard.

"You know what? I just had me a little midlife crisis. I had a lot of trouble working. I really hit a wall. Bad. So I decided to take a year off and go back to art school. I'm only just now coming out of my slump, working with the same intensity I was working with fifteen years ago. Drawing had become a job, but now it's also a passion again."

She is looking at my daughter while she says this, but I feel like she is staring inside of me. Colleen burned out creatively and needed a recharge. My creativity has lain dormant. I'm at midlife, to borrow a word from Colleen, but I don't know if I'm mentally strong enough to upend that life.

"Can I talk or what?"Colleen says. Perhaps I appear lost in thought. I smile and nod. She talks some more, I film it, and then I tell her I have more than enough and turn off the camera.

"Want to see something I'm working on?"she says after I put the camera away. I say yes. Marisa sits up, craning her neck. "Come on over, honey," she says to Marisa, "I don't bite."Colleen slides open a drawer and pulls out an illustration with three frames stacked vertically, each showing a ship arriving in New York harbor, the first from the 19th Century, the second the 20th, and the third one in the future. It's from a graphic novel she's illustrating for a highly successful author. She points to the top illustration, a three-mast sailing ship. "Every detail, every sail and every rope, is authentic. When I draw, whether it's historical or fantasy, I want to capture it on paper exactly as if I'm seeing it firsthand."

"It's... beautiful,"Marisa says.

"Well, that's a great reaction," Colleen says. "Yippee! Your daddy tells me you want to be an artist."Marisa nods. Colleen liberates Marisa's sketchbook from her hands and I steal a peek at the contents as it passes. It's been quite a while since my daughter has shared her art with me. In the sketch Marisa has captured Colleen, not just her appearance but her fiery spirit. Every detail of the scene is rendered vividly in spare but telling strokes.

"This ain't bad, sweetie," Colleen says. "What pencil did you use?"Marisa holds up a yellow Dixon Ticonderoga No. 2. "Oh Lordy, girl, a proper artist must have the proper tools."Colleen slips a hand into a basket mounted under her drafting table and emerges with a bundle of black pencils wrapped in a green rubber band. "Here, this will get you started. There's a good assortment in there, professional drafting pencils for all types of shading."Before handing the pencils to Marisa she thrusts the sharpened tips in my face. "Come on, Dad, help a girl out here."

Marisa looks at the pencils, then back at Colleen, and says thank you with a note of tenderness I haven't heard in a year.

We head back to the car. This time my daughter leaves her ear buds in her purse, a worn bag decorated with Tim Burton-sketched skeletons. She opens her sketchbook to a blank page and quickly leaves me again for a world she creates with her new pencils. I am left alone with my thoughts, of how I arrived here viewing Colleen as a future Marisa—and still do—but I also see the professional who decided to reboot her life as a would-be me. I watch for a sign that will lead me back to the highway. Three interviews await us tomorrow, if I can think of me and my companion on this trip as a collective pronoun.

AUGUST 19: NORTH CAROLINA

Elliot Mazer won't work with me. The music producer has been in the business for decades, so he knows what language my funders want. But every time I bring up copyright he changes the subject back to himself and his past glories. In fairness, however, he does this with every other question I ask him as well.

I thank him for the interview and imagine the edited version. I'll include some discussion about how he's produced many of Neil Young's seminal albums, but perhaps—because viewers might think him arrogant—I'll leave out the part where he says the singer and guitarist wouldn't be where he is today without Elliot's expertise with a sound board. I'll include discussion of his life now, here in Reidsville, North Carolina, just south of the Virginia border. How he's converted the stately dining room of this grand old home into a state-of-the-art studio. And how he's using that studio in his semi-retirement to produce albums for clients who find him online.

I'm okay with this interview being a disappointment, because I have another one to shoot, here in this home with his wife, Diana Reid Haig. Elliot and I leave the high-ceilinged front parlor and walk down the home's front hallway, across the worn oak floors, past the antique brass gas-style wall lamps, below the dental plaster molding framing the pressed tin ceiling. Halfway down the hall he slips into his studio and I keep going. As I enter the kitchen, a wooden floorboard creaks under my foot. Marisa, seated with Diana at a small round table, slams her sketch book shut. One of the pencils Colleen Doran gave her yesterday rolls off the table onto the parquet floor.

"Oh here, sweetie, let me get that for you."Diana slips gracefully out of her chair and retrieves the pencil as she stands. She reaches down and presses straight the skirt of her blue sundress. Marisa takes the pencil from her.

"Thank Diana," I say to Marisa.

"Oh, that's not necessary. Your daughter is so charming and polite,"

Diana says, as if boasting about a favorite granddaughter. She's describing the Marisa I once knew, not the teenager I live with now. I decide to celebrate the fact that Marisa did not alienate our host during the hour I was interviewing Diana's husband. "How did it go with Elliot?"

"Great," I lie. "Are you still up for an interview?"

"Oh, why not," she says with a smile.

When it was decided I would interview Elliot first, Diana immediately volunteered to "entertain" Marisa in the kitchen. Elliot clearly won't be playing the same role during my interview with Diana. I recall how quiet Marisa was during my interview yesterday with Colleen, and how much she seemed to get out of being present for it. "Marisa, do you want to join us?"

Marisa looks down at her notebook, and then shakes her head no.

Diana places her hand gently on Marisa's right shoulder. "I think she probably just wants to keep sketching. She's a brilliant artist, Patrick. You should see the still life she just did. Show your father, Marisa."

I step forward. Marisa would in the past show me some of her drawings, but the person she most wanted to share with was my mother. I don't know who she shares her art with now, or even what art she is producing. I've had opportunities to peek at her work—like everything else she owns, she leaves her sketchbooks all over the house —but I've resisted. It isn't the same if she doesn't show me. I'm not sure this counts, with Diana insisting she do so. But I'll take the opportunity nonetheless. I see on the page the fruit bowl centerpiece. Two bananas, a peach, and an orange emerge from the blue ceramic bowl. The fruit is depicted accurately, but there's more to it than that. It's as if Marisa has added some spark of life to the display. The banana in the foreground appears to be calling to me to choose it over its bowl mates.

"Marisa, that is quite good. Diana is right."

"Oh, your daughter is so talented. She told me all about her love of drawing, and especially of photography. And she's so thrilled you're taking her to Savannah to tour the art school there. She's lucky to have a father like you."

Now my discomfort level matches that of my daughter. I nod to Diana to join me in the hall.

"Marisa," Diana says as we leave the kitchen, "don't forget that I'm sending you two on your way with blueberry muffins. I won't take no for an answer."

We return to the front parlor. I had seated Elliot in a wing-back chair, but I want to film Diana in a separate part of the room. She suggests the bench in front of the upright piano.

"You said this house dates back generations in your family," I say as I set up the camera. "And I can't help but notice that your last name is Reid, and the town's name is Reidsville."

Diana laughs. "Yes, I am local royalty, if you will. But my branch is the black sheep. My grandmother built this house at what was then outside of town. We're still viewed as the splinter line."

I nod knowingly, but don't inform her I also grew up with black-sheep parents. We begin the interview. Diana discusses her early career as a songwriter in New York, Nashville and Los Angeles. She grew up surrounded by music, and it was in that professional world that she met Elliot. She turns and places her left hand on the keys behind her. "I remember when I was young, my piano teacher, at this very piano, told me that when I play, I'm putting my hands in the same position as that composer's hands. That made the music come alive to me. It's like a living link to the past, stepping into someone else's shoes."

Diana has written a series of travel books that guide the reader along the same paths followed by famous people in their cities of origin. If you've ever been curious about where Napoleon or his wife Josephine passed the time in Paris, her books will take you there. I've been reading a fair amount of travel literature as I've prepared for this trip, and I didn't come across any other works that are so original in concept.

"That's not unlike the books you write."

"Yes, you're right, although I've never really thought of it that way. You know, that first book about Napoleon grew out of a personal obsession. I love Paris, and when I was there I'd seek those places out. Often they're very hard to find, so I'd jot down directions to share with others. But believe it or not, I found the people I knew, in the music business, weren't that eager to talk about Napoleon. I'd bring him up and I could see my friends kind of back away and say, 'Oh there she goes again.'"

That's my experience when I try to share with Washington lobbyists my passion for antique maps. With these books, Diana found a way to convey her passion to like-minded readers. A perforated ulcer laid her up in bed for close to a year, she tells me, so to keep busy she compiled her travel notes into a book. It didn't take long for her to find a publisher, and she's since written more books about Paris. Her new project is a book about Jacqueline Kennedy Onassis' lifelong love affair with New York City. The Kennedy family has given her access to some of the former first lady's personal records.

I tell her about meeting Michael Swanwick in Philadelphia, and how he turned a personal obsession about a poet into a published biography. Then I ask what her friends in the music business think of her books.

"It's been very interesting to see how people perceive different forms of creativity, the songs I've written and my books. It's a different reaction. It seems to me that people really admire it when you can make something up, like with my songs. But I love writing nonfiction. It's my passion now. It's what I think about when I wake up in the morning. You just need to find your own compass."

I like that metaphor, and not just because I love the artistry found in an antique map's compass rose. I picture Diana, an artist who reinvented herself late in life, gliding along the cobblestones of a tucked-away Parisian lane, sunlight glistening on her copper hair. I see her bursting with excitement, a skip in her step as she explores, then her stopping to pull out a notebook from her purse so she can jot down her latest discovery.

We discuss the mysteries of the creative process some more and then I wrap up, not distressed that we haven't really discussed copyright law. I secure the camera in its bag. Diana remains on the piano bench, a mischievous gleam in her eye.

"I assume you're writing a book about this trip, right?" she asks.

I feel as if she's caught me stealing a banana from her bowl. I realize now that my subconscious has been toying with the idea since that first day in New England. My resistance stems from the fact that I can't figure out how to write a book about my travels without putting me in it. I think of other road-trip authors like John Steinbeck and Jack Kerouac and William Least Heat Moon and Robert Pirsig. They invite you to join them in their journey. Steinbeck, an old crank longing for an America he feels is lost. Kerouac, living without fear of consequences. Heat Moon, learning and healing from those he meets along the way. And Pirsig, who slowly reveals his struggle with mental illness. That last one hits perhaps too close to home.

"You absolutely must write this story," she says. "What you're doing is so, well, different. I'd love to be Marisa, to ride along with you, even if only for a few days."

We head back to the kitchen. Rain pelts the bay window over the sink, a barrage of liquid bullets. Marisa and I will have to brave a run across the street to the car. Diana offers us umbrellas, a gesture I immediately reject. I don't mean to dismiss Southern hospitality, but we'd have no opportunity to return them.

Elliot remains in his studio, but Diana offers us a farewell. She thanks me for the interview before I can thank her. Then she gives Marisa a full-body embrace. I watch for my daughter to flinch, but she does not. Her arms go up, and her red sketch book wraps around our host. Then Marisa and I dash to the car. Once safely inside the vehicle, only moderately drenched, Marisa says, "Um, Dad," and points out my driver's side window.

Diana is rushing across the street, a bag in one hand and a red umbrella in the other. I lower the window.

"You forgot the muffins," she says over the sound of the sheeting rain bombarding the umbrella's nylon.

"You didn't have to do this," I say, but I take the muffins.

"I wouldn't let you leave without them," she says. "It's the least I could do, after your gift of letting me talk about my creativity."

Diana heads back to her family home, I close the window, and then turn to Marisa. She's smiling and shaking her head.

"What the hell was she thinking?" Marisa says. "That is so nice, and so ridiculous."

"You know," I tell her, "I've stopped being surprised by things on this trip."

. . .

We slice west through the rain toward Asheville, North Carolina. I'm taking Marisa tomorrow to the Biltmore Estate, a summer home for one of the Vanderbilts. It seemed like a good place to give Marisa a tourism experience and, perhaps, make up for having done so little with her during our family vacation on the Jersey Shore. To justify the drive, I booked an interview with an artist nearby.

Marisa and I chuckle over how sweet Diana is. She then tells me that Diana spent most of their time together in the kitchen encouraging Marisa to pursue her passion for art. That was unnecessary. Art is the only thing that motivates Marisa to apply herself. Then Marisa falls silent, and I see her eyes are focused on a highway sign. It tells us we have forty-seven miles to go before we reach Asheville. But it also says we are one hundred and sixty-three miles from Knoxville, Tennessee. Marisa emits a low growl, puts her ear buds back in, and then flips open her sketch book.

I didn't realize that this highway could lead me to my parents' home. I consider the possibility of pushing on to Knoxville for a surprise visit with my parents. Perhaps that is the way to mend this latest rift. I ended the last one, after all, by calling them with news of Marisa's impending birth. Maybe this time having Marisa in tow would do the trick. Since we left their house in the middle of the night a year ago, Marisa has finished her first year of high school. She's knocking at the door of womanhood. But my mother knows that without me visiting. That call fifteen years ago delivered news unknown to her.

I almost drove another route to Knoxville in January of this year. I was attending a conference hosted by one of my funders at the Gaylord

Opryland Resort in Nashville. While seeking a quiet moment under a palm tree in the resort's glass-enclosed garden conservatory, my mobile phone rang. It was my mother.

"Your father's having a hard time breathing. I'm taking him to the hospital now."

Somehow I had been expecting a call like this. And here I was, I thought, back in Tennessee for the first time since that August night five months earlier. "I'm in Nashville, Mom. I can rent a car and be there in two hours."

"I doubt your father would want to see you, but hold on. I'll call you from the hospital."And she hung up.

I felt as if the marrow had been drained from my bones. I made my way to a hotel bar, a dark, low-ceilinged establishment that cocooned my fear. An hour later the phone rang again. I quickly put down my scotch and answered.

"He's fine. False alarm."

"I'm glad. I can still come."

"I don't know why we'd want you here."

I took a sip of scotch. How often had I held this conversation in my mind? Hundreds, probably. Each time I tried a different approach. The only commonality was that each ended disastrously.

"Mom, I think we should talk."I forged ahead. "The last time we found ourselves like this, Marisa's birth brought us back together. Well, Marisa and Parker still need grandparents."

"She'd have to apologize first."

Already I was thrown off-script. "You mean Marisa? What would she be apologizing for?"

"For starters, she defriended me on Facebook."

I placed the phone down on the bar, careful not to disconnect the call. I needed a moment to process my mother's demand, and the reason for it. My motion caught the bartender's eye, and he pointed at my near-empty glass. Ordering another round had not been my intent, but I nodded.

Two weeks after the kids and I returned from Knoxville last August, Laura took me to a psychologist she trusted. I wanted to better understand my mother, to learn how I could repair this latest rift or, at a minimum, discuss with my children what had happened. It didn't take him long to assess my situation. He mapped out our relationship on a whiteboard. Various boxes represented me, Laura, Marisa, Parker, my mother, and my father.

"Your mother is a classic narcissist. This is how she views her world," he said. He drew circles that placed all of the boxes in orbit around my mother. "She is basically frozen as a child, the center of everything and all drama magnified. Perhaps some trauma when she was young locked her into that mindset. It's an appealing place to be, the center of attention and no responsibilities. You've empowered her mindset your whole life, and it sounds like your father began to do so when she let him back into her life all those years ago." He then erased the circles and drew straight lines connecting various boxes. Only one line extended from my father's box. It connected with my mother. Laura, Marisa, and Parker were all connected to me via dry-erase marker strokes. These two clusters—my parents and my nuclear family—were joined by a single line between my mother and me. I couldn't reach my father separate from my mother. And she couldn't reach my children separate from me.

"You're the nexus, Patrick," the psychologist said.

"I don't want to be."

"It's not a matter of want. If your children are to have a relationship with your mother, it has to go through you."

In that Opryland bar I took a sip of my new glass of scotch and thought of that whiteboard diagram. Before that night, my mother had a line connecting her with my daughter. It was social media. Marisa had erased that line, and I knew she had no interest in re-drawing it. I picked up the phone again, assuming the responsibility I was evading. "Mom, I hear what you're saying. But I think Marisa would want something from you as well. Not an apology," I said quickly, anticipating an objection by my mother to a word she associated with surrender and defeat, "but perhaps an explanation. You could explain to her you didn't mean some of the things you said, some of the things she heard you say."

"What? That I wanted to keep her safe from her crazy father, who could snap and hurt her in a heartbeat?"

There are a number of fathers who could have been in her mind at that moment other than me. My father, who never physically harmed me but had on several occasions committed significant damage to inanimate objects such as drywall and bathroom doors. My mother's biological father who, like mine, left when she was young, but unlike mine did not return. Or her stepfather, of whom my mother spoke with an unsettling combination of love and disgust. I couldn't know where my mother's mind was at that moment—I never knew such things—but what was clear was that she had spent the last few months completely recasting in her memory the events of that night. She was the saint who had struggled valiantly to protect her grandchildren from a demonic father. I knew my father would have retained a memory of the evening's actual events. But the only box he was connected to on the psychologist's whiteboard was my mother. I could not expect him to support a more accurate version of events. He would do everything he could to keep from having that solitary line erased.

I did not drive to Knoxville that day at the Gaylord hotel. I stayed in that bar. I do not recall how many drinks I had, but it was not enough to fill, for even a moment, the places where my marrow had been drained.

We pass the highway sign directing us to Knoxville and I look over at my daughter. I've never told her about that January call with her grandmother. I consider acknowledging the sign, using it as a way to get her to talk to me about that night, and about the loss she has suffered the last year. She's trapped in the car now, no way to walk away from my questions. But I'm feeling a connection with her that is rare and refreshing. I don't want to ruin it by bullying her into confronting a pain she is actively avoiding.

As I reach the outskirts of Asheville, I develop another plan to engage her. When I booked the interview with percussionist Paul Babelay, he told me he lived in a wooded area on a steep mountain slope, and the road that led up that mountain was extremely hard to spot. The GPS tells me I'm getting close. I hand Marisa printed directions provided by Paul. "Marisa, I need you to play navigator."

Marisa removes her left ear bud and takes the paper. "There's supposed to be a turn on the right," I tell her, "but he says it will be hard to find."

The road I'm on hugs a cutout of mountainside. On the GPS screen it appears as a solid patch of green, no black lines penetrating the block of color. Marisa leans forward, squinting.

"There it is!"Somehow her artist's eye has perceived a thin break in the pines. I come nearly to a stop, then wonder if it was wise to lose the car's momentum. The slope is steep and the road isn't paved. I press the car forward. As we move under the tree canopy, the sound of pelting rain is replaced by pings of gravel kicking up against the car's undercarriage. My distress is lessened when I see the smile on Marisa's face, a rare sight in the last year.

"Marisa, that was fabulous. I never would have spotted that on my own." My compliment has the added advantage of being sincere. As we climb, we pass one mailbox, then another. Thin strips of clearing extend left and right past each one. Then I see Paul's house, tucked away in the pines. The main floor extends out off the mountain into space, with a basement level supporting the right half of the house. A wide porch extends the length of the home in front of us, then turns a sharp left to extend along the drop-off. We step out of the car.

"You just missed a bear. Tiger is still a bit freaked out."

A thin man about my age places a fat tabby down on the porch. The cat shakes slightly, looks directly at Marisa and me, then walks off, tail erect, twitching slightly. We head inside, and I interview Paul in his living room in front of a massive stone fireplace while Marisa sketches. Her subject is Tiger, who stares at us through a glass door. Paul discusses his choice to pursue a musical career here in Asheville rather than Nashville. He and his wife have built a good life here for their children, and he is willing to take the work he can get so as not to disturb that life. I can relate. As a single father I turned down reporting jobs that would have had me covering Capitol Hill debates long into the evening because it would have caused havoc with my custody schedule.

Paul says his life choices have not prevented him from exploring his true passion. It's called a vibraphone, which he says is similar to a xylophone but more compelling. I ask him to elaborate but fail to listen to the response. It's as if my mind is being tugged out of my head, pulled west into a different orbit. I am in my mother's office in Knoxville. I am in the Gaylord bar in Nashville. Boxes and lines swirl on a whiteboard. I look again at Marisa. Somehow Tiger has re-entered the house and is now on Marisa's lap, forcing her to hold the sketchbook in the air above him. She doesn't appear distressed by this inconvenience. What terrible act would Marisa have to perform that would lead me to cut her out of my life? What harm would she have to inflict to have me turn my back on her, a person I have dedicated my life to fostering? I come up blank.

Marisa has been unwilling to speak of that Knoxville night with me. But what have I really said to her? Have I shared with her the depth of the pain I feel at losing my parents? No. Because I haven't fully admitted it's there. I have been performing the family tradition of denying what is right in front of me. Sabra Field told me the art-committed life is a difficult one, and many choose the easier path. The easy road—in creativity and in family dynamics—is one with which I am all too familiar. I know without looking at the camera's diagnostic display that I have enough footage. It's time to leave. It's time for Marisa and me to spend a little more time together, to search out dinner and the hotel in our respective roles of parent and child. I'm eager to do so.

AUGUST 20: NORTH CAROLINA
AND SOUTH CAROLINA

I am content. Marisa is not. This library fills me with warmth and comfort despite its cavernous size. The Biltmore Estate tour guide tells me the forty-feet by sixty-feet room holds ten thousand books written in eight languages. It is the largest privately owned library in the country. But what speaks to me is not the volume of books. It is the reverence in which the room holds them. The tour guide focuses on the ceiling painting, an Eighteenth Century mural by Giovanni Pelligrini that George Vanderbilt actually paid to relocate from a palace in Italy. But my eyes are not drawn to gods and cherubs dwelling in a cloud. Nor are they directed to the massive fireplace that runs the length of the two-tiered room, its black mantel blending in with the dark walnut bookcases running on both levels. No, my focus is on the multitude of books, leather-bound with gold-lined spines. Did Vanderbilt realize that by creating the grandest possible private library, the room itself could serve to humble him, showing him as just one man surrounded by the mental output of thousands? Whatever the answer, he is long gone, but the books remain.

Marisa fell into a funk once the tour began and the docent said no photographs were allowed indoors. As we've entered each room, I've watched as her hand flicked to her camera bag then slowly lowered, as if the bones in her arm had liquefied.

The docent tells us that Vanderbilt owned nearly thirty thousand books in all, three times what we see here. I understand the challenge of being able to display all of the books you own, even the modest number I've accumulated. In fact, I came close to solving that problem once by intending to rid myself of most of them. It took nearly two years for my ex-wife and me to resolve our custody battle. I managed to secure three nights a week with Marisa and Parker. To approximate as closely as possible a family experience for them, I moved us from my bachelor apartment to a three-level, three-bedroom detached home in a quiet northern Virginia suburb. In what I now recognize as a bout of manic spending—always a risk for someone with my diagnosis—I furnished every room. But the legal cost of securing that custody schedule produced unanticipated debt. After a year I couldn't afford to keep renting the house. I knew things needed to change when I found myself acting out a cliché, actually digging under couch cushions for loose change so I could buy bread and milk for my children. I did in fact produce enough change, and ignored the fury of the woman behind me in line at the supermarket as I slowly counted out what I owed.

The only way to begin the climb out of debt was to relocate to a small apartment. That meant nearly all of the furniture I acquired had to go, but I hoped to make a little cash by selling it at a yard sale. I gave the kids the apartment's one bedroom, yet it was still too small for their two beds, so I sold them at a severe loss and bought a bunk bed. Marisa played the older child card and took the top bunk, but Parker seemed to like the cocoon-like environment formed underneath when Marisa's sheet hung down over the side. I placed my bed in the living room in the space meant for a dinette set, something else I had sold. I purchased a collapsible card table and folding chairs that I would set up by my bed for meals. My first year in the apartment the custody agreement had the children with me for Thanksgiving. I gathered up a number of my coffee-table books of antique maps and placed them on the bed. Each held one of the sides—mashed potatoes, peas, candied yams, the fruit ambrosia my mother always made for that meal—and my nightstand held the turkey.

I found a use that day for books I ended up not selling. When I conducted the yard sale—a key element of what I called The Simplification, the initial caps visible in my mind even now—most of my books were on display, from suspense novels bought on impulse at airports to first-edition biographies acquired through extensive explorations of used bookstores. The books were of course cheaper and more portable than a 7-piece dinette set or a set of beds, and began moving quickly. As a customer brought to me for purchase a cherished biography of the English clockmaker who made possible the calculation of longitude at sea, I realized there are only so many sacrifices that are acceptable in life. About thirty minutes into the official time of the sale, I covered the books in sheets to ensure they were off-limits. They traveled with me to the small apartment, but were not displayed in two-story walnut bookcases. Instead I stacked them on any free section of floor. My display aesthetic may have been lacking, but my reverence for those books was no less than Vanderbilt's was for his.

We are ushered out of the library to make room for the next tour group, and soon enough we are back outside, walking down the wide stone steps to the gravel drive in front of the mansion. I squint, adjusting to the sunlight after an hour spent in near-darkness. When my vision clears I see Marisa has already removed her camera. In front of us is a large expanse of green lawn. To the right lie acres of flowers and fountains we had darted past on our way to the mansion. Marisa looks at me, I nod, and she is off to the garden.

I catch up with her a few minutes later. She is shaded under a vine-covered trellis, standing precariously several feet up on the edge of a fountain. It appears she's trying to capture a close-up of a cherub pouring water. She's resting her left hand on the wet stone behind the cherub, and I imagine several scenarios that have in common a disastrous ending.

"What are you doing?" I call out.

"I'm trying to freeze a drop of water against the contours of the stone behind it," Marisa says without looking. "It's tricky with this camera, I'm stuck with the built-in lens, there aren't a lot of settings and it seems to have been designed by chimps. But I've struggled with it enough to sometimes fool it into getting the exposure level I want with the focus range I need."

I rush to her side while she takes a few more photographs. Then she permits me to support her by the arm as I guide her back to the ground. She turns instantly to her camera's screen to examine her handiwork.

"Can I see?"

She pauses, then turns the camera display my direction. I see an image too real to be real, a glistening drop of water broadcasting a hint of rainbow from the morning sun. The photograph's tranquility momentarily washes away the scorching August heat.

Marisa's latest passion is photography, and for her fifteenth birthday she had asked for a something called a digital single-lens reflex camera, or DSLR. They turned out to be pretty expensive, nearly as pricey as the laptop I'm using to edit these films. I couldn't pull the trigger on such an expensive gift. So after I said no she gathered up her cash and bought this camera used. It's not a true DSLR, but apparently she's spent the last few months trying to figure out how to get it to do what she wants anyway.

I like to think I have done my part to foster her creative development. But that has mostly been through encouragement. As Colleen Doran said two days ago, an artist needs the right tools. But Marisa's will to create trumps her technical limitations. And perhaps it is will that is the most important thing. I no longer sleep in the living room of a one-bedroom apartment. I cut expenses and took on extra work, and clawed my way out of debt. My parents helped with that, in part by adhering to my request to honor my birthday and Christmas by making donations to college funds I had set up for Marisa and Parker to which I could no longer afford to contribute. I remain grateful for their assistance, even if the amount they provided has continued to balloon in my mother's mind. Then, after I knew I would not be a financial burden on a partner, I remarried. Two years ago Laura and I purchased a three-level, three-bedroom home in a quiet northern Virginia suburb. We bought Marisa a new bed, but Parker insisted upon keeping the bunk bed. He still sleeps on the bottom, and keeps a sheet on the unused upper bunk, which I sometimes find hanging down, cocooning him. It's good that Marisa experienced that life arc, seeing her father fight his way out of a personal setback. I suspect she has focused a fair amount in the past year on what genetic inheritance she may have received from her grandmother, both artistic and mental. I don't know what questions she asks herself about genetic hand-me-downs from her father. She overheard my mother that night. She knows I have struggled with bipolar disorder. She knows I impregnated a girl as a teenager, and paid for it to be aborted. But she has also seen something in both her father—and her grandparents— that should hearten her. Resiliency. Or perhaps stubbornness. My mother has always demonstrated an unwavering determination to overcome obstacles through sheer force of will. I have never ceased to admire that about her. Perhaps unwavering fortitude is part of Marisa's genetic destiny.

. . .

As we leave the Biltmore estate a road sign informs us that turning right leads to Charleston, South Carolina. A left brings us to Knoxville, Tennessee. I glance at Marisa, who smiles in agreement as I make the right turn. As the driver, I control the car speakers, so I fire up my portable music player as I start down the interstate. After a minute of not hearing any music I glance down at the player and see the screen is frozen. I fiddle with it, turning it on and off with my right hand while my left holds the steering wheel. Such multitasking is reckless, I know, but I am compelled to bring this device back to life. It is unthinkable that I am facing three weeks of lengthy drives with no recorded music to distract me. I filled this player specifically for this trip, hundreds of hours of rock, blues, and gospel to provide energy and classical to wind me down. My record-label and music-publisher members would be pleased to know that all of the music was acquired legally. But now that is all gone.

Thoughts race. Bile rises in my throat. I hear my doctor's voice reminding me of the importance of staying calm in the face of the unexpected. I do not feel calm. I want to take this thin metal contraption with its brand name frozen on the front screen and hurl it out the car window. I want to whip the car into a violent U-turn and thread through the oncoming traffic so I can smash the unfaithful plastic player under two tons of unforgiving steel. Instead I glance at Marisa. Lost in her own music, she has not detected my growing rage. Nor do I wish her to. I focus on the road ahead, counting the white highway dashes whizzing by on the left the way I used to count letters when I would pyramid as a child. The repeated flicks of paint dance across my mind in a rhythmic staccato. My heartbeat synchronizes with the beat, then my breathing joins in harmony.

When my father would realize he was on the verge of a manic

outburst, he often would flee to his car. My mother and I would wait, sometimes for hours. When he returned, he was back to his calm, medicated self, and we would all pretend that life was normal. I am approaching an approximation of normalcy now, at least well enough that I can fake it with my daughter. I point to the music player on her lap, then speak loudly.

"Do you want to play that through the car speakers?"

She pulls out her left ear bud, I repeat the question, and she smiles.

"Really? You don't mind?"

"I'd like to hear what you're listening to."

For the next three hours she flicks through her music library, informing me of when she discovered this song or that artist while explaining how her musical tastes have developed. I tell her what I like about what she's playing, as well as what I dislike. I'm surprised at how much of it I enjoy. There's a darkness to a lot of her music, minor chords and lyrics dripping with pathos. It is a stark contrast to the music popular when I was a teenager, bouncy pop tunes by Boy George and Cyndi Lauper. But then again I didn't listen to those artists. Some of the music from my childhood is on that dead music player, including moody works by Pink Floyd. And, from what Marisa tells me, her music isn't what is popular now.

"Oh, you've got to hear this song," she says, repeatedly pressing a button. "It's a giveaway tune that was already on the player."

An acoustic guitar opens to a wholesome male voice.

"The world... is made of energy. And the world... is electricity. And the world... is made of energy. And there's a light inside of you, and there's a light inside of me."

The dark complexities that have filled the passenger cabin are washed away by this sunshiny folk tune. I wince, and begin to seriously question my daughter's musical taste. Then I hear it, rising above the music. Marisa is actively suppressing laughter. I glance at her and see those blue eyes squinting as a smile extends upwards from the edges of her mouth, the same expression she had a year ago as we watched that dancer on my mother's television.

"What a lovely song," I say. "I can see why you like it so much, Marisa. It's so moving. So insightful. And so true!"

Marisa's laugh finally explodes.

Music was central to our time together when she was young. When I first moved out of her mother's house I bought her a pink cassette player to have at my apartment. She would fall asleep to Disney soundtracks. Of course, kids can listen to the same music over and over again, at least as much as I listened to *Dark Side of the Moon* as a teenager. The tapes weren't just her bedtime accompaniment. They'd play in the car when I drove her to school, or at the table when I fed her dinner. Those tunes burrowed into my brain without invitation, and sometimes I would snap. Unlike my father's pre-lithium explosions, I instead embraced a more creative response. I would make up goofy lyrics and sing them loudly over the Disney talent.

I find myself doing that now: "And the world… is made of angry bees. And the world… is made of nasty fleas. And the world… is full of underpants trees. And there are leafy shorts on you and there are leafy shorts on me."

Now she's bent over, gripping her side. Apparently she didn't mind that the word "underpants"has too many syllables to perfectly parallel the song's meter. Then she pulls out her phone and begins to text. I had her, for a moment, but now she's fallen into her virtual world, a place without fathers. Yet, after some frantic typing, she resurfaces.

"I just got a text from Brian."

All I know about Brian is what little intel Parker has provided me. Brian is one of Marisa's classmates. From what I gather she is fond of him, but he is like many boys in his early teen years, not fully focused yet on girls. I am very pleased with this and hope he stays that way for some time. But she has never spoken his name around me.

"Brian," Marisa says, "wrote that any dad who imagines underpants trees has to be the coolest dad there is."

I fix my eyes on the road so Marisa can't see how close I am to tears. "Text Brian that he is an excellent judge of character."

Before I know it I see a sign reading CHARLESTON 18 MILES. But my focus is on the sky above, which has turned black as night even though it's still a couple of hours away from sunset. We're scheduled in an hour to interview John Smoak, a jack-of-all-trades photographer. He wants to be filmed outside his home on a small island in

Charleston Harbor. I question the wisdom of that desire when a clap of thunder rips over the car. Traffic slows. Moments later we are under assault.

"Is that... hail?"

Marisa's right. It's August, in the South, and yet, somehow, frozen rain is pelting our car.

I hand Marisa my phone. "Could you find John Smoak's number and give him a call? We're probably going to be late, and we'll have to film him indoors."

Marisa takes the phone, flips through my directory, and calls. I don't know where the shy girl is who sat quietly on Colleen Doran's rug two days ago. I only hear her side of the conversation, but they talk as if they're old friends.

"Dad, he says he'd like to do the interview tomorrow morning, say around nine. It's supposed to be clear then, and we could still shoot outside."

I run the math in my head. Tomorrow is all about Savannah. We're meeting Meghan Woodcock, an instructor at the Savannah College of Art and Design, in the early afternoon. But the drive from Charleston isn't that long.

"Okay, Marisa, tell John that's fine."

The exit ramp drops us onto the edge of old Charleston. I find myself driving through flooded streets. The water level rises on either side of the car.

"Oh my God," Marisa says. "Can we get to the hotel?"

We're only three blocks away, but it's a reasonable question. This rental is a basic sedan with no ground clearance to speak of. And it's a hybrid. I know little about these kinds of cars, but it's generally not good to get batteries wet. I refuse to fail, however. This day has been perfect, and I'm not letting a literal freak of nature—frozen rain on a hot summer day—destroy it. We press forward, deeper into the water. Marisa squeals, I believe more in delight than fear. Waves erupt from both sides of the car like a crystalline angel's wings. And then we're clear, the road rising just enough to allow us to emerge.

The motel parking lot is a lake. At least three dozen parked cars soak in water, the tires very nearly submerged. I locate the highest

93

ground, far from the building, and park. Fortunately the hail has shifted to rain. I offer Marisa an umbrella but she declines. Instead she leaps from the safety of the car and runs straight into the lake, kicking the water with her sandal-covered feet. "Come on, Dad!"

She'll be drenched. She must know that. Now Marisa runs in circles near the entrance of the motel. I watch her, experiencing the secondary buzz of her joy, soaking it in the way I do the creativity-driven enthusiasm of my interview subjects. I'm still holding the umbrella. I'm still safe and sound in the car. And then I'm not. I leave the umbrella behind. Rain soaks my shirt as I run to join her. My pace slows as the water level reaches my calf. Then I reach her. In one smooth motion she guides her arm down to the water and up again, splashing toward my face. I smile and return the favor. An older woman with well-coiffed hair glares at us through the lobby window. Let her judge.

AUGUST 21: SOUTH CAROLINA AND GEORGIA

Everything is a blur. I don't see John Smoak, or the marsh behind him. The screen shows nothing but white. The humidity this Saturday morning is as thick as grits, and it has enveloped my video camera's lens. But John remains calm. It will take a few minutes, he says, for the camera to adjust from the climate-controlled environment of my car to the humid outdoor Low Country. I take that to be a sign that we should film this indoors, but John will not be dissuaded.

When I booked this interview, I was pleased to have another visual artist for Marisa to meet. John is a self-employed photographer and is young, I'm guessing late twenties. His business isn't mature enough yet for him to offer specialized services. Whatever you need—portrait, wedding, architecture—he's your man. But in a few hours Marisa will be taking a tour of the Savannah College of Art and Design, known as SCAD. She confessed to me this morning that the upcoming tour is all she can think about, so even though we are in the presence of a professional photographer—someone living a life Marisa dreams of—I know this interview will be lost on her. I don't tell her that I am already looking ahead to Savannah as well.

When the camera acclimatizes, I position John on the small deck that extends out into the marsh. Marisa sits behind me in a damp director's chair, sketching John's bloodhound lying unmoving at her feet. I start the interview, and John launches in. I watch the timer on the camera display. When it hits thirty minutes, I'll wrap up, and Marisa and I will move on. John talks about one thing after another that should be able to capture the attention of me, or Marisa, or both. He's getting married, and is fixing up his house to accommodate his soon-to-be-bride. He studied ceramics in art school, and wants to return to that once he builds a separate studio. He says he admires the fact that I've managed to get somebody else to pay for a cross-country trip, and tells me how when he was in his early twenties, he and a buddy spent a summer driving from town to town in an increasingly smelly van promoting an energy drink.

Then the time is up. I thank John, glance over at Marisa, and see her first smile since we stepped onto the dock. A few minutes later we're back at the car. I open the trunk, dig out a clean white shirt, strip off the dark blue polo I'm wearing, and put on the new one.

"That's not fair!"Marisa exclaims. "I'm dripping wet in this thing."

"You can change in the back seat. I'll make sure no one sees you."

"I'm not doing that!"she says, then pauses. "Actually, I don't have anything clean to wear."

"I'm sorry we were trapped in this humidity, but you look great."And she does: a white cotton dress, skirt breaking just below the knee. It's simple and professional at the same time, and completely unlike her normal look.

"I want to make the right impression with Ms. Woodcock."She's referring to Meghan, my interview subject for Georgia who also is a SCAD instructor.

Because we haven't yet gotten a good look at historic Charleston, I take her to White Point Gardens, a park that juts out from the peninsula into Charleston harbor. It's lined with elm trees, with the occasional gazebo that I suspect is popular with weddings. I wonder if John has photographed any here.

The park is flanked on two sides by water, the other two by striking antebellum homes. I'm tempted to encourage Marisa to stroll them with me, but I know we'll see similar architecture in Savannah.

"Okay, Marisa. We can say we saw Charleston."

I stop at a station before leaving town to fuel up the car with gas and myself with coffee. Moments later we're headed south. We're no longer on the interstate, which is to the west of us, but instead on a local highway that cuts through marshes. The road is empty before and behind us. After a while I need a restroom, and Marisa informs me she does as well. My GPS tells me the "Low Country Convenience Store"is ahead. We almost miss it, a decrepit wooden shack fronted by a porch shaded with a rotting-timber overhang. No cars occupy the gravel lot. No neon "Open" sign welcomes us. A screen door hanging loose on its hinges is covered in paper. Foreclosure warnings? Notices from the local Board of Health?

"Absolutely not," Marisa says. "It's abandoned."

"It could still be in business."

"Well, I'm not going in. I'll just hold it."

"Fair enough, but you've got to clean the upholstery if you fail."

I park, lock Marisa in the car for her protection, and step up onto the porch. The wood creaks beneath me. The papers on the screen door are flyers for various local events, posted over the top of each other. They advertise Bible readings, prayer groups, a traveling evangelist who has already come and gone.

The door is ajar.

I push it open further, attempting to focus in the dim light. I can make out two short rows of free-standing metal racks, the kind I use to store paint cans in my garage. The shelves boast a random assortment of sundries, from single-serving bags of potato chips to small boxes of off-brand laundry detergent.

On my left is an old-style deli refrigeration counter. It's hard to tell what meat is being offered for sale, as the glass is opaque with age.

"Welcome, good sir."

I hadn't processed that anyone was in the room. I turn to the sound and find a petite woman with a silver-specked afro and pearl eyeglasses. She's seated behind the deli counter on a stool, her face glistening from the humidity. A simple gold cross lies just below the top button of a white cotton blouse.

"Hello ma'am," I say. "I hate to bother you, but do you by chance have a restroom I could use?"

"That I do, young man, in the back. It's marked 'employees only,' but don't you mind that, just go in and take your time."

I thank her for the offer and for calling me young. The bathroom is tiny, with plumbing easily fifty years old, but very clean. Hanging on the wall in front of me is a poem informing me that a man's aim isn't as good as he might think, and he should be considerate with his stream. The message is depicted in a tight cross-stitch, framed in pine.

After I leave the bathroom I go in search of something to buy to justify my use of her facilities. I see nothing I need, but I choose a bag of barbeque chips made by a mystery manufacturer and bring it to the register.

97

"Honey, the bag is torn. Fetch yourself another one."

She's right. There's a slight perforation at the bottom of the bag. An orange chip is sliding its way to freedom.

"Thank you, I will," I reply. As I turn to select a new one from the rack sunlight strikes me. Marisa is entering.

"Ma'am, this is my daughter, may she…"

"Chil'," the woman says to Marisa, "my door is always open to angels straight from Heaven. Head to the back, hopefully your daddy left it clean enough for you."

As Marisa thanks the woman and slips past me, I whisper, "Thank you for trusting me."

Marisa slips her left hand around my right, gives it a squeeze, and then heads for the bathroom. How long has it been since my hand touched hers? A year ago, I think, when I pulled the children into my car, our last moments in my parents' house.

"Humid enough for you?" the store proprietor asks.

"It's a perfect day," I reply.

When we arrive in Savannah, dampness presses against my every surface. I long for the indoors, for air conditioning, for the dry Arizona desert of my youth. For escape. But Marisa is all smiles, the humidity no longer a nuisance. She is quite nearly skipping as we cross one of historic Savannah's tree-lined squares. Meghan Woodcock assures us that Savannah is delightful most of the year, but few students brave the summer humidity. Then she warns us not to touch the Spanish moss hanging down over our heads. It descends enticingly from the tree branches like spun taffy in the window of a beach boardwalk store. Chiggers live in the moss, she says, and will burrow their way into your skin. Once they're in there it's nearly impossible to lodge them free, and you'll believe you'll never stop scratching.

Meghan is younger than I would have expected. I'm unsure of her exact age, but I know she is only a couple of years out of graduate school, a SCAD alum who teaches graphic design. She looks as young as one of Marisa's high-school classmates. But I'm now at a point in life where it's hard for me to guess the age of any female between the ages of fifteen and thirty-five. Disturbingly, once they stop buying clothes in the kids' department and try on makeup, they all look the same to me.

Meghan leads us to the photography building, a three-story sliver of glass and concrete that clashes with the surrounding antebellum homes bedecked with spreading ivy, marble columns and wrap-around porches. We tour the empty building, and Marisa admires some of the darkroom equipment, revealing a knowledge of the photographic arts I was unaware she possessed. Next up is the illustration building, housed in one of those antebellum homes. We spend a little extra time there, as Meghan's security card allows us to enter the building but doesn't permit an exit. While we wait for a security officer to liberate us, I admire the mosaic floor in the majestic foyer, and Marisa examines a supply closet filled with pencils, pens and charcoal.

"We should see some students on our next stop," Meghan informs us once we're back outside, blessed by shade thanks to a tree canopy that covers this cobblestone street. "We're offering a late-summer printmaking class, so some students should be there because they'll need to use the presses."Meghan drives, and I savor five minutes of air conditioning. We arrive at a large warehouse seated near the bridge Marisa and I traversed a couple of hours ago when we arrived here from South Carolina.

We are greeted in front of the building by a young man with a shaved head, skinny jeans and Vans sneakers. His face is lined with piercings, including studs on either side of his lower lip. He flashes Marisa a grin as he unlocks the building for us.

After we're inside I lean over to Marisa. "Did you see his lip?"

She giggles. "Those are called snake bites, Dad."

"If you ever mutilate yourself like that I will hunt you down and rip them out."

Marisa smiles as Meghan guides us past a series of small rooms filled with easels and paint, which she says are personal studios for upperclassmen. The art works are incomplete, as are the rooms themselves. The walls extend up about eight feet, but then meet air, as the warehouse roof is at least thirty feet higher.

Finally we find them, the elusive SCAD students. The well-lit room is a slightly larger version of the printmaking studio Sabra Field has in her South Royalton, Vermont, home. Three large wooden presses sit to the far left under paned windows. Filling the rest of the room are a number of square tables lined with stools and covered in large sheets of illustrations. There are about a half-dozen students in the room, only one operating a press. Marisa takes a step back into the darkness of the hallway.

I slide past Meghan into the room and march up to the woman at the press, who doesn't look a day older than Marisa. She is removing a large sheet of paper depicting an intense interweaving of flower outlines. "That's quite a print you're working on."

"Thanks," she says without looking up.

"Would you mind telling my daughter what you're doing? She's considering going to school here."

She looks over my shoulder to the door. "Of course!" she says, flicking her head in a gesture of invitation. Long black hair sails over her right shoulder. Marisa makes her way to us, and I feign a sudden interest in an unused press at the other end of the room.

Marisa won a regional art award a year ago for a print she made in eighth grade. The ceremony was held at the local community college, and I recall Marisa appearing to float as her name was called. I was sitting with her mother, who immediately whispered to me after Marisa left the stage that the award would be framed and displayed in her house, not mine. I was disappointed but did not object. Marisa didn't enter the contest this year. When her mother and I both pestered her to submit something, anything, Marisa insisted that all of the art she had produced in the last year was crap.

I watch Marisa and the student talk. They take turns pointing at things in the room, back and forth in animated conversation. Meghan watches with me.

"She looks comfortable here," she says.

"She looks at home," I reply.

Marisa finally returns to us, saying she didn't want to keep the young woman from her work any longer. So I say it's time to interview Meghan, which is of course the technical reason I'm here today. As I film her, I learn she's in her early thirties—she spent seven years between undergraduate and graduate school working for an architectural firm in Virginia—and recently won an award for a modular-construction prototype that would allow quick construction of schools in areas devastated by natural disasters. The idea came to her when she read about all of the children in New Orleans who found themselves without any place to return to class after Hurricane Katrina. But Meghan, seeing Marisa on a stool behind me, keeps returning the conversation to the merits of attending SCAD.

I surrender. "What does someone need to do to be admitted?"

"Well, our admissions process is highly competitive. We have applicants from all over the world who are exceptional artists. So you have to have an impressive portfolio of work with a lot of originality." She looks over my shoulder to Marisa. "You mentioned you love photography."

Marisa nods.

"So you'd submit a collection of your best art, photographs of course but also other works. Illustrations. Perhaps a painting or sculpture. But you also need to have pretty good grades. This is a rigorous academic institution and we need to know that you can handle a heavy workload from a variety of subjects."

I'm glad Marisa is behind me so I can't see the disappointment on her face. This was not a good year for Marisa academically. Her grades have never really reflected her intellectual abilities, but in her first year of high school they dropped precipitously. Her motivation appeared to have vanished, particularly at the beginning of the year. Her mother called it a "lost year." I do not believe it to be a coincidence that the school year began mere days after we returned from our last trip to Knoxville.

I wrap up the interview, making sure to get in a few more questions that will elicit answers I can use in my video. Marisa and I thank Meghan for giving us an entire afternoon with her, then as we leave the building bid goodbye to the guy with the snake bites.

We dash back into the heart of town, reaching a small pizza joint named after Vincent Van Gogh. Just as we step under the entrance's red-and-white striped awning, rain pelts at the canvas above our heads. The young hostess has crimson-dyed buzz-cut hair that competes for attention with a nostril ring. An open book rests on the podium in front of her. I glance over and see it is *One Flew Over the Cuckoo's Nest*.

After the hostess seats us, Marisa asks me about the book.

"It ain't beach reading," I say. "I've never read it myself, but the movie is about a criminal who thinks he's gamed the system by getting himself sent to an insane asylum. It doesn't turn out so well for him, though. A psychotic doctor and nurse give him electroshocks and turn him into a drooling vegetable."

"Wow," Marisa says under her breath. "Dark stuff." She's looking over my shoulder, and I realize she's watching the hostess, who has returned to her book.

Even in this last year, when she has changed so much, Marisa has remained a reader. Her literary taste has trended to dystopian futures in which teens and young adults overcome unimaginable odds. I have been troubled by their dark themes, but they're full of heroism as well, young people defying a system geared against them.

"Dad?"

"Yes?"

"If I went to school here I'd be surrounded by people just like me."

She'd be surrounded by kids with piercings, but maybe she'll have some by then.

"Well, yes, I assume the hostess is a student here. It's true that if you go to an art school, you'll be surrounded by artists."

"It's more than that," she says. "I don't know how to describe it. But, well, I could be myself here, talking about art, doing crazy creative things. No one would judge me."

"I suppose that's true." This is the closest Marisa has come to opening up to me in a year. I want to know more, to understand what she means about being judged, about being forced not to be herself. Do I judge her? Do I force her to hide who she is? The spell is broken by the arrival of a waiter, a gangly young man who looks at Marisa in a way that I'm not happy with. He scratches his left arm as he greets us, and I wonder if he made the mistake of touching some of the Spanish moss. We order our pizzas, and then Marisa comments on how hard the rain is coming down. I agree, but I'm not focused on the weather. The moment has passed. I'm already planning how I can achieve another, but in twelve hours I take her to the Savannah airport for her first-ever solo flight, a nonstop return to D.C.

Back in our motel room, Marisa disappears into the bathroom and seems destined never again to emerge. What uses of that space have teenage girls discovered that the rest of us survive without? I could be editing, but like other nights on this leg of the trip I have resisted, not wanting to be the first person to hide behind a screen. Instead I am sitting on one of the motel room's two twin beds. This room is even more worn than the others we've stayed in. The dark olive nape of the carpet nearly hides various dark patches, stains also masked by the dearth of light. Much of the quilted threads on the brown bedspread beneath me have long since migrated, but the paisley impressions left behind still struggle to raise themselves. One of the ways I was able to sell my Board on this trip was by pitching how little I'd spend. I'd stay in cheap motels on the fringes of town. I probably should have started with a higher price tag and let them negotiate me down, the way they haggled with Hill staffers when drafting economic returns on legislation. But Marisa hasn't complained, and I'm grateful for that.

Finally she emerges, face and hair still wet. I jump right in.

"I think you've got a real shot to go here someday, Marisa. But you heard Meghan. You've got to get those grades up."

It's as if I've stripped the muscles from my daughter's legs. She stops, then slides down the wall to the floor, sitting cross-legged beside the bed. The father in me wants to tell her to get up off of that carpet, you don't know the last time it's been cleaned. But I'm sitting on a bedspread of which the same can be said, and besides, I've already upset her with one fatherly admonition.

"You sound just like Mom," she whispers.

"Well, Mom's right."

Marisa plays with a string emerging from the waistband of her cotton pajama pants. "All she does is ride me. If I get a C, she says I should've gotten a B. If I get a B, she says 'Why didn't you get an A?'"

"When have you ever gotten an A?"

I should hold my tongue, but I'm not happy, being lumped in with her mother. I want to be the cool dad, the one showing her adventurous futures, not the partner to someone she perceives as a dream-killer. I've seen the way the two have been the last year. I can hear them from the driveway when I walk up to her mother's house

103

every other Saturday morning. They fight. A lot. And I know how quickly Marisa's mother can escalate a conflict, and how when I met her as a young man straight out of college I found that intensity in a woman nine years my senior strangely comforting and familiar. My perspective changed, and after a decade I left. Marisa doesn't have that option.

"Your mother," I start, then fall silent. I need to handle this right, this moment, this opportunity. This is a conversation I should have had a long time ago, years perhaps. "Your mother, Marisa, loves you. A lot. It's because she loves you so much that she gets so intense about things, like your grades. But yes, I'll admit she's not really good at praise. Well, what she thinks is praise isn't the way we'd like to hear it said. But when she pushes you to get higher grades, she's showing confidence in you."

"I can't believe you're taking her side."

Why, because I divorced her? I respond in my head. But I keep the words to myself. I understand, in a way Marisa doesn't, that her mother and I can be united as parents even with the marriage disunited. "I'm on her side on this, and I'm also on your side. There shouldn't be any sides here. Your mother and I want the best for you, just like you do. And we know now, thanks to Meghan, that the grades you get do have consequences, even if your art continues to be brilliant. Which it is."

Marisa lifts her head, but not to engage with me. She looks across the twin bed I'm on to the other one. I follow her glance and spot what she's looking for.

"Can you please leave your phone alone for just a few minutes here? You were on it almost the entire time we were at the pizza joint."

"I was texting my friends about SCAD."

"And you'll be able to text them more. But I want to share your excitement with you, Marisa. Pretend you're texting me right now, only you don't have to type."

"But my artist friends. They, you know, get it."

"Get what?"

She points out the window, in the direction of historic Savannah. "Art. Passion. Obsession. Creativity."

"Really, Marisa? Have you not been listening to the conversations I've been having with the artists on these interviews?"

"Yeah, but my friends, they make art."

I see myself as someone who used to be creative but put it aside. These artists consistently perceive me as a fellow artist there to connect with them, just like Marisa is longing to. But my daughter apparently doesn't see the creative me. I do the math, and realize the last time I was actively pursuing creative writing, she was probably nine or ten. And as I look back, I recall that I rarely wrote on days she was with me. I wanted to maximize my time with her and her brother. I would save those moments of creative writing for when she was with her mother. "I used to write, you know. Fiction. I even wrote a novel a few years back."

"I know. I remember you talking about it once with Gramma. But you stopped."

The word "Gramma"emerges almost like a growl. My mother hasn't been on my mind today. It was as if driving the opposite direction of Knoxville yesterday gave me more than geographic distance. But now I see a bit more why Marisa is so driven to connect with her artist friends. For most of her life, her artistic confidant was my mother. It strikes me that my mother has no idea that Marisa is here today, in Savannah, seeing clearly for the first time a possible future full of artistic promise. It's an experience I know my mother would have loved for herself, a college dropout who, like some of the artists I've interviewed on this trip, is largely self-taught. Regret consumes me. If I were standing right now, I likely would slide down a wall the way Marisa did with my mention of her grades.

"I may not be writing anymore," I tell her. "Well, not that type of writing. But surely you see the passion I have for creatives, how I'm their cheerleader."

"I know that, Dad. I tell all my friends what you do. They think it's pretty cool."

"Thank you," I say, surprised but heartened.

"I don't see why you don't write any more, though."

The answer to that question is complicated, and more so than I realized before starting this trip. Unprepared to answer it I play reporter, shifting the focus back to my interview subject.

"You miss being able to talk about art with Gramma. I'd love to be that person for you."

"Well, it was a little different with her."

"Because you could bitch about your mom and dad with her as well."

"Actually, yeah."

I asked for that answer, but I'm furious with it anyway. "Great, Marisa. I'm really glad your grandmother, who could hardly ever be bothered to visit you, who never had to pick you up from school or fix your dinner or take you to the doctor, was always there for you so you could bitch about what mean parents you have. I'm sure the two of you could really go on and on with that subject."

For the first time Marisa makes eye contact with me, but I don't like what I see. I imagine it's the way I used to stare at my father before one of his rages.

Shit. I slide off of the bed on the side opposite Marisa. Three steps later I reach what appears to be a discarded dining-room chair, tucked under a Formica-lined shelf the motel claims is a desk. I swing the chair around and sit with my chest against the back rest. I hope the physical distance I've created doesn't sever the emotional connection I feel we've been gaining, but if it's gone, it's not because I walked across the room.

"I'm sorry. That was out of line. This is exactly what Gramma would want: us fighting."

"I wouldn't let her, you know."

I don't know. "What do you mean?"

Marisa looks down again. "We talked a lot. Mostly texting. And yes, I'd complain about you. And she'd listen. And she was sympathetic. And she'd complain about you too. Some pretty bad stuff. But shortly before that last trip to Knoxville, I told her she wasn't allowed to talk to me about you like that anymore."

I'm proud of my daughter for coming to my defense, but also horrified. Eleven years ago Marisa's mother, still my wife, was lighting in to me about how poorly I had cleaned the bathtub, or something like that. What is crystal clear in my mind is what my four-year-old daughter did. She walked into the room, stepped between the two of us, and said to her mother in a soft voice that she didn't like it when Mommy talked to Daddy like that. I knew at that moment I had to leave. It was one thing to choose emasculation when it was just the two of us. But I couldn't be that kind of man and raise children. I couldn't have my children thinking of me the way I see my father.

"Marisa, thank you for that," I say. "Really. But I'm sorry she put you in that position, where you needed to say that to her."

My senior year in high school I worked as a technician at an animal hospital. I often took X-rays of dogs and cats, and the regulators required me to wear a badge that absorbed ambient radiation. If it reached a certain level, I was not allowed to take any more X-rays for a designated period of time. I would picture that badge on me when I visited Knoxville, knowing my mother needed to vent her toxins, and the imaginary indicator filled faster with each visit. It reached maximum on that last visit before I was able to spot the change. I believe I now have a better understanding of why. By removing my mother's ability to release her frustrations with me to my daughter, Marisa had cut off another opportunity for my mother to scratch her perpetual itch.

A good scratch provides my mother a temporary release. But I understand, in a way I do not believe she does, that it doesn't address the source of the itch. That is burrowed too deep inside her psyche, and there's nothing I can do to liberate her from it. As long as she denies that reality, she will continue to feel compelled to dig nails into flesh.

"Gramma," Marisa says, "would tell me that she was the only one who really understood me. You didn't, because you weren't like her, an artist. But I was. We both were. And we thought the same way."

I should be upset at my mother telling Marisa I wasn't an artist. But she has said far worse things to me. What appalls me is my mother telling my daughter they think alike. "You figured she was right."

Marisa nods.

"Do you still?"

Marisa doesn't answer. Instead she sniffles, and then wipes her hand under her nose.

I walk to the bathroom, reach under the sink, remove the aluminum plate that hides a box of tissues, and bring Marisa the box. Marisa wipes her nose, and then uses another one to dab her eyes. I sit on the edge of the bed. "Marisa, just because you're creative like Gramma, that doesn't mean you think like her. Look at the artists we've met on this trip. Look at how caring Colleen was, giving you pencils. Look at Diana, who ran out into the rain to make sure we took her muffins with us. These are good, talented people who allowed us into their homes with no hidden agendas. Now as for genes, I'll confess I've wondered about that a fair amount myself. I don't know what you may have inherited from Gramma, or Grampa, or from me for that matter. We are who we are. Maybe some of your artistic talent comes from her, and you know what, that's great. She has a lot of it. But we don't inherit actions. We make choices every day. We can choose to act differently from our parents. Sometimes we have to."

"I'm never going to yell at my children."

She could be referring to my mother yelling at me, or her mother yelling at her, or me yelling at her. All three apply. "That's a good commitment, Marisa. And you might start practicing now, by not yelling back at your mother when she yells at you."

"You didn't yell back at Gramma that night. A fat lot of good it did you."

"I hoped remaining calm would encourage her to calm down. It didn't. But that's an important lesson. You can only change your own behavior."

"You're saying I should just put up with having a crazy Gramma and a bitch of a mother."

"I wouldn't have chosen those words. But basically yes."

"You didn't just put up with it. You aren't talking to Gramma. And you left Mom years ago."

I've wanted this conversation for a year now, but I now find myself wondering why. "You're right, Marisa. You know, you're stronger than me. You always have been. You'll find a way to deal with your crazy-ass family, me included. And I know you'll have your act together more than all of us." I keep going, not sure where the words are coming from. "You don't have to be like me, avoiding conflict. I've only tried once in the last year to reconnect with Gramma, and when it didn't work I moved on. I could have pushed harder, but I chose the easy path. And yes, I did decide a long time ago not to listen anymore to your mother's constant disappointment with me. But you don't want to copy me any more than Gramma or your mom. I run away. Even this road trip is running away, from my funders. And I ran away that night last year in Knoxville."

Marisa puts her hand on my left knee. I meet her red, puffy eyes. "Dad, you didn't run away that night. You rescued Parker and me. That's behavior I'd copy any day."

Now it's my turn to sniffle. Marisa hands me the tissue box.

"Thank you, Dad. For taking me here to SCAD. For letting me see a future for myself, a future I'm going to work hard to make happen. And thank you for being my defender."

I take Marisa's hand in mine and give it a tug. She stands up, as do I. And we embrace. How long has it been since I've hugged her, really hugged her? It strikes me how few opportunities I'll have for this, how three years from now we could be here in Savannah again, except I'll be hugging her goodbye as she starts her new life as a college student. This past year we've been pushed apart, at a time in our lives when we needed each other more than ever. This hug will have to end at some point, but its memory won't.

PART FOUR: THE SOUTH

AUGUST 23: ALABAMA

Twenty-four hours have passed since I dropped Marisa off at the Savannah airport for her flight back to her mother and normalcy. I'm holding in my mind my last sight of her, a moment after she cleared security when she turned, smiled, and waved. The rest of the day involved a long drive to a motel outside Atlanta and a marathon film-editing session. Now I've arrived at the Alabama visitor's center just west of the Georgia border, stalked by an older white woman in an ankle-length plaid dress. I managed to evade her on my way into the men's room, but when I return to the lobby she positions herself between me and the exit. I cede to her insistent Southern hospitality and accept her assistance, inquiring about a large motorsports museum I've been told is outside of Birmingham. She practically sings the highway exit number while sliding over to a display rack to produce a brochure. I head back to my car, grateful but unnerved, and then am disturbed by a tombstone-like granite slab near the parking lot boasting the words "ALABAMA WE DARE DEFEND OUR RIGHTS."I am a middle-aged white man driving an air-conditioned rental car to Birmingham. Forty-five years ago a group of young black men sought to march from Selma to Montgomery to promote equal treatment under the law, but while crossing a bridge they met the wrong end of night sticks and tear gas from hastily deputized young white men. Both sides said they were fighting for their rights that day. I wonder whose rights were in mind when this monument was commissioned, and if the woman inside applies the same degree of hospitality to all of her visitors.

My defiance of authority is far less noble as I violate Alabama's speed limit of fifty-five miles per hour, a significant drop from the seventy in Georgia. I avoid any encounters with highway patrolmen and arrive at the exit for the Barber Vintage Motorsports Museum, exactly where my staker told me it would be. This should be a perfect introduction to my interview subject today, photographer Marc Bondarenko. He is a self-described "gearhead"who loves all motor vehicles, but particularly motorcycles. Some of his photos found their way into a Guggenheim catalog. When that New York museum put on an exhibit of motorcycles as works of art, about twenty percent of them came from Barber, and the photos came from Marc.

I park in the empty lot of a building that resembles a mega-church built by a TV pastor, a massive house of worship celebrating man's boundless ambition rather than God's infinite love. But I am happy to pay homage, given that I belong to the Church of the Wheel. As a teenager I longed for a motorcycle. My mother, however, said she'd prefer not to be childless, and my father told me not to push it. I still lined my bedroom walls with centerfolds of chrome beasts. As I started my own life as an adult, I continued to long for the freedom of a motorcycle, but my first wife assumed the veto. Once divorced, however, I wasted no time. For about eight years I was a motorcycle owner and rider. But a bike does not suit a single father picking up kids at school or making supermarket runs for milk and bread. Also, although I feel a sense of connection with Robert Pirsig's struggle to achieve Zen-like tranquility in his memoir *Zen and the Art of Motorcycle Maintenance*, I proved far worse at the mechanical element of his book title. I sold my bike a year ago, and still feel its absence. The open road on this trip in a rented hybrid sedan isn't quite filling the void.

I look every bike up and down. I read every sign, learning about the evolution of this grand machine, which in many respects has not changed much in a hundred years. As I discover something amazing I turn, expecting to ask if Marisa also sees it, and then remember I no longer have a travel companion. I abandon my effort to capture the museum's collection with my point-and-shoot camera, imagining how much better Marisa would be at the task. After admiring the long-handlebar chopper from the iconic motion picture *Easy Rider* I move on.

Marc's studio is located in an industrial area with train tracks in one direction and a decaying factory in the other. He greets me at the steel-plated door wearing a worn olive V-neck shirt and jeans on a tall, thin frame. He's a bit older than me but in better shape. A dry-walled section near the front of the studio features a sofa and a few framed poster-sized photos of bikes and women, both glistening and inviting. Beyond that waiting area is a warehouse filled with easel tables, light stands, umbrella reflectors, and various shelves lined with cameras and lenses. The ceiling and walls are a compelling fusion of wood and steel. Developers in gentrifying downtowns are creating spaces like this as residences for the upwardly mobile, but the neighborhood suggests this industrial appearance is authentic.

Marc asks me about my drive. I bitch about the low speed limit and he congratulates me on avoiding a ticket. We chat while I position him below two posters of his photos. One depicts a long-handlebar bike tripped out with chrome, emerging sans rider from a gray mist. In the other, a striking young woman in a gold one-piece bathing suit stretches by a beach chair beneath a startlingly orange-red sunset. When I start filming I compliment him on the photos.

"I have an emotional connection with automotive subjects," he says. "Cars. Trucks. Bikes. I'll admit to getting an emotional boost from photographing them, lighting the subject and composing it in the frame. But bikes and cars are pretty static. They don't really give back. That's why I love photographing people so much."

I take in the bathing beauty over his right shoulder. I'm only familiar with his motorcycle photography so I ask him to elaborate.

"Well, I love the experience of photographing people. You really have to break down social barriers, and pretty quickly, because you're only going to be with them for a few hours at most. I've found that people enjoy when someone is genuinely interested in them. It lets you get past their physical—I don't know—I guess their physical husk. They give something back, and it's a real gift if you're receptive to it."

Marc is the first person I've had a face-to-face conversation with since Marisa's departure. My itinerary the next few weeks is tight. Social interaction on some days, I realize, may be limited to the artists I'm interviewing. I'm doing with these film sessions what Marc does with his professional shoots. I am genuinely interested in my subjects and their stories, and they have been responding to that enthusiasm by giving back energy and encouragement. I vow to appreciate their gifts.

AUGUST 24: MISSISSIPPI AND TENNESSEE

My itinerary on this trip charts a convoluted circumnavigation of Knoxville, Tennessee. That was not my intention, at least not consciously. The pattern of the southeastern leg on a map resembles a pyramid-shaped glass beaker, with Knoxville the inert but toxic gas hovering in its center. Here in Oxford, Mississippi, I am located along the beaker's base. I'm hoping a stroll across the sunlit University of Mississippi campus will clear my head of such thoughts. I approach the school's imposing football stadium and am passed by three smiling sprites, each with teeth blinding white and teased hairstyles in various shades of the Caucasian spectrum: yellow, red and brown. Giggles accompany their aerial skips while crimson gym bags sporting a familiar corporate swoosh swing at their sides. I assume they are cheerleaders. A sign says the stadium is named after two men, Vaught and Hemingway, but I'm disappointed to learn the latter is not the late, great novelist. I peer through chain-link fencing at sixty thousand empty seats and think about how all I heard on the radio into town— being trapped as I am at listening to local radio stations with my music player dead—was hyperactive discussions about the impending start of the college football season and how this year Ole Miss' fortunes would turn around. I stand before the uniting presence of Oxford, Mississippi, and almost hear the cheers.

While in college I studied abroad at the other Oxford, in England. I had not yet been diagnosed with bipolar disorder, but it had manifested years earlier. My time in England consisted of deep depression punctured by an occasional burst of angry mania. I had arrived a young man raised under the blue dome of the Arizona desert. In England the days grew shorter while the sun remained hidden behind a perpetual blanket of clouds. I now know, thanks to my psychiatrist, that I also suffer from a condition called seasonal affective disorder, or SAD. Lack of exposure to sunlight triggers my bipolar symptoms. Unlike my bipolar diagnosis, I no longer make an effort to hide my struggle with SAD. I have learned it is a condition accepted by society. Many boast of having it, diagnosed or not. But we do not similarly embrace bipolar disorder. I no longer watch police procedural TV shows because all too often the serial killer shares my disorder. I've never seen a show in which a madman slits the throats of beautiful young women because cloudy days are activating his SAD.

At Oxford I self-medicated with repeated pints of bitter at the Rose and Crown pub. One night in a stone hall similar to what King Arthur would have used to meet with his Knights of the Round Table, I shocked and embarrassed my fellow students by loudly accusing one of the Oxford dons sponsoring our program of conspiring to send me back home. I stormed out before he could respond and didn't stop until I reached a fountain, where I engaged in dry heaves, too wound up to vomit properly.

Here in this Oxford the sun is brilliantly bright. I'd like to see more students, but the fall term is not yet in session. I make my way back to the car and head out of town into the Lafayette County woods to interview painter and photographer Amy Evans Streeter. I discover her driveway is a barely perceptible slice in a thicket of oak and spruce trees, and soon am bouncing along rutted gravel on a curving road lined with trees and shrubs. A clear spot in the hedges on my left provides a quick glimpse at a small pond featuring lily pads and geese. A low-slung, natural wood-paneled home appears before me and I park in a gravel clearing. As I open the car door a dog's large, black nose presses into my crotch.

"Jackson! Let the man breathe!"

I flash back to my job as a veterinary hospital technician. When it comes to dogs, the key is to mask your fear and establish dominance. I place my hands on either side of Jackson's head, then slowly pull his head away from my pants while rubbing under his ears. His tail beats even faster.

"He likes you," Amy says. "It's settled, then, I'll do the interview." She's wearing a white cotton shirt, a bit billowy, with a coral scarf around her neck. There's a bit of color in her cheeks, consistent with the glow found in new mothers, of which Amy is one. I follow Amy and Jackson into her kitchen and encounter a tall man in a red-plaid flannel shirt with hair short and straight like a dog's wire brush.

"You must be Kurt," I say, anxious of his reaction to a strange man from an Eastern city wanting to spend time alone with his wife. I remember a detail I learned from Amy while setting up the interview. "I can't wait to see the studio you've built for Amy," I tell him.

"Thank you," he says. They offer me coffee, I accept, and we gather at a rustic kitchen table with an empty baby car seat in the center. Amy does most of the talking, lightning fast, her Southern accent softer than I had expected. She discusses her day job working as a photojournalist for a nonprofit documenting Southern culture, such as mom-and-pop restaurants that are being shoved aside by Cracker Barrel franchises. I think of how on this trip I am documenting a pre-digital art culture in its death throes. Alabama photographer Marc Bondarenko told me he has all but given up working with film. Most of Brenna Lyons's fiction is published solely in ebook form. Even old-school printmaker Sabra Field in Vermont confessed she almost never gets her hands inky with her own wooden press, instead outsourcing her final work to a digital printer. If Cracker Barrel is Amy's Moby Dick, is digitization mine? If so, I'm documenting the transition with a digital camera.

"Where's Sophia?" I ask.

"Oh, she went down for her afternoon nap a few minutes before you arrived. The timing is perfect." Amy then regales me with stories of their infant daughter, whose many exploits suggest she is some kind of superbaby. I decide it's time to start the interview, and Amy enthusiastically agrees. We head through thick woods to her studio, led by Jackson, who clearly knows the route well. The space is a modest, single room, lined with windows with shiny-new glass and bookcases housing hardbound collections of painters and photographers. In the corner is a two-story dollhouse next to a miniature easel. Amy's desk isn't an artist's drafting table but rather an imposing wood beast that appears to have been liberated from a 19th Century law firm. The surface is covered with coffee cans filled with paintbrushes and various bottles of ink. A large palette is its own work of art, swirling colors covering the surface.

On the easel to the left of the desk is one of Amy's paintings titled

Ethel loved breakfast in bed. Too bad she had to make it herself. In the painting, set against a mustard-yellow background, a can of Carnation condensed milk provides a resting place for a bird-shaped green plastic pipe. Also visible is a pink hair curler, bobby pins, and a white lace doily under a plate holding a slice of cherry pie. Amy has painted directly on a block of wood, no canvas.

"I want to have that easel and desk behind you in the shot. I love that painting. And that spot is where the real energy in this room exists."

"Thanks. And I'm not surprised you feel that energy," she says, taking a seat in the chair in front of the desk. "I feel it too. In fact, I'm really feeling the creative juices flowing right now, so it's a good time to talk to you."

When I start filming she tells me how she came to paint directly on wood. After abandoning printmaking for want of a press, she took to drawing and mounting the work on wood. She loved the tangible essence of her chosen mounting surface, and soon abandoned both pencil and paper for brush and wood. She considers her paintings three-dimensional art in line with a sculpture, so it surprised her to learn a recent purchaser of one of her paintings had it framed. "I haven't seen it but I'm very curious, because I feel like that will totally change the vibe of the piece. Not necessarily in a bad way," Amy adds, not completely convincingly.

I ask about the subject matter of her paintings, this seemingly random assortment of objects paired with a whimsical title.

"In my mind, I guess, my paintings are landscapes and still lifes and portraits all in one. I assign narratives of people to the pieces—I make the people up, of course—but they all have a back story and the titles of the pieces reflect that story. You know," she says, pointing to the painting beside her, "I see a landscape in this one because there's a horizon line, and the cherry-pie plate is kind of a sun."I see how the doily's curves are like arching light from a star. I'm not sure what role the pie slice plays. Perhaps a sunspot?

Amy says she brings her love of surrealism to her paintings, the idea of combining dissimilar ingredients with an unconventional narrative. "I like to make little head scratchers that make people look at them a bit funny. When people look at art they're always trying to figure it out. But it doesn't always need to be."

I've never been a particular fan of surrealism, and now I realize that it may be because of the discomfort I feel at being unable to discern what the artist is trying to tell me. I like being liberated from the detective work. I'm attracted to the notion that what matters is my reaction to the work, that in that reaction I find satisfaction, and the artist does as well.

Sophia comes up again, because you can't talk to a new mother for long without the child being mentioned. "I want to share this studio with her. She already has a little apron and easel."Amy points to the small easel that Sophia won't be old enough to use for some time. "Once she's really expressing herself on canvas and paper, oh my will that will be inspiring to me. I see her asking me questions about my work, and me maybe reassessing my art as a result. I want to be an Artist Mom, and I want to hear her say, 'Hey, my mom paints.'"

It's true that this space is charged with creative energy. Perhaps it is that volatile field that sparks my pain. I'm back with Marisa in our motel in Savannah, when she told me she misses describing her father as a creative writer. As a child I certainly was proud of my mother and her writing. I'd only pretend to be embarrassed when my sixth grade teacher would read aloud to the class my mother's latest newspaper humor column. I rushed to high school to tell all of my friends the day my mother received a contract offer for her first novel. And my mother encouraged my writing, dutifully filling a box with my childhood prose. Those included a picture book from first grade called "The Runaway Rabbit"about a hare that didn't want the burden of being the Easter Bunny, a short story from fourth grade about a school nurse who turns kids into zombies, and a sonnet from high school titled "Senioritis"that won twenty-five dollars in a local writing competition.

I know those pieces well, because I've had many opportunities to re-read them. Nearly twenty years ago that aging box arrived unannounced on my doorstep when my mother cut off contact with me for the first time. It came while I was reading Julia Cameron's *The Artist's Way*. Actually, I had put the book down once I hit Week Two and read the section titled "Crazymakers."A *crazymaker,* Cameron wrote, is a walking storm center, full of charm and inventiveness but destructive to creatives around them. Crazymakers are divas, the star, the center of attention. The nexus. They "triangulate those they deal with," pitting one person against another. They are expert blamers. They deny their crazymaker status. And they struggle with their own blocked creativity and fear the possibility that someone else could be unblocked. There was no doubt Cameron was describing my mother, but when I read the author's advice—isolate myself from the crazymaker's toxic influence—the solution seemed too harsh.

But the box's arrival marked that break. After spending a few days with the items in that box I resumed Cameron's lessons. For three years my mother and I didn't speak. In those three years I wrote three novels. I doubt now they were any good. Likely they were the junk prose Michael Swanwick said we have to write before we can write well. But they were a joy to produce, the creativity leaping from my fingers through the keyboard to the amber screen of my clunky 1990's personal computer. Then, with Marisa's arrival imminent, I reconnected with my mother and began anew the dance of crazymaker empowerment. It was around that time that I stopped writing fiction.

Amy is just beginning her dual role of both creative mentor and mother. "What Kurt and I can do for Sophia, for her future, is to make sure she's not stifled creatively," she says. "My father and I used to play the Doodle Game. One of us would make a doodle and hand it to the other one, and they'd have to add to the doodle. We'd do that for hours."

My mother's passion was Scrabble. She always won, but would praise my use of an unusual or unexpected word, even if the point yield was low. I looked forward to Scrabble battles and those moments of praise for a word well-constructed. If only people could be summarized as easily as Julia Cameron would have us believe. Is it as significant a crime if a crazymaker undermines your creativity, but you owe that creativity to her to begin with?

When the interview is over, Amy plays the dutiful local and gives me highly detailed directions on how to get to Memphis. I nod my head and smile but don't listen. I plan to let the GPS direct me. There is too much on my mind to recall her verbal guidance. Soon enough

I'm in Memphis, and exit the highway into downtown. I've got a little time before my next interview, so I make my way toward the Mississippi River and stop at a park offering a clear view of the Arkansas shore.

I take in the arched Hernando De Soto bridge, which I crossed twenty-two years ago this month. I was a college graduate heading from L.A. to Washington, D.C. Young, eager, and naïve, I believed I had found my own path. I would not be a creative writer. I would instead worship at the High Church of Democracy, serving my country by working on Capitol Hill.

I imagine how that twenty-two-year-old would have reacted to the news that he would one day launch an influential D.C. lobbying coalition. He would testify before government agencies and advise Hill staffers and White House political appointees. I suspect that twenty-two-year-old would have been thrilled. But that young man left his first job on Capitol Hill crushed and disillusioned, having seen the ugliness of our political system up close. Yet he stayed in D.C. because he married one of the players. Then kids arrived. My parents like to stay on the move, but I have grown deep roots in a place where the person I wish to be has no place.

I step out of the car onto the edge of a steep slope that climbs from the shore up to Riverside Drive. Tired, I sit on the newly mowed grass. A boy throws a tennis ball to the top of the slope, allows it to start rolling back down, then at the last minute runs to place himself in a position to catch it. His father sits at the far end of the park from me, watching approvingly. The boy throws again and again, catching the ball even when it takes an unpredictable bounce. The roll of his toy reminds me of the soothing motion of a metal ball moving down a Pachinko machine, the toy my child psychiatrist would allow me to play with after I agreed it was not my fault my father had left me.

As I watch this boy again catch the ball I spot an older man walking a beige whippet. The dog struggles against his leash as he strains to chase the ball. The boy, I suspect, would love to say hello to this dog were he aware of its presence, but he is engrossed in the game. To him, nothing exists but slope and ball. Not even the mighty Mississippi just behind him, the sprawling river that divides East from

West and will live forever in the telling of another young boy by the name of Huck Finn. I want to be the boy with the ball. Or I want to be Huck Finn, floating without a care. In my fantasy I ignore the fact that Huck was on the run from an abusive father.

I stand up, confirm my black Dockers aren't sporting grass stains, and head to the car to get my camera equipment. I have another interview to conduct.

. . .

As I walk to the Memphis Music Foundation I pass the entrance to Beale Street, that blocked-off stretch of downtown pulsating with live music and sexual possibility. An operator of a horse-drawn carriage smokes a cigarette while offering his beast of burden a carrot. The carriage is straight out of *Cinderella*, a hollow wrought-iron white sphere strung with white lights. I disappear quickly from the horse's view due to a large blinder by his left eye. The animal's owner ignores me. I am fine right now with not being seen.

I reach the side entrance of a three-story brick building. After pressing the buzzer I am met by a tall man with a gray beard and mustache and matching hair pulled into a pony tail. Steve "Voice of Golden Eagle"Cox leads me up the stairs to the foundation's office and introduces me around. So as not to disturb the others I set up the shoot in a conference room, placing Steve against an exposed red brick wall. He opens a velvet bag and pulls out several wooden flutes, his instrument of choice, and arranges them on the mahogany coffee table. As I set up the camera he shows me a 1986 issue of *Electronic Musician* magazine. "There's an article I wrote in here," he says while staring at me with squinted eyes. "It was about technology I was involved with, new at the time. It allowed musicians to sample other people's recorded music. I am the person, I must confess, who helped give birth to the sampling revolution."

He's testing me. Steve knows I'm here to film him on behalf of major record labels, who have fought aggressively the unauthorized use of copyrighted recordings by other musicians. My organization's position is that the law clearly states a musician wishing to record a song that uses someone else's recording must pay for that use. Few up-and-coming rappers and hip-hop artists do that, and there is a significant movement among lovers of technology to support the musicians in what my funders call theft. Steve has agreed to be interviewed by me, but is letting me know I may not like his answers.

I finish mounting the camera to the tripod. "It must have been exciting," I say, "to be on the cutting edge of technology in the music industry you love so much."

I perceive a slight nod, followed by another smile. I have passed his test. "It was indeed, Patrick." He tells me about working with Michael Jackson and Cyndi Lauper as a sampler of others' works while I perform a sound check. Even though we haven't officially begun yet, once I turned on the camera Steve begins speaking in a very deliberate manner, with clear articulation and dramatic pauses. He also looks directly into the camera.

"Steve, I need you to look at me during the filming. We're having a conversation, and I film your profile. I'm not seen in the film, but you still talk to me."

"Oh, okay," he says, turning his body to me but maintaining his pose, which features a straight spine and a head that leans forward at a slight angle. We start the interview with his passion for technology, since he's already begun on that subject. He tells me that from the time he was five years old, reading *Popular Science* magazine at his grandfather's house, he dreamed of what the future would hold. "I wanted a computer that would see the sky overhead and tell me what the traffic and weather was going to be like. I was one of those guys waiting for the Internet to get here, and it finally did!"

AM radio could give the five-year-old Steve traffic and weather, but I know the Internet has had a far more profound impact on our culture and, of course, on artists. Colleen Doran is waging a battle against those who would steal her graphic novels. Steve is using online media to promote his music; it's how I found him. "I'm older now, in my fifties," he says, "but I work to keep up with technology."

"How did you come to be called 'Voice of Golden Eagle?'"

"During the '70s and '80s I spent most of my time trying to chase a hit. I then ran into a gentleman, an elder with the Southeastern

Cherokee by the name of Silver Cloud. I'm part Native American myself, you know. Well, Silver Cloud invited me to participate in a naming ceremony, and the Council of Elders explained that I was basically a bear with an eagle on my shoulder. That eagle had a golden voice that needed to be heard. And the eagle's music was pure, not driven by commercial gain but by the power to communicate from the heart."

It's clear he has told this story many times before. It's as if he's performing a reading while auditioning for a community play. But despite the theatrics and the borderline corniness it resonates with me.

"I find a lot of artists feel a compulsion to put their art out into the world," I say, "as if they have no choice."

"It's true," he says. "But many artists suffer because they aren't doing it. They've put their creativity in a closet. A creative person who doesn't have the guts to put their work out there—and it's not easy to do—can spend the rest of his life with some part of his heart feeling empty." He reaches over to the table beside him and grabs one of the half-dozen flutes he has spread out on the table next to him. "I have a need to play because I want to give to others. Forgive me if I sound too 'New Age' here, but to be able to reach people through music is a magical gift."

Someone watching this video later might think Steve arrogant. But his face, and his voice, and his aura convey not unbounded superiority but sincere gratitude. "Can you play something?" I ask.

He opens his eyes wide. "I'd love to."

I'm not much of a fan of wood flutes. I associate them with an annoying Peruvian pan-flute ensemble that I often hear outside D.C. metro stations, hustling for donations while I'm hustling to work. But that memory departs when Steve starts playing. His piece is short, and beautiful. When he's done, he takes a short breath, turns to me slowly, and smiles again.

"Thank you for sharing your eagle's voice with me," I say.

He doesn't pause this time before he speaks. "That was indeed the eagle. I just channeled him." He leans forward. "I'm going to get all New Agey again, but every time I perform or record, I say a prayer. I ask that, as the flute is hollow, as I form breath I become spiritually hollow, so the Creator's breath can flow through me."Now he pauses, then speaks again. "Boy, do I need to get back on the road."He has been focused in recent years on raising his two teenage boys, but now they're both in college. "Don't get me wrong. Raising children was the finest thing I've ever done in my life. But now it's time to go be a musician."He tells me that he senses "possibility"of travel, then repeats the word "possibility.""Don't talk about things that don't yet exist, Steve," he corrects himself.

My children are not quite grown. What they are, however, is used to not having their father there on days he doesn't have custody. And they're used to their father being on the road for business, including this trip right now. I can't cite them as an excuse for not engaging my creative muse.

"It's hard," I say, "to fully engage yourself creatively."

"It's a big challenge for anyone," he says. Again that deliberate pause before speaking is gone. "I haven't just taken a sabbatical from touring. I've put aside my songwriting. It wasn't totally voluntary. The inspiration simply hasn't been there."Suddenly he sits up again, and his voice rises in pitch. "Here's a tip for artists who are in it for a lifetime. When the tide is in, write. Wake up at two in the morning if you have to and write. But if the tide is out, don't sweat it. That's when you get your busywork done."

"How do you know when the tide is in?"

He pauses, presumably to formulate his answer in a complete sentence. "You'll know when the tide is in the same way you knew when you fell in love. But Patrick, creativity is very temperamental. If you let it keep knocking on the back of your mind and you don't answer, it will quit knocking."

I've been feeling that knock on this trip.

"Let me tell you," Steve says. "By allowing myself to be open to possibility, my life has unfolded in a way that I celebrate. You just have to make yourself available, and see what life brings you."

I am open right now to possibility in the same way a defeated prey is open to a predator's jaws. It is an openness grounded in passivity. But perhaps the very concept of being open to possibility is passive, a lean-back approach. One of waiting. I'm more comfortable doing things, to

124

making things happen, like this road trip. I find myself thinking that perhaps Steve needs to go beyond being open to possibility. Perhaps the reason he was free for an interview today, when every other Memphis artist I reached out to was on the road performing, is because he is being reactive rather than proactive. He is waiting to see what life brings him. It would seem all he has received lately is me.

I have enough footage and begin to pack up. Steve asks if I want to join him and his friend Jimi Jamison, the former lead singer of *Survivor*, for drinks. "I could call Jimi," Steve says, holding up his cell phone. "He may say, 'Steve, I think I'm going to stay in tonight,' but he's usually up for a good time."It's a very generous offer, but I feel I've spent enough time with Steve. Like a good play, after a couple of hours you've received enough of a performance to leave satisfied.

A few minutes later I'm free from the obligations of the day. After storing my gear in the rental car I join the throng of tourists on Beale Street. I walk its full length, stopping to take in the music that pours out of each club. None of the clubs' performers are playing classic Delta blues, the simple melody lines with a lyric rhyme pattern of A, A, B, A. That's fine with me. As someone who discovered blues through the creative interpretations of the British rockers Led Zeppelin, I prefer a bit more complexity. I choose a corner joint with a brick facade lined with a red-and-green striped awning, the Rum Boogie Cafe. A large man with a round face framed in a curly black beard plays the keyboard and croons into a microphone, performing solo. His harmonies are nuanced, but his lyrics are as raw as a classic Delta blues artist, tales of woe both pocketbook and heart.

I soak in the music as I devour a half-rack of ribs. His name is Victor Wainwright, and he's good. When it's time for him to take a break, he announces that his CD is for sale, and holds one up. I walk up to him and purchase one. I'm the only bar patron doing so, and he happily hands me, in exchange for a ten-note, his CD *Piana' from Savannah*. I inform him I was in Savannah a few days earlier. He says he grew up there, and while it pained him to leave, he has a greater chance of succeeding in the music industry if he's based in Memphis. Unlike Steve, Victor isn't waiting for a new possibility. He is proactively seeking it.

I return to my seat and Victor begins playing again. He will go home later tonight knowing that at the very least, he sold one CD. I will head to my motel reflecting on the choice an artist faces, of waiting for inspiration or seeking it out.

AUGUST 25: TENNESSEE

When I told my father twenty-two years ago that my cross-country drive to Washington, D.C., would take me through Memphis, he insisted I visit Graceland. It would prove to be one of many times I left him disappointed. On this trip, without my father knowing, I am finally honoring his request.

The estate Elvis purchased when he was about the same age as I was on that drive years ago is not in Memphis proper. When Elvis lived there he was surrounded by open land, but times change. I find Elvis Presley Boulevard lined with retail establishments selling used cars with no-qualification financing and fast-food restaurants offering drive-through windows for those cars' new owners to buy a celebratory meal. I'm disappointed not to see a Burger King, as that would seem fitting on a street named for the King. Then on my left the iconic wrought-iron gates leading to Graceland appear, featuring quarter- and eighth-notes flanked with matching pelvis-swinging guitar-playing silhouettes. They block a driveway of modest width, not markedly wider than the one that leads to my parents' five-bedroom Tennessee home. Jammed just to the left of the gates is a squat brick souvenir store with a banner that reads like a middle finger to the Presley estate and the massive visitors center across the street. "We have 10 years left on our lease! Thank you for your business."

I pay $10 to park at the visitors center and shell out still more cash for a ticket to the house itself, and then am transported across the street in a van filled with half-alert senior citizens. The actual home is remarkably small, less imposing in some respects than my parents' McMansion on the other end of this state. As we exit the van the driver tells us to make sure we take our time in the adjacent racquetball building, which has been converted to a museum featuring Elvis' collection of gold and platinum singles and albums.

"The record display is amazing," an elderly man tells me in what he probably thinks is a whisper. "But the best part is the last room, where you get to see some of his sequined jumpsuits."

We enter Graceland itself. I'm anticipating tacky decor, and I find it, but the living room has touches of taste, with a white sofa on white carpeting that almost forgives the two floor-to-ceiling stained-glass peacocks. The room attracting the most clicking of cameras is the Jungle Room, which appears to be a rear porch that was walled in and stuffed with furniture in the shape of wild animals.

I came prepared to play the role of snob, appalled by the King's poor taste. As I've found myself working among the upper strata of Washington society, I've experienced elite living. I've savored single-malt scotch on a satin divan in the salon of a political maven's Georgetown mansion. I've devoured a three-pound lobster at D.C.'s Palm Restaurant. And I've pleasured in the smooth draw of a three-figure Cuban cigar on a terrace atop the Grand Hotel Duomo in Milan, Italy. That five-star landmark, built in 1860, overlooks the stunning Duomo Cathedral, with which it shares the same marble. Many of the hotel rooms are decorated in motion-picture themes, and the poster outside my room on a business trip five years ago depicted a robed Peter O'Toole with the words *Lawrence D'Arabie* below it. The room's walls were white stucco with faux-candles holding flame-shaped light bulbs tucked into grottos. Tiger and cheetah-print pillows adorned the bed, and an intricately detailed cloth embroidered with a vaguely Middle-Eastern pattern covered a table in front of a wall-mounted cushioned bench. Elvis would have loved it, without knowing that the hotel ownership was going for irony. Yet this desert boy who grew up with modest means savored that room.

I progress along the tour. The King's garage is a fence-lined carport capable of preventing perhaps a half-dozen cars from getting pelted by rain. The horse pasture doesn't appear large enough to host a softball game. The pool is no larger than the one my parents had installed in our back yard when I was in junior high school. The aforementioned racquetball building is the only place where my expectations are exceeded. The hallway lined with gold and platinum records appears to continue forever. The King was before my time, but his appellation seems reasonable as I admire each award. How could one man so dominate his artistic field? In our modern lean-forward society, where with the tap of a screen we can find whatever niche entertainment will please us at that moment, it's hard to imagine anyone could today. But while Elvis may have been presented with a technological possibility of domination, there was no guarantee he, or anyone for that matter, would achieve it. My admiration grows with each colored piece of vinyl. By the time I reach the jump suits, I don't see the butt of jokes. I see a man who lost touch with how special he truly was.

I offer him silent praise at his grave. I discover he is buried between his mother and father, and rather inappropriately only a few feet from the swimming pool, a location where one might expect a homeowner to station the pool's pump equipment. A menagerie of items has been left around his gravestone in homage, including a male and female pair of dolls dressed in Swiss attire, a white plush bear, and a handmade satin heart pillow with Elvis' photo in the middle above stitching that spells out "The King."All of the flowers are plastic. One could make a joke, to say that they match the tackiness of the home and the man. I choose to celebrate the fact that their beauty will last, like his musical legacy.

The shuttle bus back to the visitor's center winds through The King's front lawn. I sit on the van's left, facing not the house but the estate's spread of grass and trees. The trees were planted in a pattern clearly meant to simulate randomness. I see that each tree has a ground-mounted spotlight aimed up at the trunk and branches. I ask the driver if those lights are original to the house and he says of course, in a tone suggesting offense. The flood lamps aren't on right now—it's a bright, sunlit day—but it is clear from looking at the bulbs that each is a different color, namely red, blue, or green.

I know those colored bulbs. I was friends in high school with a boy who attended a fancy Phoenix prep school. Troy owned a boat, and if you were lucky he would let you join him on water-ski trips to nearby Lake Pleasant. His back yard was lined not with a crumbling wood-slat fence like mine, but a grand concrete wall covered in white stucco. Fronting that wall was an impressive array of desert plants—cholla, ocotillo, barrel cactus—rising out of a bed of river rock. The first time I was there at night was when Troy was throwing a party. Tiki torches surrounded the pool. Kids went back and forth in swim suits from the

Ping-Pong table on his porch to the pool table in his father's den. I sat on a love seat in Troy's sweeping pool, attempting without success to woo a bikini-clad prep-school girl. After she slipped away into the warm water, I took in that stucco-covered wall. Troy's parents had just flipped a switch; the wall was now awash in lights. It wasn't the soft white accent lighting you see adorning the homes of wealthy and powerful D.C. power players. Emerging from these lamps were bright beams of red, blue, and green. They were called "Malibu" lights, after the manufacturer. It seemed such an extravagance, wiring one's yard with electricity to provide illumination serving no purpose other than colorful amusement. Now I imagine Elvis sitting on his front porch, looking past the two stone lions that lead up to his home, taking in the light show in his front yard and smiling, satisfied that he had reached a place in his life where he could have Christmas all year round. The lights Laura and I put on our Christmas tree are white, like a lobbyists' yard accents. It's simply more tasteful, I say every year when I place the strings on the tree. But I understand the King's desire for a little color.

AUGUST 26: KENTUCKY AND OHIO

Yesterday afternoon I completed my circumnavigation of my parents' home. Driving east on I-40 from Memphis, I felt no temptation to press on to Knoxville, instead turning north short of Nashville to press on to Bowling Green, Kentucky. I finished off a rare day with no interviews by editing more video and calling Laura from the motel's indoor hot tub. This morning I completed an interview with photographer Clinton Lewis. He was a nice enough young man. A devoted husband and father, he dropped out of Western Kentucky University to support his family as a full-time photographer for the local newspaper. Now, at twenty-nine, he has finally completed that Bachelor's degree and works as WKU's official photographer. He brought a photographer's eye to our interview, setting us on an outcropping of large boulders that sits at the center of the school's hilltop campus. His dedication to his wife and children resonated with me. But he is young. Many of the stories he could have shared with me have not yet happened. Perhaps that is why I kept the interview short and returned to the road.

Or maybe it's because his last name reminded me of Meriwether Lewis, a brave explorer who traversed this continent long before me. He suffered from what his mentor Thomas Jefferson called "melancholy," what many historians today have posthumously diagnosed as bipolar disorder. On that drive yesterday on I-40 I was within a short distance of the place where in 1809 Lewis shot himself in an apparent suicide attempt, and then took several hours to die.

Now entering Ohio, I'm two states removed from the scene of that tragedy. I cross the Ohio River into Cincinnati on a steel-trussed bridge near an attempt at a modern downtown boasting a few modest-sized structures not quite scraping the sky near a tired football stadium. I was right to book my Ohio interview for tomorrow not here but instead in the Toledo Botanical Garden.

A little over an hour later I arrive at my motel. I spend the next three hours editing Marc Bondarenko's video, hearing the passion in his voice for photographing individuals and motorcycles. Perhaps that is why I felt flat in my time with Clinton this morning. His photography puts food on the table, but he spoke most passionately about rock climbing. I'm sure creative thinking is required to avoid falling to your death, but I'm seeking artistic passion. I can relate to Marc's love of both people and bikes.

It's time to eat. I go spelunking up a narrow country road and after a few minutes am rewarded with a biker bar. I am careful to park far from the stunning display of well-loved bikes lined up one after another, not wishing to topple them like dominoes. A thin man with a trim beard sits on a parked black Harley. An even thinner blonde faces him, her rear on the gas tank and her lips on his. I walk past the couple into the bar.

I'm sporting a green polo shirt, khaki cargo pants, and Timberland sandals, not exactly biker attire. But I'm not concerned. I learned long ago that in the type of bar that my wealthy funders would disdain as much as colored Malibu lights, the only requirement for acceptance is a complete lack of airs. And I accept everyone in this bar. We share a passion, if not a uniform. I take a seat on a worn wooden bar stool and order the most exotic brew they have on tap, a Yuengling. Minutes later the couple from the Harley enters. The man takes a seat to my left.

"Nice Fat Boy," I say to him. I'm referring to his Harley model, but I realize as I say it out loud it's an easily misinterpreted line.

"Thanks, bro," he replies, his toothy grin revealing sharp canines. "Had her about three years now, good times."

"She looks brand new."

"I take good care of her. You ride?"

I nod. "In between bikes right now."

"What were you riding?"

"Not a Harley, I'm afraid. Honda Shadow ACE."

He slaps the bar's lamination, which covers up a display of beer coasters. "Don't apologize for an American Classic Edition, that's a damned fine bike. V-twin engine. Good pipes. Hell, probably more chrome than mine."

The bartender returns and I offer to buy my companion his beer of choice. He also chooses a Yuengling. We go deep into the weeds, comparing bikes we love and long to someday ride. The blonde spots a pair of girlfriends at a nearby table and wanders off.

"So what is it about a bike that truly speaks to you?" he asks.

I'm not a gearhead like Marc Bondarenko, so I don't say the elegance of its mechanics. And I also don't speak to aesthetics, although I did enjoy Marc's photographs from the Barber collection, in which he captured their aggressive beauty.

"The freedom of the ride," I say.

He nods. "It's something, isn't it? No steel cage around you. Just raw power beneath and the world around. When I ride, I don't think about anything but the tire's grip and the gear's hum. You read about these city boys, doing their yoga and repeating mantras. And nature boys, climbing mountains and shit. I mean, more power to 'em, whatever works, right? But if you've got a good bike and a nice winding road with a few good banks, you've got all you need."

"That's poetry," I say.

"Thanks. You know, I lied to you just now. I think about more than grip and gears when I ride. Lately I've been thinking about this whole freedom thing, what it means. I don't think freedom really exists."

For the first time I take a good look at my companion. He is built like Marc, one of these men who is lean of frame, the opposite of the beer-gut motorcycle stereotype. He's sporting a leather riding coat free of adornment. His T-shirt is simple white. And his eyes are a striking gray, like the sky before a refreshing rain.

"What do you mean, 'Freedom doesn't exist'?"

"Well, how can I put it? It's not something that is tangible, you know, always there. It's like something that you can create and hold on to before it goes away again. What are those scientists looking for, that God particle? The Higgs boson?"

It doesn't seem at all odd to me that he would bring up particle physics. I want to prove I am also well-informed on the latest in science and technology, and search my mind for what I've read on the subject. "I think I know what you're talking about. Some scientists say their model of the universe requires it to exist, that it's all around us, but we can't see it."

"Right. They're trying to create this particle in a lab, but as soon as they think they've got it, it goes away. But they're still willing to go through all of that effort, just for a single solitary moment with the particle. Freedom is like that. I love my Fat Boy, but I had to spend money to buy it, and I had to work a crappy job to earn that money. When it's just me and the bike and the open road, I can sometimes, for a moment, grab that freedom by the hair, swing her on the back of my bike, and give her a good ride. But the ride has to end. I've gotta return to my house and think about my next rent payment. I've gotta figure out what the hell I'm going to buy Kirsten for her birthday this year, because I blew it last year with a new hair dryer. Not a good choice, bro, not at all. But even though I know that I need just the right conditions to grab that freedom from her hiding place, and I know I can only hold on to her for a moment, I still try."

What am I searching for? Some questions have manifested momentarily during my drives. Why am I obsessed with others' creativity? Why did I drift from the creative path? Can I return to it? Should I? And how can I free myself from the yoke of my funders? I've been frustrated that the freedom I've found from them on the road can't last. But this man understands something I do not. We shouldn't mourn the eventual surrender of freedom gained. We should understand that freedom belongs to the universe, yet it's always there. Perhaps it is the fundamental building block from which all other elements of life derive.

"Have you only been able to capture that Higgs boson particle on a bike?" I ask. "There have to be other ways. Perhaps when you kiss Kirsten."

He looks over at the blonde. She's deep into conversation with her two friends. "She may find the particle in a kiss. I don't think she finds it when she rides with me. Have you ever been the passenger on a bike?"

"No."

"My daddy used to ride me around a lot as a kid. It's not the same thing. It's passive, you know? But when you're operating it, you have that illusion of control. And that's critical. You have no such illusion on the back of a bike. I think that control—deciding whether to keep going straight or turn, whether to speed up or slow down—that's a condition you need to capture freedom. Kirsten and I have a little routine. I give her a crazy-big kiss at the end of each ride. It's my gift to her for letting me be the one in control, the one capturing that freedom."

"It ain't so bad for you, either. She's a fine woman." I feel safe saying that. In my polo shirt and shorts, I hardly come across as someone who would move in on a biker's girl.

"That she is, bro, that she is. And maybe that kiss is a place for her to find that freedom. You know, I've never really talked about this with her. Haven't really talked to anyone about it, actually. Anyone ever tell you you're easy to talk to?"

"I hear that sometimes," I say, but now I'm not really listening. I'm focused on what my conditions are for capturing the Higgs boson. I've been filled with troubling thoughts on these empty stretches of road, experiencing emotions that are both familiar and distant. My drinking companion might say that being surrounded by a ton of steel prevents me from obtaining the particle while driving, but he is not me. I find driving a car can create the optimal conditions. Until now I hadn't realized that this must be part of the reason I so like to drive, why when I conceived of producing these films, I knew it had to be a road trip.

And I know that just as his girlfriend has a ritual with a post-ride kiss, I have a ritual with a white, round pill. When I take my lamotrigine each morning, I'm reminded that I'm bipolar. But I also know I have just set in motion the possibility of a day free of symptoms. My adult life has largely been free of mania-inspired incidents. Because of a pill taken that morning at my parents' house last year, I kept myself together sufficiently to resist taking my mother's bait, allowing me to project calm to my children as I took them to a hotel. It is a stretch to say lamotrigine equals freedom. After all, I am yoked to the pill far more so than I am to my funders. But I do accept that yoke with gratitude.

A burly man with a thick gray beard walks over and slaps the philosopher beside me hard on the back. I wave off the need for an introduction and let them converse while I turn my attention to my beer. It's almost empty, so I signal the bartender for another. Alcohol, of course, is an anti-node to finding the sanity particle; it counteracts the magic of the morning pill. But while my lamotrigine may be a gateway to possible freedom, I don't want to allow it to enslave me with rules. I'll be taking another one in the morning. Tonight my embrace of freedom involves living a little.

AUGUST 27: OHIO

The only outlet available to charge my phone is near the motel room's modest desk. Thus I am forced to get out of bed and cross the room when it goes off at 5 am. As I go to silence this disruptive device I see that its screen is casting a bluish glow on the white laptop beside it, and I remember why I have to get up so early. I have a schedule to keep with video uploads, and having too many beers the night before is no excuse. Over the next three hours I down two pots from the coffee maker provided with the room; edit my footage of Oxford, Mississippi's Amy Evans Streeter down to a rough-cut five-minute video that needs only B-roll of her wood-sheltered cabin; shower and put on my last clean outfit; confirm the motel I'll be staying in tonight in Ann Arbor, Michigan, has a clothes washer and dryer; load up on waffles and more coffee at this motel's free breakfast; and pack up what little had been unpacked the night before. Then I'm back on the road, heading due north toward Toledo and an interview with musician Leah Martensen.

Leah is unique among my interview subjects in that her artistic inspiration is explicitly her Lord and Savior. She visits churches across the country, performing original songs with her guitar as part of her ministry to help people recover from life traumas. I like bluesy rock sung by angry women who've been done wrong, but Leah's songs twang with sunshine and major chords.

I will do my part to prevent Leah from asking me about my own faith. Consistent with someone who has earned a living asking questions, the lack of definitive answers in religion has led me down the path of agnosticism. When I was fourteen, however, my faith was unwavering. Having been raised for most of my childhood without religion, my mother's love-hate relationship with Rome had shifted back to love three years earlier and we began to attend Mass each Sunday. She enrolled my father, a Presbyterian, and me in a crash-course so that he could be baptized and we both could receive communion. The first time I took that wafer I felt the Holy Spirit fill me. I was determined to catch up with my Catholic peers, and soon became an altar boy. Wanting to honor God by appearing as holy as possible, while on the altar during mass I would position myself in a beam of sunlight piercing one of the church's upper windows, allowing the Lord's warming rays to illuminate my white robe as bright as Christ's halo.

My mother then began taking me to mass daily. Often the only other parishioners were a small handful of white-haired retirees. But a few months after that my mother began her predictable swing back to her default position of railing against the Pope while telling ever-more-dramatic trauma stories of her Catholic school upbringing. Her manic swing was complete, but I was determined to stick with this new life even without her participation. I joined a revival-style group that met at the church on Wednesday nights and insisted my mother drive me there. At those meetings we would take turns sharing how the Lord had moved us that week. I was tempted when driving by a liquor store, but God's hand kept me moving, one would say. Praise the Lord, we would answer. I've found myself lusting after my boss, another would say, but my Lord and Savior has kept me from responding to his flirtations, another would share. Praise the Lord. My offerings as a fourteen-year-old were less profound, but the love-filled responses from my fellow worshipers were no less enthusiastic. Even though our membership never varied, we would always wear name badges we filled out with colored markers. Those badges soon covered my closet door. Each label seemed another point accumulated in my race for Heaven.

One night, however, a young woman who rarely spoke demanded to be the first to testify. She rose to her feet and placed her arms up, palms outstretched. Her washing machine had broken, she said. With no money to fix it, she turned to prayer. Three times she worked her way through her rosary. Before each Hail Mary, she said, she asked Jesus to fix her washer. Before every Our Father, she promised to live a life without sin. When she was done, she went to the washer and tried it again. It was now working. We all raised our arms and praised God. I was happy for her good fortune. But I couldn't see myself worshipping a god that would trifle with an Arizona woman's broken appliance while declining to answer the prayers of starving Ethiopians. I had been throwing myself into being a Catholic not due to blind acceptance of the church's tenets and principles but out of a driving determination to outperform peers, a trait I so admired in my mother. I didn't testify that night, and said nothing to my mother on the drive home. Once in my room I peeled all of the name badges off of my closet door. I was afraid to leave my bed the next morning, knowing that I was walking away from the Lord of the Catholic Church yet unclear as to what punishment would befall me for doing so. My mother finally came into the room to force me out of bed and saw the door covered only with the sticky remains of the labels' glue. "It's about time," she said. "Tell you what. I'll make you a nice breakfast today, perhaps some French toast or pancakes, and call the school to tell them you're going to be late."Once again, I had fallen in line with her, and I was to be rewarded for it.

I arrive at the Toledo Botanical Gardens and thank whatever power is responsible for the lack of rain and cloud cover assuring me a perfect shoot. I rule out filming at a Japanese gazebo nestled against a pond covered in lily pads because it is near the main entrance and there will be too much pedestrian traffic. I stop at the Herb Garden and set up such that Leah will be seated on a mount for a now-missing sculpture. She finds me not too long after that, floating into the garden a shimmering vision. A billowy blouse reflects against the sun nearly as many shades of green as are found in the garden. Further catching light are numerous gold chains adorning her neck, framed by bleached blonde hair feathered like a 1980's pop star. Her motion is smooth and graceful, as I imagine she looks when taking the stage. I wave and she makes her way along a path through low-growing shrubbery toward me.

"How great to meet you!"she says, her voice rising dramatically on the word "meet.""You have fantastic energy!"

For a minister her powers of perception are poor. I feel like I was run over by a dozen motorcycles. But perhaps she is detecting a different kind of energy, something inside me I myself am not fully in harmony with. I thank her for a fantastic location for our shoot, and she laughs—a deep roll of a laugh—saying Toledo's frequent appearance as the butt of jokes is undeserved. When I start the interview Leah ramps up immediately into full storytelling mode. Telling her story is, I remind myself, how she ministers. She informs me people in recovery may have some sort of addiction, but her focus is on their deeper motivations. "A lot of people have a strong need to get their lives back together after some pain or hurt from their past," she says. "Sometimes there's something that we're holding on to, something that could be embedded in your brain or your heart, and you just can't let it go." She has worked with prostitutes, drug addicts, alcoholics, and victims of sexual abuse. When I ask why anyone would want to do this, she says simply, "It's what God wanted me to do, so I did it."

To Leah, God and music are one and the same. "God, I realize, used music to reach me at the age of five." She stops, blinks, and continues. "I came from a household with some, well, problems. When I was scared I'd lie in bed and sing church hymns in my head until I fell asleep." I wait, expecting more, but she has stopped. So I ask a question borne from my own experience putting together a road trip, how she finances her travel.

"Money is something I don't like to talk about," she says, but she keeps going. "Churches also don't like to talk about it, either." I learn she doesn't charge an appearance fee up front. "I go out on what I call love offerings. I love living off fate." She asks God to help her receive what she truly needs. "If I tell the event organizer ahead of time what I think I need, I'm going to be cutting God short."

That seems the very definition of faith, I think, launching a road trip and counting on the generosity of those to whom you're ministering. While I am covering some of the costs of this trip out of my own pocket, I only moved forward with this trip once I had secured financial assistance from my funders.

When in her thirties, Leah took her ministry on the road. She said she faced a crisis, not of faith, but of questioning her life purpose. She knew she needed a change. "I think there is always this time in our lives when we come to some kind of stop. We re-evaluate where we came from and where we're going."

Was it only a little over a week ago that Virginia illustrator Colleen

Doran shared a similar story, in her case a mid-life crisis that led her back to art school? I have been hearing Colleen's story daily in my mind.

"I realized there was a lot of stuff in my life I hadn't yet dealt with," Leah says. "God was calling me into a different kind of ministry. As I worked through it, I realized that he was calling me to go back to where I first began, to my music."

I couldn't believe in a God that fixed washing machines. But I am envious of Leah, whose God gives her a little nudge toward what she knows deep down is what she really should be doing with her life. Colleen, however, said nothing about God guiding her back to art school. She worked that out herself. Colleen and I didn't discuss religion, but perhaps her supreme being is a lot like the one I imagine, a Creator that gave us the gift to find answers in ourselves, and then said "Good luck with everything"before squeezing in eighteen holes before the sun set on the seventh day. Whatever role God plays—directly, indirectly, not at all—Leah found the answer she needed, when she needed it.

"Can you tell me about a person you feel you've really helped?"I ask.

"What I hear in meetings is confidential," she says. "But I can tell you that I share my story of how I felt as a child, living with alcoholic parents, in a house with a bipolar mother."She pauses, and I take that moment to break eye contact, staring at the gravel path under our feet. "I share how that left me in the dark a lot of times, and how there was a lot of insecurity there. And when people come up to me and say 'Can I talk to you for a minute?' and they share their story with me—they open themselves up the way I just did—well, it doesn't get any better than that."

I look up to find Leah bent over. She sucks in air, then dabs tears with her right hand. Her mascara remains intact, enough that it will still look fine at the low resolution this will be displayed online.

"Sometimes, when I tell my story, someone will come up to me and say, 'I was that child.' And sometimes I'll tell my story, and someone will come up to me and say, 'I was that parent. I was the one who did that to my child, and I had no idea...'" Now the tears are really flowing.

Leah is now the one to break eye contact. After a minute or so she regains her composure, straightens her blouse, and once again looks at me. Looks through me, actually. "They say, 'Now I know what I did. Now I have to go back and fix it.'"

This is too raw. It's too raw for a video meant to spur legislators to crack down on copyright theft. It's too raw for me to hear now, and yet I know as I edit it, I'm going to have to replay the footage four or five times. I suggest we wrap up the interview, and turn off the camera before she can say a word. As I do so I notice for the first time a young girl in a white dress and matching hat staring at Leah, at her vibrant blonde hair and her shimmering green blouse. Leah follows my gaze, spots the girl, and gives her a wide smile. The girl giggles, then runs off through a slice in a hedge.

As I fold up my tripod, I ask Leah how she feels the interview went.

Leah is now completely composed. "It was great!" she says. "You know, Patrick, I knew you'd want to talk to me about my music, but what's really cool is that you let me share God."

As a film editor I have the power of a Creator. I could edit this footage to create any Leah I wish. With just a few clicks of my computer mouse, I could delete the presence of her Lord. I could, but I won't. "It would seem difficult to convey you without mentioning Him," I say.

She laughs from her belly and slaps both of her knees. "Well, you just never know, you know? But that's okay, because I take every opportunity to share in any way that I can. I'm not one of these people who feels everything needs to be inside the church. God is all around us," she says, surveying the garden with her hands, "wherever we need Him to be."

Leah and I walk together toward the parking lot. Interviews drain some people but charge others, and Leah is positively electric. I sense she isn't ready for the conversation to end, and I'm surprised to find I'm not either. Knowing the camera is off is liberating to me, so when we reach the lily pond I suggest we sit on a bench and chat a little bit more.

"I'd like that," she says.

"Would you mind," I ask when we sit, "talking a bit more about your childhood?"

She places her hand on my knee, holds it there for a moment, then withdraws. I tingle, but not the way I usually might if a woman were to touch me. It evokes something deeper in me, some childhood memory of love and tenderness and spirituality. "Of course, Patrick," she says. I realize that when the camera was on she was in performance mode, because now, on this bench, her voice is so soft as to be almost elusive. She doesn't tell her story the way a creative writer would, with dramatic scenes designed to heighten tension and highlight a moment of awareness or trauma. Her words, rather, paint broad strokes of a girl who didn't understand why her mother would suddenly "turn dark."It was years before she became aware of her mother's diagnosis, but by then she had already found comfort in the Lord. He was her Rock. But most of her narrative is not about God. It is about herself, the person she has come to peace with. She understands now, she says, that her mother wasn't responsible for her own mental condition. That doesn't excuse her from complete responsibility for her actions, Leah says, but it provides context. Leah still loves her mother, she tells me, even if her childhood memories are colored with regret.

I speak even more softly than Leah. "I grew up in a bipolar household as well."

I watch for some sort of change in Leah, perhaps eyes opened in surprise, or narrowed in sympathy. But she maintains her same measured demeanor, reacting no differently than if I had told her I was enjoying the seventy-degree weather. "Mother or father?"she asks.

"Father."

It's not as simple as that, of course. His dark moments could be terrifying, yes. And I have inherited his diagnosis. But my undiagnosed mother birthed the center of the legacy that haunts me.

I have long since given up hope my mother will seek psychiatric treatment, but at one point when I was young she actually did so. The doctor did what many of his profession had done with their female patients in the 1970s; he wrote my mother a prescription for Valium and told her to get a grip. Years later my mother had a built-in excuse for not seeking help from the medical profession. She would cite a memoir by Barbara Gordon titled *I'm Dancing as Fast as I Can*, published just a few short years after my mother's thoughtless treatment by the medical profession. Like the author, my mother would say she too had been tossed aside with nothing but an addictive medication to help her get through the day. She was right. But then my mother would say she was done with doctors, even while insisting my father receive treatment. When my mother cut off communication with me for the first time I read Gordon's book. It was heartbreaking. It helped me understand my mother a little more, how angry and hurt she must have been, a struggling mother reaching out for help and instead being handed a bottle. And it filled me with pain, wondering what kind of life my mother might have lived had the doctor actually listened to her, actually cared enough to try to help her work through her problems rather than simply drug her. But then the target of my anger shifted as I continued to read the book. Gordon's story, like many memoirs, is a tale of darkness followed by triumph. The author finds her way back to sanity, and back to happiness. She does so with the help of a sympathetic mental-health professional, an individual who demonstrates that not all caregivers resist caring. My mother's story, at the time of my reading of Gordon's book and now, is incomplete.

I want to tell Leah this. I want to explain that I have lived my adult life fearful of my genetic inheritance. She likely would tell me to turn to the Lord. I believe I have to first turn to myself. I'm starting to understand a bit more on this trip how I came to be where I am, a writer who doesn't write and a son who doesn't communicate with his parents.

I realize that Leah doesn't ask if I am also bipolar. Given her own personal experience with the diagnosis, she must know that it often runs in the family. My father, when he was diagnosed, reflected long and hard on his family tree. He became convinced his late mother had been bipolar, describing her periods of mania when she would be up for three days straight, followed by days where she wouldn't get out of bed. He believed his oldest sister was bipolar as well. I had never met her, but I knew she had moved to a remote cabin deep in the Canadian Rockies, just she and her husband and her son, cut off from civilization. She called my father once when I was a teenager. He said little during the conversation, and told my mother and me afterward that she had been extremely animated. Among the delusions my aunt had shared with my father was that her son, who was around my age, was being recruited by the Montreal Canadiens professional hockey team. That last story is another my mother loves to retell, always with a smile on her face. But while my mother is only connected to these individuals by marriage, they are part of my genetic history. The humor was lost on me.

I wonder if Leah also is diagnosed bipolar. Given her inclination to share—that is her life mission, to expose herself fully to others—I decide she is not. Or perhaps she doesn't share every detail of her own life, choosing what will be effective and withholding the rest. I can relate. I've only shared my diagnosis with two other people in my life—my ex-wife and Laura. Leah fills the silence that has descended upon us with a sermon on how all of our lives are blessed. We can take everything from our childhood—the good and the bad—and make of it whatever we choose. She is right, but I am back now to where I was while filming her. I don't wish to be ministered. I've had enough skin peeled back already today. I tell her I must be going, we hug, and I return alone to my car. I sit in the seat, hands on the wheel, unmoving. I must move forward. I have a schedule to keep. But I fear what lies ahead.

. . .

This chili-cheese dog is not agreeing with me. That is, of course, a chili-cheese dog's reason for existence, but now it is only exacerbating the acid already set churning a short while ago in the Toledo Botanical Garden. The actor Jamie Farr stares at me in a reverse image, as I am seeing his face from inside the restaurant. Packo's was a restaurant Farr's character Klinger pined for on the TV show M*A*S*H, and that cultural legacy is now a major marketing tool for what has become a Toledo tourist attraction. I'm alone in a red vinyl booth, but the table to my right is fully occupied by a father, mother and three small children. The oldest, a boy of about seven, moves as much as one possibly can while remaining in one's chair. The mother is ignoring his conversion of potential energy to kinetic as she secures a bib on her high-chair-bound infant girl. The father is engrossed in conversation with the middle child, a boy I'm guessing is five. The father's hands slice the air as he emphasizes his narrative. The son is mesmerized, as still as his older brother is mobile.

There were no siblings for my parents to manage. As someone who had experienced the burden of being the "man of the house," I never possessed the freedom to wiggle in a chair. I was like the middle child at that table, the quiet one. My mother was the animated one, the storyteller, the center of attention. All those years of listening to my mother's stories, I know, contributed to becoming a professional storyteller as a journalist and advocate. But that is not the parental inheritance on my mind right now.

I watch the man's arms gesticulate. His motions are soothing. My father's weren't always so. He never struck me in a way I didn't feel I deserved, but inanimate objects were always on notice. Throughout my childhood he wrestled with his condition without diagnosis or treatment. I came to realize as an adult struggling with my own moods that my father had developed a coping method. Sometimes his instability would surface when under assault from my mother for some perceived fault or wrongdoing. Other times there appeared to be no trigger, at least one not visible without seeing into the neurochemistry of his brain. He'd dash to his car and drive away. Sometimes he'd be gone for an hour, sometimes twelve. With no husband to combat, I would avoid becoming a default target by retreating quietly to my room. Invariably, my father would return, and we would all dine together and listen to another of my mother's stories. Nothing would be said of the cause of that particular fight, my mother's threats of divorce, or my father's angry departure. We were a happy family and that was all that mattered. The only occasional evidence that anything out of the ordinary had occurred would be olfactory. My father professed to be a non-smoker, but often after one of my dad's disappearances the white cloth upholstery in his burgundy Monte Carlo would reek of cigarettes.

As a child I viewed my dad's disappearances as evidence of

cowardice. But I believe now my father was trying to protect my mother and me from himself. I don't know where he went when he left, although I often wanted to ask him. That would, of course, have required acknowledgment of his departure, which just wasn't done. Perhaps he just drove around. Maybe he went to a strip bar. He might not have been able to give me a good answer. My own memories of my actions when I am shaking off a dark mood are often unclear mere hours after the experience.

Discarding the remains of my chili-cheese dog in a nearby trash can, I bid a silent farewell to the family of five and return to the road. I quickly cross the Michigan border, but I bypass Ann Arbor. I have two interviews scheduled there for tomorrow, but my motel for tonight is outside of town near a small body of water called Whitmore Lake. The motel itself is a typical eyesore, a long two-story row of doors and railings resembling a cell block, but the lake proves calm and inviting. I step out of the car to examine it through a chain-link fence. Development surrounds much of it, stately homes with bay windows facing the water. But I enjoy seeing the water through the metal links. My mission now is laundry and video editing, but I vow later this evening to circle the lake until I can find a way to reach its shore.

In my room, I begin in the final stages of editing the video of musician Steve Cox. The Voice of Golden Eagle appears on my computer screen, and that eagle voice fills the motel room. "You'll know when the tide is in the same way you knew when you fell in love. But Patrick, creativity is very temperamental. If you let it keep knocking on the back of your mind and you don't answer, it will quit knocking."

My muse knocked for many years while I was on lithium. The drug muffled that knock. During the period my parents and I weren't speaking and I was dabbling in fiction writing I would answer, but moving toward the door was like walking in a swimming pool, an action that is deceptively laborious. It was easy to ignore the knock once my mother was back in my life. For twenty years, under the care of the same psychiatrist, I have been on various medications in different combinations, a changing cocktail to keep my angry flashes and deep depressions in check. It has seemed the last year or so that she has finally hit on the right treatment. For one, I went through my first winter in as long as I could remember without dipping into a severe depression. Not even that troublesome January conversation with my mother, when she demanded an apology from Marisa, sent me to a place I didn't want to go for more than a few hours. The strongest evidence, however, is how I find myself interacting with my own mind. My doctor has always told me to watch out for "racing thoughts." As Laura knew when we spoke on the beach in Cape May a few weeks ago, it is one of the stock questions my doctor asks in each session. Have you had any racing thoughts? While on lithium it sometimes seemed my mind was occupied by few if any thoughts, racing or not. In the last year, while on this new medicine, my mental synapses have lit up like a yard full of Elvis' Malibu lights. But I would not characterize those thoughts as racing, at least not in the sense my doctor means, undisciplined and erratic. No, these neuron lights illuminate more rational mind maps of paths to all sorts of new and creative possibilities. The conception and execution of this road trip is but one example.

In an effort to tighten an editing transition I replay Steve Cox's discussion of our knocking muses again and again. My mind map on this trip, I now realize, called for me to be open to possibility. Perhaps I am at a place in my life where I can take on a creative adventure without fear of mental consequences. But I still have the matter of my funders, who have paid me well to purchase the rights to my creativity.

I reduce the video to a rough cut of the right length and call it a night. I leave the room determined to explore the lake but hear music. It's a Friday night, I realize, and the bar that shares a parking lot with the motel has a live band playing. It's two guys on guitar fighting their way through an Aerosmith cover, poorly. But the idea of distraction among musicians and an anonymous crowd speaks to me. The lake can wait.

The bartender is a vivacious young woman, with shoulder-length red hair, full lips highlighted with crimson lip liner, and lime green rectangle glasses. She's the perfect embodiment of a naughty librarian. When she smiles and tells me they're offering a special on Cuervo Gold margaritas, I say yes. When she asks me if I'd like a large one I say yes. A voice reminds me that alcohol is to bipolar disorder like kerosene to a fire, and that infidelity is a common result of a manic outbreak. But when the drink arrives I take a large sip. I focus my attention away from the bartender, staring instead at the Steven Tyler wannabe on the microphone. Steve Cox said that when he plays his flute, he asks his Creator to make his form hollow, so the music can flow through him. My hollow places are filled with fear and regret. The abandonment of my art. The loss of my parents. The paralyzing fear my diagnosis casts upon my life actions. Tonight I'll replace them with classic rock covers and discounted tequila.

I check in with my wife by phone, but she has a hard time hearing me over the din of bar patrons and overly amped guitar music, so the conversation is short. I hang up and order another large margarita. Salt-rimmed glasses come and go. The rockers finally stop playing. A young man in an apron begins resting chairs atop all unoccupied tables. I've reached that point in my drinking where I am forgetting where I am, and that is where I want to be. I ring up and gently guide myself off of the bar stool, not wanting my imaginary ginger mistress to know how inebriated I am. I then head for the lake and try the gate I saw earlier. I'm not surprised to find it locked. I walk to my right, looking for access to the water. A series of homes thwart my path. I spot a cross street that cuts between two homes and terminates at the lake. This stretch of lakeshore is also lined with chain-link fencing, but it allows approach almost to the water's edge. I walk up to the fence and grab links with each hand. Leaning forward, I press my face into the wires and gaze upon a thin slice of moonlight cutting its way across gentle ripples. I can't reach you, I say silently. Can you hear me? I can't get through.

PART FIVE: THE MIDWEST

AUGUST 28: MICHIGAN

A throbbing headache is my only companion as I locate Lillian Cauldwell's driveway, tucked in amongst crops and trees in Michigan farmland. In her driveway I find a Cadillac sport-utility vehicle with an older man sitting in the driver's seat. He informs me he is the husband of Rowena Cherry, the other author I'm interviewing here this morning. I shrug and head to the house along a concrete path lined with the petals from a stretch of elderberry bushes, and inform Lillian —a short woman about my mother's age with a bent spine and thin orange hair—of her outside guest. She darts past me with deceptive speed and returns moments later with the chagrined husband, ordering him down to the split-level's family room where he can wait with her husband.

"Men," Lillian tells me with a heavy sigh. "It's nice to have a husband, I suppose, but they can be such a pain. I've always thought a woman should have more than one husband anyway. One for financial security, one to play around with, one as a lover to make her feel special, and one to procreate."

I chuckle as Lillian leads us into a large living room in which every surface, from tables to walls, bears something to catch the eye. Books. Framed photographs. Ceramic figurines. The only backdrop I can film them in without distractions behind them is the brick fireplace. Then I meet Rowena, a much taller woman made larger by prominent shoulder pads in her black jacket. She welcomes me with a highbrow British accent I recall from my time in Oxford, then defends her husband, saying he insisted on bringing her here from Detroit because he didn't trust her driving.

This is a new challenge for me on this trip, interviewing two people simultaneously. I first reached out to Rowena, who has been active in our grassroots network and could be expected to say provocative things about people who steal others' writings online. Not having time to drive to Detroit, I suggested a meeting in Ann Arbor and she agreed on the condition I interview her friend Lillian, a fellow fiction author, as well. I inform them they can pass a handheld microphone back and forth. Rowena quickly takes it from me, and before I can ask her a question she launches a soliloquy. "I've lived the life of a romance novel," she says. "My life has been so good I feel compelled to share it in my books."She grew up wealthy on the British channel island of Guernsey, she says, proud of being the deputy head girl at her school. She won something called the Duke of Edinburgh Award, and seems to think I should know what that is. That led her to study at Cambridge followed by "teaching the children of the powerful"at a prestigious boarding school. Then her husband enters the narrative, a now-retired auto-industry executive she met and won over. "I left teaching and joined the glamorous corporate ex-pat life."

I'm rescued by a wooden bird that pops out of the wall clock about three inches above the clock's face and creates a racket. The bird's yellow head bobs up and down, as if nodding. I decide he is telling me the disdain I'm feeling right now is okay, and I take the opportunity to direct my interview to Lillian. I ask Rowena to hand the microphone to her, but instead she holds it in front of her friend, reporter-style. Lillian does not compare her life to a romance novel. "I brought up my son in a public housing project in Houston, Texas, a single mother below the poverty line," she says. Her books feature young heroines overcoming obstacles. "My protagonists show girls that you don't have to dumb yourself down, you don't need a boy to solve your problems."

I look again around the room. Now I don't see clutter, I see reminders for Lillian of how far she's come. I want to hear more, but Rowena turns the microphone back to herself. She goes on for a while about how imaginative her fiction is, what she calls "space snark"because her books are set in outer space and involve clever characters with biting senses of humor. When she pauses I think of something interesting I read about Lillian, and ask how a former welfare recipient found herself running an Internet radio station. Rowena reluctantly redirects the microphone.

151

"My first book did really well, and I was interviewed all over the country on TV and radio. Most of the interviewers were terrible. They'd go off on some soliloquy about whatever nonsense was on their mind and then they'd mention my book and we'd be done. I decided they were full of it."Lillian sought a career in traditional radio but found it a closed club, she says, so she conducted some research and learned about opportunities in Internet radio. I'm charmed by her telling me she learned of this budding online industry not through Internet searches, but from books and periodicals at her local library. My question about financing is left unasked when Lillian fills me in. "Rowena's husband invested, actually," she says, pointing off toward the study.

Rowena's left arm is twitching, the microphone beginning to drift back toward its holder. I quickly ask Lillian a follow-up question. "How did you learn to conduct a good interview?"

"By raising my son, bless his heart. When he was little he'd ask these extraordinary questions. I'd give him a simple answer and he'd put that answer into another extraordinary question. So I do that with the authors I interview. One of my goals is to become another Larry King, the one before he became famous and got really lazy."

Rowena appears about to launch herself out of her chair. I offer her relief, asking her if she's working on any books right now. "Well, I don't want to give my ideas away, but I have a lot of things in the works."She's imagining a series of short stories she describes as "Gulliver's Travels with sex"; a book about a hot, young, wealthy woman who hooks up with some aliens; and a "'Miss Marple in Outer Space' book with a sleuth empress."First up, however, is ghostwriting her husband's autobiography, detailing his powerful role in the auto industry. "I don't know if he'll choose to use it, but I want to call it *Autobio: A Life Around Cars*."But Rowena says her husband has been reluctant to work with her on the book.

I ask why, if he's resistant, she doesn't work on one of her novel ideas.

"I have to keep my promise to my husband first."

Lillian lets out a snort.

"How did you two become friends?"I ask.

Lillian says she interviewed Rowena on her radio station and, discovering how saucy and engaging Rowena could be, invited her to host her own show.

"But you know," Rowena tells Lillian, "I remember differently how we met."

"Oh I'm sure you do," Lillian says.

Rowena says a mutual friend passed along a manuscript by Lillian, asking Rowena to review it. Rowena agreed, in exchange for an interview on Lillian's station.

"Yes, I do that a lot," Lillian says. "I try to barter. I have a tendency to open my mouth and just ask. I learned a long time ago, the only thing someone can do is slam the door in your face, throw the phone down on the hook, or tell you to drop dead twice."

A wall phone in the kitchen rings. Lillian shrugs. "Don't worry, my husband will get it."

The interruption reminds me it's time to get some footage about copyright. Rowena gives me plenty, much of it clearly rehearsed. It will more than satisfy my funders. I shut down the camera, and after hugs all around I head back to the car.

The dashboard clock tells me I have time to have lunch in town before my next interview. It also tells me that I spent nearly two hours in Lillian's house. When she was speaking it felt like no time at all, but with Rowena it was an eternity. Rowena was the one I had wanted to interview. Like Lillian said, she can be saucy and engaging, and I'm sure that will come out in the video. The two of them are both authors, like my mother, and both from my mother's generation, it would seem. I realize that Lillian reminded me of the mother I so admire, the scrappy one who climbed up out of whatever dysfunction she suffered in a next-to-nowhere Oregon town and made herself into a bestselling author who doesn't need anybody but herself to succeed. Rowena, on the other hand, appeared to be channeling the mother I find myself resisting, the narcissist who chafes anytime the spotlight isn't bright upon her. We are all, of course, many people in one, but I never figured out how to be with the Lillian in my mother without the Rowena present as well.

. . .

If you find yourself blessed with every possible advantage in life, you should at least express sincere gratitude for it. Perhaps that is why I have not completely tuned out James Aikman despite my envy of his good fortune. Lillian Cauldwell fought her way out of a public housing project, and her decor spoke of a woman who cherished mementos of life's unexpected triumph. James, a fit and handsome white man in his fifties, it seems, does not appear to have known economic hardship, and his home reflects that. Sunlight shimmers off the living room's white walls, the sheen broken only by the occasional oil painting of fields and flowers. Lines of polished pine floorboards lead the eye past a black leather sofa to an equally black grand piano positioned just to the left of a white stone fireplace. I'm filming James at his piano, the sheet music to one of the symphonies he's composed spread open above the ivory. The home belongs to someone who appreciates clean lines while favoring a fusion of classic and modern. That is certainly how I interpret his music.

James has spent the last hour telling me of his many lucky breaks. There was the elementary school music teacher completing her doctorate in music who taught him to differentiate Tchaikovsky and Stravinsky. There were the private lessons with a neighbor who herself was training under a master of Mozart. Then there was his master's course taught by Leonard Bernstein. Still more encounters came his way while pursuing his doctorate, including an opportunity to work with Aaron Copland. His charm dents my instinct to resent him, my desire to champion Lillian and her distinct lack of exposure to creative mentors. James appears to have been born on the center line of an art-committed road, atop a Harley-Davidson Twin-Cam with no opposing traffic. Every mentor James has had can tie his or her instruction back to the great masters of composition. Now James is teaching the next generation as a university professor. He shares still more stories of his learning path, from private study in Amsterdam to a Master's class in Aspen. I wonder if he's simply starting in the A's.

"Let's talk a little about your compositions," I say.

"Well, my work is now clearly symphonic in nature. I write music that people say should be in movies, but my father says you can't sing it in the shower."

When I ask him if he'd like to write a motion picture soundtrack he pauses for the first time. He confesses he'd very much like to if the opportunity arose, but so far it hasn't. It becomes clear he's given the prospect a lot of thought when he says he would be ready to agree to allow the film producer to call the shots. "Patrick," he says, "I'm old enough to know when to surrender creative control."I realize I too am blessed, with my videos being funded by Hollywood studios that have not sought to exert any editorial control over the content.

James finds his way back to his musical legacy, and I ask him if he considers his path triggered by that elementary school teacher, whose last name, James delightedly reports, was Fiddler.

"No, it was definitely my mother."James was one of three children, he says, and each night their mother would play the piano for them. "She would sit at the piano, with a small task light illuminating the sheet music. I still remember that light. All we would see was the warm light over that music. And her performance of Chopin created in me a sense of mystery and warmth and beauty."

When I was young my mother played the piano for me. Her score of choice was Beethoven's *Für Elise*. But when I remember my mother's upright piano now I do not see her playing it. Instead I see a ten-year-old me coming home from school to find his mother waiting for him on the sofa. She tells him that she has a secret to share, and walks over to the piano bench where she keeps her sheet music. She knows her husband, who has now returned to the marriage, would never look in there. She knows her son wouldn't either, because he gave up the piano once he realized how much practice was involved. She opens the bench, lifts up the scores, and pulls out a few sheets of typing paper hidden below. The mother asks her son to read a short story she's written. He hadn't even known she had a desire to write. He reads each page while his mother watches. He is afraid, knowing he cannot hide his emotions from her, that she will read it in his face if he finds the prose atrocious. But he has no need to fear because the words guide him along, as entrancing as a Beethoven sonata. The mother has found the courage to share with her son what he would come to know

155

to be a core element of her being, her passion for creative writing. He would never be as proud of her as he was at that moment.

"James, that sounds like a beautiful experience for you. You've led a charmed life. But one of the things I hear from the artists I interview is that there's always an obstacle they've been forced to overcome. Have you encountered any?"

"Oh sure," he says quickly, "there are daily obstacles. Finding time to compose." Then he pauses again. The ever-present smile fades. His broad shoulders, so crisp in his finely tailored chocolate-brown blazer, slump. "You know, Patrick, it was especially hard to write for, well, many years, while I was the sole caregiver of my wife. She contracted ALS. That's Lou Gehrig's disease." He takes a deep breath, then another. Throughout the interview we have maintained eye contact, but now he is looking down at his polished hardwood floor. "Patrick, it's a horrible disease. It gradually takes away everything but your mind. You're able to think but not move. And so, with three young children—seven, three, and six months old at the time—I was caring for them and for her. I was taking care of Deanna's every need. Feeding her even, every gesture we take for granted I was providing. It stalled my music career, but I knew caring for Deanna was more important."

I have been unfair to James, assuming he has not known hardship or struggle. But what do we ever really know of another human being? We are all tested. He is quiet again, and I have a burning question to ask him. He is using the past tense to refer to his wife. But before I can ask the question he answers it.

"She's still alive," he says. "She was a great pianist, so stubborn at her craft, and somehow that stubbornness combined with her positive spirit has kept her alive all these years."

This is a large house, comparable to my parents' five-bedroom home. I wonder where she is now. Upstairs in a back room? In a custom suite here on the first floor, with easy access to the garage in case a sudden need to be driven to the hospital arises? Then he answers my unanswered question again.

"Deanna lives just down the road, about half a mile away in a home we set up for her. She's got round-the-clock helpers, and my oldest daughter lives with her. When I wound up with a hernia I couldn't do all the moving and lifting required. It's been something, the chronicles of a book perhaps one day. But it just proved to be too much. We had to divorce."

I don't think James' revelation was planned. It's one of those moments born of a mutual connection and trust quickly formed, the way photographer Marc Bondarenko told me can happen. I allow the silence to settle in. I want to ask him about the divorce, whose idea it was, why he felt that was necessary. Yet I've made a lot of choices in my life that I believe were right but would not want to have to defend.

"You know," he says, looking up, shoulders squared again. "We've been talking for two hours now, and you haven't once asked me about copyright." And off he goes, giving me great footage about how important it is that artists have a chance to pursue financial gain for their hard work. He also tells me he's an optimist who believes we'll sort everything out. I want to believe him.

We part warmly, with a hug. And then I'm back on the road, marveling at how the day has transpired. I woke up hung over and despondent, wrestling with the knowledge that I could no longer blame my many inactions in life on my diagnosis. The last thing I wanted to do today was interact with other people, but instead three artists have helped me to put my struggles in perspective.

AUGUST 29: INDIANA AND ILLINOIS

I know now that an airplane hangar is not an ideal space for an art show. The Indiana Visitors Center in Hammond, Indiana, does not in fact store commercial jets. But with aluminum and steel walls lifting fifty feet into the air to form an arched roof, the similarity is uncanny for this way station wedged between Michigan and Illinois. The space swallowed the several dozen paintings mounted around the room. Everything was white—floor, walls, beams—everything, that is, other than the dots of color representing the community art show arranged by Maria Braun-Perez, a woman about my age who came to the interview with her parents in tow. I am grateful Maria was willing to meet me at eight am on a Sunday morning, allowing me time to conduct another interview in Illinois before spending the night in Madison, Wisconsin. Maria's initial discomfort, however, was both frustrating as well as surprising, given the openness of her art. The works she had on display comprised various personal photographs and other memorabilia from her childhood. Yet she remained frustratingly resistant to talking about herself. Every question designed to elicit more insight on who she was would be deflected to broader topics such as the Hammond art scene or changes in the graphic design industry. Perhaps she is only comfortable revealing herself through her art, or more likely, the awareness of her parents seated on a bench nearby chilled her ability to share.

As I review the interview in my mind now while winding through this Rockford, Illinois, neighborhood of post-war ramblers and split-levels, I recall one moment where she opened up a bit. She talked about how one of her favorite activities as a child was playing with alphabet magnets. She would make all sorts of artistic shapes with them on the side of her family's furnace. She also loved her Etch-a-Sketch. To Maria, creativity is the ability to erase and begin again.

I wind the rental car around yet another gentle curve. I'm guessing this subdivision was designed a developer who wanted to produce a sense of flow by eschewing right angles. It creates a sense of peace for residents but invites confusion for visitors.

The neighborhood looks as tired as I feel. The modest homes I pass were likely quite striking when built, before the sun ravaged their siding and their owners grew too old to maintain the grass and hedges. The commercial road I just navigated on my way here struck me as frozen in the 1980s. The Tex-Mex bistro where I braved lunch—a cantina-style establishment with red Formica tables bearing sticky bottles of Cholula sauce next to plastic-sealed menus meant to resist the sauce when spilled—squatted along a wide road next to a strip mall boasting a mom-and-pop video rental store and a baseball playing-card trading shop.

I park across the street from the home of Bob Kurtz in front of a house with a concrete porch occupied by an elderly man wearing wide-brimmed fishing hat and wrap-around sunglasses. I can't see his eyes, but his gaze is fixed upon me. An oxygen tank on wheels sits beside him. The man breathes in deeply when I exit the car, but when I cross the street to Bob's house he visibly exhales. As I walk up to Bob's front door I pass a large picture window but can't see inside. A thick, red velvet curtain blocks my view.

I knew when I started this trip that I would interview Bob. He is a musician and composer, with a focus on what I would call modern chamber music. When I listen to his pieces, heavy with violin and piano, they remind me of my youth. My mother had failed to teach me the piano, but as a teenager I embraced classical music as a singer, a creative path she had never followed. I performed everything from Bach's B-Minor Mass to Duruflé's Requiem. Bob's music reminds me of the traditional Bach rather than the unpredictable Duruflé. Bach constructed sublime harmonies, but he did so with serious deliberation. He was a pyramid engineer, placing perfectly shaped blocks atop each other, building both for strength and for height. Duruflé introduced early 20th Century unpredictability to Bach's structural integrity, generating spontaneous harmonies as surprising and startling as the many wars and government upheavals he witnessed during his life in France. It would be an extreme stretch to say that Bob Kurtz is the next Bach—I'm sure he wouldn't claim that himself—but he embraces traditional chamber-style structure far more than most composers who came later.

The reason I chose to interview Bob is not my appreciation for his music, however. It is because he knows exactly what needs to be said on copyright. Bob discovered my organization about a year ago and has been an aggressive online promoter of our cause ever since. Bob seems to spend a lot of time online, seeking confrontation in the comment fields of blogs and news sites. He pushes back against those who would dismiss the rights of artists, who insist that musicians should play and write for the love of it without expectation of payment.

Bob welcomes me in, telling me how pleased he is I found him. I tell him his directions were thorough, and they were. I follow him into his kitchen, which is just off of the front door. It too has curtains drawn closed, but they are a bit sheer, and a little sunlight breaks through to join us. He offers me a cold beverage, rattling off many choices. He starts, oddly enough, with milk, but I stop him at lemonade. It proves incredibly refreshing, even with some instant crystals floating undissolved.

Bob is in his fifties, a man of modest height and modest weight. His hair is moderately long, and moderately gray. What strikes me is his voice, which has a hint of the accent Frances McDormand used in the movie *Fargo*. He combines that with a fairly high pitch that puts me a bit on edge. We've spoken a few times on the phone, but that medium hasn't fully conveyed the voice's distinctiveness. If you wanted to find Bob in a crowd, you wouldn't look for him, you would listen.

I sip my lemonade and Bob talks. Then he talks some more, telling me all about the neighborhood and his neighbors. The man with the oxygen tank is an original owner of his house, I learn, and my suspicion that this is a post-war development built for returning GIs and their families is confirmed. Bob tells me his mother bought this home in the 1970s and that he spent part of his childhood here. As an adult he moved back into this house—I gather it was after Bob found himself divorced, but he rushes through that part and I allow him to—and he lived with his mother until she passed. Now he lives alone. He says he likes being the youngest man in the neighborhood. A blue-haired woman next door likes to flirt with him when he comes home from work, he says with a smile. But what he really likes about this place, he says, is his basement studio. I have heard a great deal about this studio, in Bob's lengthy emails and long calls leading up to my visit. He has told me he owns a lot of top-of-the-line composing and recording equipment. Bob is a one-man shop. He composes his music on a computer, records it using a synthesizer that reproduces various stringed instruments, and then seeks to sell his recordings online. I know he does not make very much money doing so, but he continues to pursue his dream. His story should be an inspiring one, and his studio should make a nice setting for the video.

Bob leads me down a set of wooden plank stairs to a paneled basement. It is sparsely decorated. A tattered brown leather recliner and a tan suede sofa with oversized arms boasting matching stains faces a small projection-style TV with a built-in VCR. The carpet is shag, and appears once to have been Kelly green. One small transom window is high on the opposite wall. Slits of light act as a frame around another curtain.

I see no studio, no equipment of any kind. We walk silently across the carpet to an unadorned particle-board door. I wonder if he's guiding me into the furnace room, or perhaps a space for laundry. But the door instead leads to his studio. It has no window, only two bare bulbs illuminating dark wood paneling. The space is no more than ten feet long from door to back wall and stuffed with metal filing cabinets, a table covered with sheet music and CD jewel boxes, and various pieces of electronics equipment I can't identify. My newly acquired filmmaker's eye forces me to tell Bob this won't work. It is too small, too crowded. The lighting is poor. I ask myself if I am being critical because I am finding myself overcome with claustrophobia. I suggest we film the interview upstairs, in his living room, which I know will be more inviting once I pull back his heavy curtain.

His face hangs. But this is my studio, he says. I want people to see how serious I am as a composer, how much money I've invested to produce my art. I fear Bob becoming angry so I succumb, setting up the camera in the small space between his desk and the door. I tell Bob we must leave the door open.

Bob insists that two computer monitors on his desk remain on, even after I explain the compositions displayed there won't be visible in the video. With Bob backlit by the monitors, his face falls under an ominous shadow. I want to get on with this interview so I ask him a question I've learned gets people to relax and open up, when he first discovered his love of music.

It begins. A litany, starting with a story about his early love of music—as a toddler he would sit by his mother's feet while she played the organ at church—and while I am touched by the answer, it is a mere prologue to a lengthy monologue. He talks about Mozart, Beethoven, and Bach. Then he talks about technology. Then we're back to Mozart, Beethoven, and Bach again, always repeated in that order, like Peter, Paul, and Mary, or Crosby, Stills, and Nash. I haven't asked a single question since the first one. I glance at my watch and see that fifteen minutes has passed. I look to the camera's monitor to confirm that time, and realize that in my haste to begin the interview I forgot to turn the camera on. It takes me a few minutes to get up the nerve to break the news to Bob, but he takes it well. I'm happy to repeat myself, he says. I push the record button and tell him that this time he needs to keep his answers short while allowing me to ask questions. I promise him I'll ask about his childhood, about technology, about Mozart, Beethoven, and Bach. He nods, smiling. We begin again.

I wriggle in my seat, visualizing the door behind me, and turn to confirm it is still open. Bob's intensity will come across well on the screen, but I find it too similar to the part of myself that I try to keep in check through self-discipline and medication. Earlier today, Maria's resistance frustrated me, but now I long for that to be the day's biggest interview challenge.

After Bob re-articulates his points, seeming to me verbatim to his first pass, I shift the conversation to copyright. I know this is one of the videos that my funders will love. Bob knows all of the talking points. "What does copyright mean to you personally, Bob?"

"Well, copyright is one of those things that became a part of the United States with the adoption of the U.S. Constitution, when the Founding Fathers decided to provide artists and inventors the right to protect their works..."He continues with his history lesson. His information is largely correct. But this is not what I need.

"I'm sorry, Bob. I should have been clearer. What does copyright mean to you, personally, as a musician and composer?"

"What does copyright mean to me?"For the first time since I have arrived he is silent. He sits a minute. Then he resumes the rote. This equipment costs a lot of money, he says, and he needs it to be able to compose. It increases his efficiency, allowing him to produce more music. If he doesn't get paid for his music, he can't afford to make it. He'll have to stop, and that would be a tragedy, because he is committed to his music. Then he smiles, an odd smile. He says he has a funny story to tell. He once sent a CD to a big-wig in the music industry. She didn't sign him to a contract, but she told him she found his music calming, and that it spoke to her heart. So he writes music that calms the heart. I wait for the funny part, then realize he believes he's already shared it.

I need to leave. I end the interview by taking a risk and asking him if there's anything else he wants to share.

"There's one thing I need to say. Every night you go to bed, and lay your head on your pillow, and at that moment you're alone, just you and whoever your idea of God is. In the morning you wake up and open your eyes, and in that moment it's just you and God. Try to live your whole life that way, and connect with the essence of who you are. That moment becomes a lifetime between you and God, the creator of all things. Tap that. That is what I do, that is the message. It's not me, it's God's music, and that's the communion that I have. I didn't choose to be a composer. He chose me. I want you to connect with that God sense inside of you."

I reach over to turn off the camera, but he raises his right hand and I stop.

"There's a second thing I want to say. If you wake up and think about writing music, think about it all day, dream about it, then you'd better be a composer. What you think about all day long should be what you do, then. It's your responsibility to give that back to the world, to give your passion."

My need to flee this windowless room is stronger than ever. I feel guilty for wanting to run from a man who writes music to provide a gift of his God, but I must. This interview is so very different from my discussion of divine intervention with Leah Martensen in the Toledo Botanical Garden. I thank him for his time while packing my equipment. Suddenly Bob squeezes past me, knocking over a stack of jewel cases on the table next to me with his rear. He is now blocking the exit. I stand, camera bag over my shoulder, tripod held in my right hand like a club.

"I really need to go now," I say.

"Wait. I have a business proposal for you."

The intensity of his eyes redirects mine to the floor. His feet squat square in the door frame.

Did you know, he says, that I work ten hours a day selling heavy machinery equipment across the Midwest? I sell tools all day and write music most of the night. But I have a plan that is a surefire success. Every morning on my way to work I see parked cars surrounding Starbucks. Do you know how much people spend on coffee every day? A lot more than they spend on music. But coffee and music go so well together. Think of the old coffee shops and the folk singers you'd hear in there. And think about Starbucks, where they're always playing music, and where they sell CDs at the register. My idea combines those two, with my music. It's a way to calm the hearts of millions of Americans. I want to launch a chain of coffee shops dedicated to my music. We'd sell coffee, but not all of those fancy kinds. People don't really want all of those, there are too many choices. And we'd sell milk. Milk is a wholesome drink, and it's good for you, builds calcium. We stop drinking milk as adults sometimes, but we shouldn't. I'd educate people on the importance of milk. And while they drank their milk, troubadours would play my music, calming hearts with violins and guitars. I'd have dozens of troubadour groups. They'd travel the country, going from shop to shop. So you'd never know, when you went into one of my shops, which troop of players you'd see. And that way I'd be employing so many musicians, and they need the work. I have a business plan all worked out. It's solid. I've run it through every scenario, and it can't fail. I just need some capital, some investors. You may not be able to give money from your organization, I don't know how the tax laws work for nonprofits. But you can invest personally.

You must make a lot of dough, a big-time Washington lobbyist. And you know a lot of people. You have connections, travel in circles with big money. I'd give you the largest ownership stake, other than mine, of course. Be my angel investor. Please.

I place my right hand on his left shoulder and push him aside as gently as I can, but there is force, and he isn't expecting it. He staggers a bit into the table. That gives me the space I need to slide through. Relief pours over me as I stand in the basement proper, only ten feet of unobstructed space between me and the wood-plank stairs.

I turn back and see Bob's face. It is the one I saw when I suggested we not film in his studio. Bob spends his days working at a job he hates. He spends his nights in a windowless room alone with God. Bob dreams big, as all creatives do. And his dreams are gentle, even selfless in a way.

I fear Bob and his racing thoughts. But what I really fear is myself, the Bob inside me. The possible manifestation of him is why I have avoided an art-committed life. I won't be Bob's angel investor, but I tell him I know I will regret turning down this great opportunity. I will be his first customer, I say, enjoying a *leche grande* while his troubadours calm my heart. He smiles, and does not seek to prevent me from ascending the basement stairs with my camera bag and my not-so-calm heart.

AUGUST 30: WISCONSIN AND MINNESOTA

The Wisconsin State Capitol—a miniature version of the one I haunt in Washington, D.C.—is almost close enough to touch. I have stayed in the same motel chain throughout this trip, earning frequent-stay points, and my reward has been a night in a historic hotel the chain improbably owns in the heart of Madison, directly across from the capitol building. The bed was comfortable, the sheets soft and inviting. But I still find myself shaken from my encounter yesterday with Bob Kurtz. I decide to clear my head after checking out of the hotel by strolling downtown. If the primary focus on this trip were still copyright, I'd look to work into my Wisconsin film the fact that the town is named after James Madison, the father of the Constitution. He wrote the provision Bob began citing yesterday, the Progress Clause that instructs Congress to give rights to authors and inventors. Madison defended copyright in the Federalist Papers, saying its wisdom "will never be questioned." If he had been right on that point, I wouldn't have a job.

Madison's streets form concentric squares around the Capitol building, finally terminating against the two lakes that frame this isthmus. I walk due north on Hamilton Street, presumably named for the Founding Father who was Madison's most bitter rival, and arrive at a park along the shore of Lake Mendota. A young woman sits under a tree reading a textbook. A thin man in a spandex shirt and shorts power-walks a collie.

The waterline is at most five feet below where I am standing. I look across the lake at glass-lined mansions sitting just up from the shore. How is this possible? Do the residents of Madison not understand that water does not always stay at the same level? It can create the illusion of a permanent state of calm, but with no warning water can rise. A wave can propel itself across formerly languid surfaces, destroying everything in its path.

No one answers my unspoken questions, so I head back to the car.

I'm meeting Bill Aicher a few miles away at his office, where he's the marketing director for an online sheet music publisher. He is only in his late twenties but is already an author, having self-published a book titled *Starving the Artist* that decries those who would steal artists' works online. His arguments lie not in legality but in philosophy. For example, he said downloading someone else's creative work without their permission is a violation of Immanuel Kant's Categorical Imperative. Kant tells us that we should treat all of our actions as if they are in fact a universal law. One person downloading becomes everyone downloading, and at that scale, there will be no incentive for the production of creative works.

Bill's company is located on the western edge of town in an industrial park filled with anonymous brick-and-glass buildings. I cross the flat expanse of the parking lot to his mini-tower and Bill greets me in the lobby. He leads me to a sterile conference room that most definitely lacks the grandeur of the historic hotel I just departed. The whitewashed walls are bare. No impressionist prints, no portraits of company founders, no posters of their two of their biggest sheet-music sellers, Chopin and Lady Gaga. My interview with a self-professed non-artist will, fittingly, be in a space without art.

"I've got a question for you, Bill," I say as I set up my camera. "I noticed when I was on the lakeshore that the water comes right up to ground level. How do you avoid flooding?"

"I don't know," he says. "I've lived here my whole life and I don't recall any floods. I think the water just stays at the same height through some natural cause."I know better. The water is level for a reason. Someone, somewhere, is controlling that water level, through dikes, levees, I don't know what.

Bill articulates the arguments in his book for my camera. When I feel I have enough for the video I wrap up and head back to my car. Bill's monotone voice bored me, I consider as I drive west, but it was more than that. I've heard all of these arguments so many times. I've made most of them. I also know that Bill is voicing them into a barreling wave of technology and libertarian individualism that will drown out his voice, and mine, and all of the voices on my videos. Making the two of us even harder to hear over the roar is the fact that we both derive our income from middlemen. My staff is working hard without me to set up the big Capitol Hill event where we'll be showing these videos. My funders are all enjoying the congressional August recess, vacationing in exotic locales far from a Wisconsin industrial park. I am enjoying moments on the trip in which I am disengaged from the fight, brief snippets where I am not screaming into an incoming wave.

It doesn't take long for me to reach a legend of prose and song. The Mississippi River first reveals itself first on my GPS screen as a blue stripe with a dotted line running down its middle. On this trip I reached the Mississippi in Memphis. I stood on the mighty river's eastern shore and watched a boy repeatedly roll a ball up a hill. But then I drove east again. Now, nearly a week later, I am finally ready to enter the West. I cross into Minnesota and immediately pull into a visitor center along the western bank of the river. What I find is not the wide and majestic transporter of Huckleberry Finn I saw down south. From a high overlook I stare at a narrow stretch of water that easily could be traversed by a troop of rookie Cub Scouts. A sign tells me I am well upstream, and that the Mississippi widens as it heads south due to being fed by other rivers of significant size. I also learn this stretch of river has in fact already been tamed, not by pre-teen boys but through a series of locks. I am done with restraints. Let the residents of the Upper Midwest domesticate their lakes and rivers. I'm entering the West, a noun often modified by the adjective *wild*. There is enough suppression of abandon in my life.

I press on to Rochester, Minnesota, where I have an interview in the morning. All I know of the city is that it is the home of the famed Mayo Clinic, where the desperate go for one last shot at cheating death. I wonder what the clinic looks like. Is it a Victorian castle evoking sanitariums of old? Or is it a modern tower of cold steel and glass that reflects the ghostly complexion of its visitors?

As I drive into town I learn that the Mayo Clinic is in fact numerous facilities scattered across the metropolitan area. Each building boasts its specialization on its exterior. Cardiac surgery. Pulmonary therapy. Neurology. I also notice a construction pattern that follows the rule of three: Clinic, motel, house of worship. Repeat.

168

Many religious denomination are represented; most are Christian, but I see a synagogue and a mosque. I don't know if they have a dedicated space for atheists to reflect, but perhaps the realities some face here lead even nonbelievers to church.

When I reach my motel I am tired from the drive and distressed that I will have to wait in line at the check-in desk. I shuffle my feet behind a woman in her fifties wearing a floral polyester blouse and tan slacks. Her hair appears in need of a good shampoo. I am a Rewards member. Why is there no express lane for important people like me?

"It turns out we're not checking out today," the woman tells the young man at the counter. "The doctor just told us that there's been a complication with my father. We're going to have to stay awhile longer."

"How long?" the man asks without looking up.

"I don't know. A week, perhaps? The doctor didn't really say."

"No problem, we're used to that," the clerk says, tapping at his computer.

I look around the lobby and take in a smattering of sofas and chairs. Each is taken, and the occupants all appear older than I. No one smiles. A door opens to a motel restaurant, with the bar immediately in view. It is not yet five o'clock, but most of the stools are in use.

Once the woman in front of me has secured her extended stay, I approach and choose not to complain about the wait.

"Okay, sir," the clerk says. "Your room is across the street in our annex. And let me tell you the shuttle schedule. They leave on the hour, on a staggered schedule. You'll find the times over there on the bulletin board. We go to all of the major clinics, but if there's one that's not on our list, the driver may be able to drop you off anyway."

"Um, okay." I don't tell him that his information is not relevant to me, because I don't want him to feel he has wasted his time.

My room is on the third floor. In true motel fashion, the doors open to a railed walkway. I walk past two older women in my path quietly smoking while seated in what appear to be banquet room chairs. I find my room does not follow the standard motel footprint. There's a living room with a tattered vinyl recliner and a couch with sagging cushions. Behind that is a full kitchen with a small table and four chairs that match the two I just slid past outside. There's a bathroom with an extra-wide door and a waist-high chrome railing running along the tub's white tile. Beyond that is a bedroom, with room for folding cots if needed. The room tells me it's ready for me to settle in for a long stay. I'm an imposter.

I set up my laptop at a desk near the window. Through a slit in the blackout curtain a wooden church steeple pierces the sky with the hope of salvation. I will be here much of the night catching up on editing, a task that grows more tedious by the day. I resent the chore that I have forced upon myself with a daily upload schedule. And I look forward to vacating this room for someone who truly needs it.

AUGUST 31: MINNESOTA AND SOUTH DAKOTA

Kevin Strauss' home sits in a cul-de-sac lined with driveways littered with bicycles and street hockey equipment. He appears to be a little younger than I am, which might be because he's pulled his long brown hair back into a pony tail. He's dressed to impress, with a snug navy suit vest over a blue Oxford shirt. I don't know what a professional storyteller's uniform is, but if my children were younger and he came out on a stage to perform for them, I would feel they were safe in his presence. Inside his home I find a welcoming array of rich earth tones, a nice pleasant contrast with the oppressively gray morning sky and Rochester's matching medical buildings. I position Kevin in front of a bookcase that appears to have been crafted from a Native American canoe. It speaks Minnesota to me.

"Would you mind, Kevin," I ask as I start filming, "telling me what the heck a professional storyteller is?'"

"It's a fair question," he says. He tells stories to children at libraries and schools, often as part of a messaging campaign such as anti-bullying. "But I don't tell the moral at the end like the Victorians did with Aesop's fables," he says. "I let them find their own message. We tell kids a lot of 'thou shalt not.' What is a lot more powerful is 'Once upon a time.'" Kevin says he began his career telling true stories as a journalist, like me, and telling true animal tales as a naturalist. He's now pushing to have storytelling considered an art form. "Like any art form we have our own canon, if you will, core stories that recur repeatedly across times and cultures. They're sort of like story DNA. There are stories of human beings facing down a giant, for example, or a small creature playing a trick on a big creature."

"So where do you find your stories?"

"I could answer by saying Dewey 398.2 of the local library, the folklore section. But you know, there's a big ethics debate right now about what stories we should be allowed to tell." I learn that some believe stories from certain cultures should only be told by natives of that culture. Others fear the stories will be lost if only natives can tell them. Kevin encountered this dilemma when he wanted to tell stories from tribes in the Midwest. "I looked at Native American stories and asked, 'What do I like about them?' I liked the animals, and I want to tell stories about local animals. It's a fairly new thing to tell a story about somewhere else; storytelling has always been about *here*. So I've looked for stories that are set in similar latitudes. I've found some from Norse mythology, for example. There's no one I know of practicing that religion to offend."

"I like that solution," I say. Kevin faced an ethical dilemma, weighed the situation, and pursued a path that followed his own moral compass. That's not something I see every day in Washington, D.C. Then I think of the novelists I've interviewed, like Lillian and Rowena and Brenna.

"Aren't authors storytellers as well?"

"They're storytellers, yes, but they only tell the story once."

On this trip I have listened to many stories. There is a strand of universal DNA in them, namely practicing creativity while living an art-committed life. What is the underlying story DNA of my trip? Perhaps it's an archetypal journey of discovery. Am I Columbus? I hope not. We don't know the exact map he used to cross the Atlantic, but a replica of the one presumed to have been his hangs in my basement, and it is an abysmal guide. The map is a portolan, popular in the 15th Century for sailing short journeys. The ship captain would follow one of the map's many rhumb lines, which extend out from compass roses like rays on a child's drawing of the sun. But rhumb lines don't account for the earth's curvature. The map might say it will lead you from A to B, but crossing the wide Atlantic will surely bring you to C. Columbus' map is even worse, however, because its projection of a round Earth depicted a gross underestimate of the planet's circumference. The map is a slap in the face to Eratosthenes, an astronomer from Libya two hundred years before Christ who calculated Earth's circumference to within two percent of the actual amount. But despite such a poor navigational guide—or because of it —Columbus' discovery was the most remarkable in the history of Europeans. It needs to be worded that way, because surely the Native

Americans already living here didn't view their land as something needing to be discovered. Yet even after his amazing accomplishment, Columbus met his death still denying he hadn't found his true destination, China. He never opened himself to the possibility that what he might discover could be even greater than what he sought.

"We can all be storytellers," Kevin continues. "I tell parents that after a few nights of reading the same book, they should try putting it down and telling the story from memory. Your kids will probably be even more engaged. And then start playing with the story, and invite the kids to join you."

Some of my fondest childhood memories are of my mother reading to me. Many were amazing stories from faraway lands, like tales of a family of trolls called Moomins written by the Finnish novelist Tove Jansson. My mother had too much respect for Jansson's craft to alter the author's prose. But when not reading bedtime stories, my mother practiced the fine art of oral storytelling, something she does to this day. She would continually re-craft stories of her own life, just as she has completely reinvented what happened the last night I saw her.

I'm brought back to Kevin's living room by a ringing phone behind me. He stands to answer it, and I quickly unplug the microphone cord from the camera so he doesn't trip. It sounds as if he's speaking with his mother-in-law. He informs her his wife is at work, even though it's her birthday. That leads to my next question when he returns to the interview.

"Forgive me," I say, "but I find it pretty amazing that you're able to do this kind of work full time."

He nods. "In terms of full-time storytellers, I'm guessing there are less than two hundred in the entire country. Here in Minnesota, maybe a half-dozen." He says it was something he dreamed of doing for years, and when his wife was offered a job here in Rochester, they mutually decided he'd make a go at it. She provides the steady income and the health insurance. "I couldn't do it without having a wife who believes in me."

Now Kevin has transported me to that moment three weeks ago in Cape May, New Jersey. I'm watching the surf roll in while Laura tells me I don't have to stay at a job that is eating away at my moral core.

I'm not sure what I would do if I left, but I could return to freelance writing. In my early twenties—when it became clear that my struggle with bipolar disorder meant I couldn't maintain an illusion of sanity over a forty-hour week—I worked as a freelancer from home while my first wife held the steady job. My income went up and down, but I learned how to market myself, and just as importantly how to tell the stories my clients wanted told.

My job now is one massive freelance project. It was my writing on copyright policy that led Hollywood studios to recruit me to lead and build an advocacy non-profit. It would be difficult to leave my organization after putting in so much effort to build it, but as Kevin might say, perhaps there are more stories waiting to be told.

I realize we've been talking for nearly two hours. I let him know I need to be in Sioux Falls for another interview.

"If you're driving to South Dakota," he says, "be sure to stop along the way at the Hormel SPAM Museum in Austin. That place is a hoot."

"I've never eaten the stuff."

"Who cares? I just love that they've dedicated an entire building to telling the story of processed luncheon meat."

The DNA strands of Kevin Strauss' story wind around my cerebral cortex as I leave Rochester. Or perhaps the DNA itself is a double helix of both his life story and that of his wife, who willingly embarked upon this risky adventure with him. Most of the artists I've interviewed have held part- or full-time jobs in addition to their artistic pursuits, often helped by supportive spouses. But those who fully support themselves through art—printmaker Sabra Field and realist painter Victor Grasso come to mind—at some point also made that leap away from traditional employment. Or perhaps I'm not thinking about this the right way. Sabra takes on the occasional commission. She is paid a pretty penny to produce works adhering to someone else's vision. And Victor isn't opposed to producing an Atlantic City casino mural if the price is right. There are many ways to balance creative pursuits and the realities of personal finances.

Also resonating with me is the fact that Kevin receives almost no benefit from copyright. The stories he repurposes are from the public domain. And yet he invited me into his home, camera and all. That has been the gift every artist has given me on this trip. Perhaps I've been in Washington too long, but I continue to find this generosity—this authenticity—surprising.

My gratitude to Kevin prompts me to take the exit for the Hormel SPAM Museum. I park in the near-empty lot beneath a larger-than-life sculpture of a farmer and a plump hog, and am greeted in the museum lobby by an enthusiastic docent. I take the museum map he offers me and tell him I'm looking forward to exploring.

A whir above me signals an endless transit of SPAM containers, gliding along an elevated conveyor belt. That round-cornered, rectangular can is iconic. Not even Andy Warhol could have seared it into our collective consciousness to any greater degree. But the product's name has a new ubiquity in the digital age, a time when Nigerian strangers promise us untold wealth if we first wire a bit of our own savings. I know from my days covering anti-spam legislation as a reporter on Capitol Hill that the etymology of *spam* as deceptive email stems from a 1970 sketch on the British comedy *Monty Python's Flying Circus*. A chorus of Vikings sang the word in repeated staccato. The painful repetition gave name to the fraudulent solicitations that continually bombard our email inboxes.

I hear the Python song now and seek its source, admiring the museum curator's willingness to embrace mockery of what the museum celebrates. A blurry clip of the scene loops on a video display fashioned to look like a 1970s television. The Python Players belt the repeated lyric in high-pitched shrieks. I find myself singing along under my breath.

I learn a great deal about SPAM from the museum's many displays. For example, one informs me that if I were to open a can of SPAM packaged in the 1970s, the contents would still be edible, but not as tasty. I also learn that one shouldn't bother to search the luncheon meat for human flesh, although in fairness the kiosk doesn't explicitly mention that particular potential ingredient. Paul Theroux once wrote that former cannibals in the South Pacific developed a taste for the mystery meat because it had a "corpsy" flavor. But the kiosk sign in front of me insists that Spam is simply spiced pork shoulder. Letters blue and bold pronounce this fact with insistence, noting that the product's name is a combination of "SPiced"and "hAM."So much for the urban legend that the name actually stands for "Something Posing As Meat."

A spotlight shines on a promotional poster for The Hormel Girls, a troupe of females who traveled the country during World War II using song and dance to promote patriotism and processed meat. Near the poster, a 1950s-style movie marquee lined with light bulbs blinking clockwise advertises the museum's feature film, "SPAM: A Love Story." The many exhibits here promote a pork product many consider a punch line, but they do so without a sense of irony.

The SPAM train above me continues its endless loop. I press forward to a new kiosk, one for the "Hands-On SPAM" interactive exhibit. I am instructed to start the timer; fill an empty can with the fake meat; "cook" it in the pretend oven, which is the same size as an Easy-Bake but lacking a light bulb; slip a label on the can; and stack it in a shipping box. When I pick up a sample of the pretend meat, I find it is a bean bag with a rubber exterior, polished smooth by the fondling of many hands. I linger, not ready to let go of the surprisingly comfortable toy. I don't question the fact that this assembly line is a fiction. It presents itself as such.

I squeeze the play meat in my left hand and migrate to a kiosk that tells the story of another Minnesota-born phenomenon. While SPAM is presented here simply as spiced pork—no more and no less—I learn Betty Crocker is a lie. A Minneapolis milling company invented the fictional baking legend in 1921 as a marketing tool. After reading her story, I examine Ms. Crocker's familiar portrait, this one her original image circa 1936. Her shoulders bespeak confidence in a perfectly tailored crimson jacket, while a lacy white collar softens her intense gaze. I look into those eyes, resting just below thinly plucked eyebrows. They tell me to dismiss the kiosk's assertion, insisting I maintain my illusion of her truth.

I know a little bit about crafting a narrative that becomes less real upon further examination. This trip is an outgrowth of my professional obligation to obfuscate. I stare back at Betty and squeeze the play meat in my hand. My middle finger reaches my thumb as I press hard through the rubber and filling. I find comfort in this spongy toy. It is real to the touch. It is real to me.

. . .

The questions come quickly as I sit in the Barney's kitchen. How many days have I been on the road? How many artists have I interviewed? When do I head home? Before I have a chance to fully answer Tara's latest question, Andrew fires off another. I do my best to keep up while avoiding the distraction of their five-year-old son Jacob, who is running circles around the table while wearing an oversized football helmet. A golden retriever named Stella lounges across my feet. I've only been in their Sioux Falls, South Dakota, home a few minutes but I've already received more stimulation than I did at the interactive SPAM museum. When I sense a slight break in the questions directed to me, I tell Tara and Andrew I'd like to start asking questions. I slip my feet out from under from Stella and we move to the living room, which is lined with some of Andrew's oil paintings.

I point at one in the corner. "That painting is called *Oxbow*, right?"

"That's right," Andrew says as he sits on a chocolate brown leather sofa, his long, lean frame stretching above and below. The retriever settles on his feet. "I'm surprised you know that."

"I saw it on your web site," I say as Tara sits beside him, and brushes back her center-parted auburn hair with both hands so it falls neatly over her shoulders. A nearby lamp highlights her strong cheekbones and dimpled mouth. I frame both of them in the camera's monitor. "It spoke to me, that spot of calm in the middle of chaos."

Before Andrew can respond, a blur flies across my camera's screen.

"Jacob Barney!" Tara says, leaping from the couch. Their son is now wearing the helmet with the solid part in front of his face. He nearly knocks over my tripod. She leads him off-camera, removes the helmet, and hands him an action figure of a pro wrestler to play with. "I'm sorry," she says to me.

I tell her not to worry, and move quickly into the interview to capture as much of them as I can before the next distraction. Just like in the kitchen they speak in turns.

Tara: "I moved to Fort Collins, Colorado, for a job."

Andrew: "And I was there as an art student."

Tara: "We met at an art show."

Andrew: "About fifteen years ago."

Tara: "I drew a lot then."

Andrew: "We would go to art shows together."

Tara: "Fort Collins is a pretty artsy city."

Andrew: "And before we would go out we would look through an art dictionary."

Tara: "We weren't all that educated in art yet."

Andrew: "We wanted to find intriguing words so we could sound like cool artists."

Tara: "So we were just friends."

Andrew: "We'd critique each other's work."

Tara: "Then I moved back here to Sioux Falls to be near family."

Andrew: "And I came out on a hunting trip and visited Tara."

Tara: "Again, just as friends."

Andrew: "Right. And I never left."

Tara: "We decided we were being ridiculous so we got married."

"Just like that?" I ask. "No courtship?"

Tara: "We knew each other's art."

Andrew: "We knew each other as much as anyone can know anybody."

We continue like this, me prompting with a question, Tara and Andrew beginning their routine. I am again interviewing two artists simultaneously, but I can't imagine filming these two any other way. Their give-and-take reminds me of a wholesome Midwestern version of the characters played by Myrna Loy and William Powell in *The Thin Man,* one of the few black-and-white movies my mother would make me watch that I truly adored. Stella is a larger version of their dog Asta, but that couple had no kindergartener to keep them on their toes.

Tara continues discussing her work at a local art gallery that sells her jewelry and other craft works. Andrew explains how he's working as a landscaper at the local high school but landed a grant to fund his mentoring of art students there.

Stella stands up, walks across the room, and presses her large snout against the side of the camera. Glad she didn't press her nose onto the lens, I dog-whisper her downward and she sprawls again across my feet. I check on Barney; he has now found a second action figure, and one is pinning the other in a play wrestling rink.

I not only fell in love with Andrew's *Oxbow* on their website, I was drawn to a line of jewelry his wife creates as well. "Tara, tell me about the Elegant Corn necklaces."

She smiles while Andrew pats her knee. "Well, I thought it would be funny to string some corn kernels with dressy glass. My first necklace sold just like that."She snaps, drawing the attention of Stella. "I made another one and it sold. So I drove to Mitchell, South Dakota, where there's a farmer who raises what we call Indian corn with seven fields of different colors. I bought a whole bunch, we shucked it, drilled it, and made a hundred necklaces."

"That sounds pretty labor intensive."

Andrew holds up his thumb and index finger. "I still get cramps," he says with a laugh.

Tara: "He's no good at the drill. He drills his fingers."

Andrew: "Well, I'm working fast."

Tara: "My dad's better because he's more meticulous, takes his time."

Andrew: "I just want to see how many I can get done."

As we talk I hear more examples of collaboration, of support, of encouragement, of compromise. They each have different creative passions, but their endeavors are intertwined. I let them know how impressed I am by that.

Tara: "Well, art is what we live for."

Andrew: "We're working toward having our whole lives be art."

Tara: "We want to retire as artists."

Andrew: "Of course artists don't retire. My grandfather was still painting in his eighties."

Tara: "We want to travel around the country selling at art shows."

Andrew: "In a Winnebago, when Jacob is out of school."

Tara: "We already sell at regional art shows."

Andrew: "We've met couples who travel the circuit."

Tara: "It's a whole subculture, traveling artists."

Andrew: "It's a really supportive environment."

I'm watching this part on the camera's monitor, to make sure it's positioned such that I can fully capture their back-and-forth dialogue. Then the image lurches. I look down and see Stella has nudged herself closer to me, jarring the tripod.

"Stella!" Andrew calls out.

"It's okay," I say, repositioning the camera. I wonder if part of what they long for is the quiet of the road, an escape from the constant distraction of their home life. But they seem unperturbed by what to me, after weeks of quiet, is chaos. As the interview winds down I consider telling them how much I appreciate their authenticity, a concept on my mind since the SPAM Museum, but I suspect they won't understand, just like a fish wouldn't understand if you told it how impressed you were that it could breathe in water. Authenticity is core to their natures. So instead I pack up my camera and Tara heads to the kitchen. She returns with a large wicker basket and hands it to me.

"I've packed some banana bread in here to give you something to snack on during your long drive," she says. "You're heading west now and you'll find there's a lot of empty road between places to eat. And I've given you one of my painted birdhouse gourds, and a corn necklace and scarf for your wife, and Andrew has added one of his prints. Oh my goodness, Andrew, it's *Oxbow!*"

"It was just meant to be," Andrew says.

I hold up the corn necklace and imagine putting it around Laura's neck. Perhaps Marisa would like the burgundy scarf, although she might be more interested if it were black. "Tara and Andrew, thank you for this. For everything."

Then they give me one more gift, a suggestion that I visit Sioux Falls. I say I thought I was already in Sioux Falls, and Andrew says he means the actual waterfalls. I hadn't even processed that the town was named after a real water phenomenon. I was born in Klamath Falls, Oregon, a town that in fact has no falls. There is only a large lake north of town that feeds a tired river. My mother used to tell me that the town's founders added "Falls" to the name to attract settlers. I'm glad to be in a place that comes as advertised.

When I arrive the falls are not what I expected. Instead of the long cascades I am used to in the Mountain West, I stand beside a lazy wide sheet of moisture flowing across smoothly polished stone. The city park offers several hundred yards of access. An elderly couple sits on an outcropping, streaks of water brushing their feet. A group of teenagers hop from rock to rock, somehow managing not to slip.

I walk first upriver, then down, soothed by gurgles and splashes. Tara and Andrew are already building their art-committed life. Given that Jacob is five, according to Andrew's timetable they're about thirteen years away from hitting the road. But they are demonstrating in their current lives an ability to maximize their position.

I step out on a dry slab of rock. Below me a small vortex has formed, water trapped in a circular flow. It strains to break free, to join its brethren in downward motion. I understand that feeling. But I can see now the bend in my river, and I vow to enter the oxbows's calmness. Like Tara and Andrew—or Lewis and Clark—I will then begin to navigate the rest of the journey downstream.

SEPTEMBER 1: IOWA AND NEBRASKA

In his travel memoir *Stephen Fry in America*, the British comedian visits most of the states but skips Ohio. The closest he comes to entering the state is standing next to a sign stating "Ohio Welcomes You." He said it wasn't anything personal he had against the state, but more a matter of logistics. "Farewell, Buckeye state, land of contrasts," he wrote. "We will carry you in our hearts forever. And sorry." My Ohio on this trip is Iowa.

I'm sure the state boasts many creative souls. It would have been easy to find a compelling writer in Iowa City, home of the highly regarded University of Iowa Writer's Workshop. Had I lived a different life I might have found myself there twenty years ago as a student. I don't have to blame my insecurities on why I won't be traveling there on this trip, however. Like Fry, I can cite logistics. A trip to Iowa City would add eight hours to my driving schedule, and that is time I do not have. So it is just a little after 2 pm and I have already crossed Iowa off my list. I spent all of two hours today in uninspiring Sioux City, half of it in a disappointing Mexican restaurant that was too cheap to give me free chips and the other half interviewing a museum curator who had landed at this modest city arts center after washing out on a bigger stage in Miami, Florida.

So it was with a smile that I crossed the Missouri River toward Nebraska, and now I'm receiving one in return from a motel clerk in Lincoln. A young man with bleached blonde hair partially hiding a single hoop earring examines me with eyes lined with black circles, the goth detail clashing with his pink scarf. "HeLLO there, CUtie," he says, dramatically emphasizing certain syllables. "I'm STANley. You're JUST in time for FRESHly baked COOKies, HOT from the OVEN!"He then looks at my registration information. "You're from D.C.? What in God's green EARTH are you doing in THIS backwater? Are you LOST?"

I assure him I am not. Then I take a cookie. It is quite good, and I tell him so. He says he knows, silly, he baked them, and then gives me a wink. I resist telling him that I admire his willingness to be himself in a square flyover state where one would not expect much tolerance for what I assume his sexual preference to be. I also resist asking him if he chooses to behave according to a TV sitcom stereotype to openly defy those who would judge him or because he has no other model for behavior. What I do ask him is how I might kill some time in Lincoln this afternoon. Stanley suggests first the motel's hot tub, then the state capitol building. I skip the bubbling germ bath and head out to explore the town named after a former president whose actions improved the lives of others facing discrimination.

Before I reach the capitol building I spot Memorial Stadium, home to the Nebraska Cornhuskers football team. I park the car so I can circumnavigate the stadium on foot and soon spot students who must be players entering the stadium, lugging large duffel bags. They are huge—the players, that is, although the duffel bags are as well. Clearly Nebraska athletes eat a lot of that corn they're husking. I wonder if one of them secretly would like a date with Stanley. When I return to the car I see a white slip of paper tucked under the windshield wiper, and notice too late a sign telling me I parked in a reserved space. The ticket is odd in that none of the blanks are filled out. Instead there is a short message written in large block print. "Welcome to Lincoln! Hope you enjoy your stay." I will, I offer silently to the generous parking enforcer.

When I reach the capitol building I find it's quite unlike the clone of the U.S. Capitol I stayed next to in Madison, Wisconsin. Rising from its center is not a dome but instead a granite-brick tower. Lincoln is as flat as I imagined it to be, with gray sky bleeding into brown soil. Yet here a giant stone rod thrusts its way toward the cloud cover. The tower dominates the entire landscape. Did Stanley direct me here because it resembles a male phallus? How amusing it would be if the University of Nebraska created a costumed mascot that emulated this iconic structure.

Next up is a much-needed Laundromat. As the few items of clothing I'm traveling with spin before me, a woman wearing flannel pajamas occupies the olive-green plastic seat beside me. She loads her laundry and then pulls a science fiction novel from her backpack. I'm

183

tempted to tell her I interviewed an award-winning sci-fi novelist a couple of weeks ago in Philadelphia, but I decide it inappropriate for a middle-aged man to strike up a conversation with a female college student in PJs. Instead I fire up my laptop to do some video editing, but soon close it after hearing the voice of Bob Kurtz. My Illinois video is due to go live in two days, yet I keep avoiding the footage. In front of me my clothes spin behind a circle of glass, occasional bursts of color flashing and then departing. There are no flashes as bright as Stanley's scarf. I envy the motel clerk for fully owning his identity.

SEPTEMBER 2: NEBRASKA

There is no Stanley this morning to offer me a toasty warm cinnamon muffin and congratulate me on leaving this backwater. Instead a young woman with jet-black hair and a rhinestone nose stud focuses her attention on a *People* magazine as I slide my room-key card across the counter. I leave the lobby with an overnight bag hung over my left shoulder, the strap to my laptop case over my right, and the large wicker basket Tara Barney had given me yesterday in Sioux Falls in both hands. My car's trunk doesn't have room for the basket, so I remove all of the items from it and find crevices to squeeze them in. The banana bread I place in the front passenger seat. Then I gently place the basket on the asphalt of the near-empty parking lot. Perhaps Stanley will find it when he arrives for his next shift.

Pippa White's neighborhood comprises stately lots shaded by thick tree canopies. Her house is on a corner, a welcoming two-story brown Tudor. A dog I can't quite see barks from a screened porch. Pippa agreed to this interview weeks ago, but it was only yesterday that she relented to being filmed in her home. When we spoke on the phone she told me her resistance was due to her dog Nutley, who could be quite aggressive towards men. I told her not to worry. As I approach the door I can see that Nutley is a white poodle mix in a highly agitated state. He springs straight up and down, occasionally attempting to go forward only to hit the screen. I reduce my height by walking in a squat, then slowly extend my right palm to the screen so he can smell it. "Hello, Nutley," I say softly. "I'm your new friend, Patrick."

He continues to bark but stops springing. In between yaps he sniffs at my hand.

"Nutley, you are going to stop barking now," I say, firmly but gently, as I place my hand flat on the screen in front of his nose. Nutley stops barking. He looks at me, tilts his head slightly, and licks the screen. I feel his tongue's moisture through the tiny openings.

"That's right, Nutley," I say. "You're glad to see me, and I'm glad to see you."

"Oh my!" a woman's voice says. "Look at you, Nutley! What a good boy."

Nutley turns to the sound of his master's voice and runs up to Pippa, pressing his body against the cuffs of her khaki slacks. The actress is the perfect combination of casual and professional, sporting a taupe button-down shirt with sleeves folded to just below her elbows, tasteful makeup, and no obvious jewelry. Her blonde hair is quite short, giving her an appearance younger than the fifty-odd years I know she is. But I suspect its length also makes it easier for her, while performing, to don the many wigs she finds herself wearing. Pippa opens the screen door, and immediately my new best friend darts between my legs, sniffing my shoes, my pants, anything he can press his nose against.

"It's remarkable," she says. "I've never seen him like this with a man he hasn't met before."

I tell her how I learned to handle dogs in high school while working at a veterinary hospital. I don't tell her how the hospital was my sanctuary, and how my X-ray safety badge became a metaphor for my interactions with my mother. Pippa leads me through a remarkably tidy kitchen as Nutley darts between my legs. Pippa suggests we film in her living room, yet another immaculate space with not an errant magazine or drinking glass to be found. But the dining room table, which we pass to reach the living room, is buried in piles of books, legal pads, and note cards. I place Pippa in front of her elegant white fireplace mantle decorated with a splay of fresh daisies, and with her permission relocate a floor lamp to better illuminate her. As I do so I am careful not to trip on Nutley, still underfoot.

Another creature emerges, eyeing me from the nearby kitchen. Pippa says the smoky black cat is named Nicky. I never did learn how to win over a cat. Nutley recaptures my attention by resting his head on my right foot. As I seek to center the camera on Pippa she leaps from her chair. "Stop that, Nicky! Look at you, what a silly boy you are."

The black cat is now at my feet as well, chewing on the lavaliere microphone's cord. Pippa takes off the microphone, picks up Nicky, and carries him out of the room, telling him that he is a silly boy, yes he is. Nutley and I watch with satisfaction as the cat is locked inside the screened-in porch. When she returns she reattaches her microphone like a pro and we begin the interview.

"I started my life as an actress in California," she tells me, performing in local theatre productions and hosting a show on a San Francisco television station. "When I moved to the Midwest, I knew it was going to be hard to work as a full-time actor. People say 'actor' for actress now, by the way."She laughs while leaning slightly forward with smiling eyes. She quickly connected with Lincoln's local arts council and then crafted a one-woman show to perform with its support on something she learned about after moving here, a so-called "orphan train"that would deliver orphaned Easterners out west to find new homes with farmers looking for a larger family. She wrote a fictionalized script and played every role, including the protagonist, a young girl braving a new life. That grew into other historically based shows she produces, all stories of females overcoming long odds. "Having started as just a little touring artist for my local arts council, I've now performed in thirty-nine states as an artist, performing my own work. One day I'll be at a conference on the East coast at a beautiful conference center, and the next day I'll fly home and be under a basketball hoop, in a gym with kids on the bleachers."

I am impressed, and tell her so. I then ask why she moved to the Midwest.

"Oh, I followed a man."Another engaging laugh. "My husband got a job at a university here. Then I started a family. As my children were getting to school age, I thought, if I'm ever going to work as an actress here, I'm probably going to have to do it alone. That's when I started writing and creating. Desperation forced me to push myself."

I don't see desperation. I see passion. Pippa was living a life many would envy, with a husband, children, and a nice home. But a yearning to be creative still burned inside her, and that yearning spurred her to action.

I learn Pippa's plays are mostly history-based, including stories of immigrants from Ellis Island; nurses such as Florence Nightingale, Clara Barton, and Dorothea Dix; pioneering journalist Nellie Bly; and women's suffragists. Much of her material comes from diaries, letters, interviews, and memoirs. She points to the stacks of materials behind me on her dining room table. I think of Michael Swanwick, telling me in his Philadelphia rowhouse of his passion for writing the biography of Hope Mirrlees. And I think of my own passion for stories of great navigators and the cartographers who chronicled their discoveries, and the pile of resources I collect on those subjects.

I hear something jingle, then the tripod begins to shake.

"Nutley!" Pippa says.

Pippa's dog is doing what dogs do. He is scratching. While lying on his left side across my loafers, he has lifted his right rear leg up and is rubbing his foot against his right ear. Appearing as he does in a state of ecstasy, I hesitate to disturb him.

"If I put him outside he'll just start barking," Pippa says.

"It's no problem." I reach down and take over the scratching for Nutley. He immediately extends himself toward my hand, a pulse of pleasure snaking through his small frame. After about a minute I shift left on the sofa, away from the camera tripod. Once my feet leave Nutley, he scrambles to follow, resettling on the loafers. That solves the issue of contact with the tripod, but there remains the loud jingling of his small metal ID tag against his collar chain. A bit more scratching from me works out his itch, and he settles into a post-euphoria haze.

I return to the subject of her profiles, her choice of highlighting inspiring women.

"That's what I hope people take away from my shows," she says, "that there are so many people who are so courageous. Take the suffragists. They endured ridicule, harassment. There's nothing I admire more than perseverance. People who are knocked down and then they get back up. They're knocked down and then they get back up. They're knocked down and then they get back up."

When I edit this video I may splice out her repetition, but in so doing I would lose the dramatist in Pippa, who clearly is using repetition for emphasis. And I share her passion. The artists I've most admired on this trip have won me over with stories of determination and grit. The art-committed life is all about perseverance. It's about creating your art when life tells you there is no time. It's about honoring your muse when there is no immediate economic return. It's about being willing to take on new challenges alone. I see Pippa reflected in the characters she portrays.

Nutley begins scratching again, and this time I take it as a signal that I have enough footage. I thank Pippa while giving Nutley a bit more love.

"Thank you for choosing me for your series," Pippa says. "I admire what you're doing, with your organization, with this road trip, with the story you are telling. I've been watching your videos. You're not interviewing rock stars or Hollywood celebrities. Most people don't realize that there is this huge strata of artists right below the big names, people who are working all the time. They're the ones who are performing at your child's school, and they live down the street from you, and they're making a difference. And you're making a difference for them."

"I think all of you are having a far greater impact on me." I'm surprised to hear myself say that out loud. Perhaps Nutley has lulled me into a state of relaxation to match his own.

I want to stay in the warm comfort of Pippa's home. I want to keep scratching Nutley's itch. I am even open to spending some time with her cat Nicky. But it is already mid-morning, and I have another interview this evening in Boulder, Colorado, with hundreds of miles of driving ahead, crossing what I think of as the ultimate fly-over state. If I set the cruise control for eighty-five miles per hour I will be out of Nebraska in less than four hours. I'm heading west, just as I did every day as a teenager when I drove from school to the animal hospital near the edge of the desert west of Phoenix. The lure of the West was so strong. I had been accepted to college in California, which would be my escape. On my way to the hospital I would feel a pull to keep driving until I hit the Pacific. Stopping that drive each day meant I would eventually be returning home.

The sky has grown overcast while I was inside with Pippa and Nutley. A gun-metal gray blanket rises from a creepily flat horizon. I turn on the FM radio to provide a distraction, and hear two men engaging in a monotone drone-off while reading ad copy. The first informs me a local sporting-goods store is running a special on bowling shoes. Be the first among your friends to get a shiny new pair in Nebraska red, he says. The other, in a voice even slower and flatter, responds that the timing is perfect, because a local bowling alley is about to start its annual customer-appreciation handicap tournament. Only able to take so much excitement in one day, I return the car to silence, and to my thoughts, welcome or not.

As I push west the car strains against a headwind. A yellow highway sign warns of high winds while a matching yellow flag affixed to it flaps maniacally. I recall a book I read as a teenager, James Michener's *Centennial.* He wrote of Rocky Mountain winds strong enough to drive one of his characters to fatally stab her children. But I am fighting more than wind. My car is climbing a steady incline; I will rise 4,000 feet in altitude today. Nebraska is as flat as a cookie sheet, but that sheet is propped on one end.

I'm following the Platte River heading upstream toward its high elevation source. When I drove across the country that first time—a twenty-two-year old moving to D.C.—I passed a sign in the flat New Mexico desert telling me I had just crossed the Continental Divide. I stopped along the side of the highway and conducted an experiment, pouring out bits of a Diet Coke to see which way the soda flowed. It merely formed a small puddle at my feet. But years later Laura and I stood at another section of the Continental Divide in Rocky Mountain National Park. The Colorado River headed off to the west, the Platte to the east. Rivers follow the path of least resistance. That is not how I would describe *this* trip.

After a couple of hours the gray blanket frays. Sheets of light break through to my left, appearing to set a field of wheat on fire. Then the ominous material unravels entirely, revealing blue sky as I cross into Colorado. It's as if I'm being lifted into that sky. But in fact something now separates horizon from heaven. At first the strip is smooth and curving, lit in a soft violet. The shade then shifts to indigo, mountains in watercolor, blurry rock formations now in varieties of brown, topped like birthday cakes with slicing green candles pushing toward the sky.

I want to cry. It's as if I am not myself, or perhaps am not in myself. It isn't just the cruise control that makes me feel detached from the car. The opening heavens before me draw me back to the day I turned fourteen. Before Mass that day I shared the news with Father Felt while we donned robes in the changing room behind the altar. He smiled and said what I already knew, that I was born on the Assumption of Mary. That was the day Our Heavenly Father lifted the Mother of God up into heaven whole, body and spirit, to ensure her Holy corpse would not have to rot on a sinful Earth. That story had always disturbed me. I was convinced Mary must have hated being the only one in Heaven who was different, a human body among non-corporeal souls.

Perhaps she felt like I did when I found myself transferred to a fourth-grade classroom when I was in first grade. I endured verbal torment from the older kids every moment the teacher was out of earshot. I know now my presence did little for their self-esteem. That is around the time I had started what my psychiatrist chose to call "pyramiding," in which someone would speak to me but I would not hear the words, instead parsing the letters into multiples of two, three, four, and five. When the classroom change led those incidents to spike, the doctor insisted my mother return me to kids my own age regardless of my perceived aptitude. I was free from my tormentors. But Mary's sentence was for eternity.

Father Felt slipped into his private sanctuary. I had never been in the room, but I knew that was where the sacramental wine was kept. I knew that because one morning a visiting priest had chosen to change in that room, and when he emerged there was a crimson stain down his white robe. When I pointed it out to him, the first thing he did was run his hand across his mouth. But Father Felt returned quickly, with a small white box. It held a thin necklace with a pewter medallion. Mary rose from the pewter in her classic pose of love; palms extended forward from her hips, face tilted in loving comfort, head framed by a halo of stars. I put the pendant around my neck, tucking the Mother of God under my robe and T-shirt. Mary's cold metal touched my bare chest and a shock went through me, followed by sublime calm.

I wore Mary every day. I even wore her while swimming, which I now believe accelerated her discoloration through exposure to chlorine. My mother grew alarmed, telling me I was going to suffer lead poisoning or some such mishap should I keep wearing her. But Father

Felt had told me that morning that I had a special relationship with Mary. She would always be there for me. And it was easier to connect with her, because God was too often full of wrath, and Jesus, well how could Jesus understand my many flaws when he was born perfect? So I would begin each day by touching the pendant while saying a Hail Mary, and I would end each day by giving Mary a kiss. If a moment came when I needed to escape—if a gray blanket enveloped our home —I would retreat to my room and touch Mary through my shirt, feeling her press into my flesh.

I understand the Assumption now. I pictured Mary bringing not just her body to Heaven, but all of her anxieties and insecurities. But God would have lifted those from her. She would dwell in the House of the Lord forever, without the petty concerns we entangle ourselves with here on the mortal realm. I think of spiritual artists I've met, like Leah Martensen with her easy praise of the Lord in song, the Voice of Golden Eagle with his smiling embrace of mystic possibility, even Bob Kurtz and his moments alone with God as he falls asleep. We all have a unique path to grace.

The Rockies emerge more clearly with each passing mile. The road grows steeper as well. A rush of ecstasy passes over me. I am being assumed, lifted into a spiritual bliss. I am being liberated. But that is a passive description. I am in fact liberating myself. My path is within my power, as much as this car is guided by my command. It is about choice. It has always been about choice.

PART SIX: THE WEST

SEPTEMBER 3: COLORADO

The cliff wall rises perhaps one hundred feet, a man-made contusion. The grooves are so perfect I can almost imagine the chunk of mountain that was removed sliding back into place. That rock may have been there for millennia, but it had to go to make room for this Boulder, Colorado, motel. Last night I paid no heed to this beautiful scar as I arrived at the motel at dusk in a state of combined euphoria and exhaustion. I am forced to cease admiring it now because I find myself blocking a red pickup truck. From the driver I sense impatience but not hostility. How long has he been waiting? Why didn't he honk? Or rev his engine? I am now in the West, the West of my youth, the West where people don't consider honking and swearing and gesticulating rudely to be part of the regional dialect. I steer my car aside, and he passes with a smile and a nod.

I felt lifted yesterday when I entered the Mountain Time zone, or MT, the strip on the U.S. map on the back of the phone book that marked my childhood home. A mere eighteen million live in this time zone, compared to nearly fifty million in the Pacific, eighty five million in the Central, and at least one hundred and forty million in the Eastern Time Zone, the rightmost strip in which I've spent the last twenty-odd years. MTers tolerate being dissed by TV announcers declaring the start times of shows while only mentioning Eastern, Central and Pacific. I know that Arizonans take pride in being further isolated by not participating in Daylight Savings Time. The two million or so in that state stubbornly refuse to ring in even more sunshine—there is quite enough already—so when the rest of the country "springs" forward every April, Arizona stays put and the Pacific Time Zone springs east. When October arrives, the rest of the country falls back, and Arizona returns to its MT home. I learned in my youth how to live stubbornly out of step.

Today's interview subject lives in Littleton, on the opposite side of Denver. But I spent last night in Boulder so I could interview a Wyoming filmmaker who was in town for a film festival. Like Steve Cox in Memphis, Alan O'Hashi came in ready to knock me off balance. Cox had cited his history with remixing, a practice frowned upon by some of my funders. Alan laid down his own challenge at the start of the interview, declaring himself a "Pied Piper" of would-be filmmakers who wished to bypass the major studios and reach audiences directly. He seemed to feel this would cause me upset, presumably because I am bankrolled by Hollywood. What he would have understood had he watched my videos is that my focus lies in empowering individual artists to pursue whatever path they choose. Work with the big boys, bypass them entirely, it's all good. I wanted to like Alan, a Japanese-American former journalist who runs a film festival in Cheyenne for amateur filmmakers. But his overheated rhetoric about evil corporate entertainment conglomerates bored me. My funders aren't evil. They are amoral entities pursuing increased returns for shareholders. Their senior executives don't share my passion for promoting individual artists' creative growth, but nor do they waste their time conniving how to crush those artists' dreams. Alan's self-identity as a savior of amateur filmmakers requires him to have something to save them from. I resisted going East Coast Time Zone on him, engaging in a charged debate while informing him of his naiveté.

In Littleton I'm interviewing someone else who seeks to help aspiring artists, but Judith Thomas wants the writers she edits as a freelancer to become published by any means, whether that is landing a contract with The Man or self-publishing. I know how important an editor is to a writer and his work. My growth as a reporter was the direct result of a wise editor who showed no mercy and rewarded my eventual success with welcome autonomy.

Judith greets me in the parking lot of her apartment complex wearing a conservative black-and-white pantsuit jazzed up a bit by her buzz-cut copper-dyed hair. She had not given me her specific apartment address, saying she'd be more comfortable filming outside.

I've actually been surprised how many of my interview subjects were willing to allow a man they had never met into their homes. As we walk toward a park bench she has suggested for the shoot I detect a hint of Shalimar, my mother's perfume choice when I was young. That makes sense. Judith and my mother are about the same age.

As we begin the interview, Judith tells me how she left the world of legal writing and editing to become a freelance editor. "I wanted my more creative side to come out." She says her mother died recently, then repeats a story her mother often told, that as a precocious one-year-old Judith would try to say big words like chocolate and appendicitis. "Chocolate I can understand, but appendicitis?" she says.

I consider asking about her mother's passing, but Judith keeps going, with more anecdotes about her love of words and writing. I ask if she still writes.

"I've been writing my entire life," she says. But when I ask her if she is doing any creative writing right now, she laughs, looks down, and says, "Let's just talk about my editing."

Alan O'Hashi's attempts to provoke a fight last night were highly annoying. Less annoying, but still frustrating, is when an interview subject is evasive.

But I press on, and learn that Judith often puts in eighteen-hour days as an editor, stopping only to watch Denver Broncos football games. She also provides clients advice on how to get their work published, lessons she learned from attending various writing conferences. She then begins to discuss the long odds in favor of landing such a contract, how hard it is to get an agent, how quickly one's work can be rejected. "Many of the novelists I work with will complete a great book, query twenty agents, and get twenty rejection letters. They get so disheartened that some of them quit writing, and the book goes in a drawer." I suspect she is not attending these writing conferences solely to learn information for her clients.

I mention the novel I wrote a few years ago that did not find an agent, surprised at myself as I hear the words come out. I don't mention that I gave up after only one agent reviewed the manuscript. Wanting to change the subject I ask about copyright. She doesn't have much to say on the subject, but I don't really care. I then ask her what her future holds. She starts by telling me that she got a late start with her education, graduating from college when she was forty. But ever since then she's been focused on making up for lost time. "I have plans," she says, stops, lets out a nervous giggle, and looks away.

"I'd like to hear," I say. Many artists I interview forget the camera as they embrace the ability to talk about their art and creativity. But I can't tell if Judith keeps holding back because of the camera, or because she doesn't trust me.

"It's too early," she says. "I don't want anyone to steal my ideas."

I conjure dozens of ideas every day, hundreds if I forget to take my medicine. Few, I suspect, are worth stealing. But I don't push her to say more. I have enough for my short film, so I wrap things up. The moment the camera is sealed in its carrying case, I sit down next to Judith on the bench. I'm close enough once again to smell her perfume, which is mixing with her perspiration.

"You've been holding back on me."

"It was that obvious?" she replies softly.

She turns her body toward me, and her left knee touches my right one. I'm suddenly reminded how long it's been since I've had any physical contact with a female. I've been away from Laura for a longer period than at any point in our seven-year relationship. "It's not a big deal," I tell her. "It will be a great video. But you strike me as a very creative woman, and I think you have more going on than just editing."

"I do," she says in an almost whisper. Then she leans in and places her lips near my ear. The Shalimar is nearly overpowering. "Are you pressed for time?"

I tell her I'm free, but as I do so I feel apprehensive, not unlike when I walked the steps into Bob Kurtz's basement.

"Why don't you come up to my apartment for a little bit? I'll get you some iced tea, and show you my secret." She stands, her face emerging from the shade. The color in her cheeks no longer appears applied merely with makeup. Her chest rises slightly as she inhales. I stand, already questioning my agreement with this, and we begin walking. "I'm not so good at trust," she says, "particularly with men. Perhaps it's my two failed marriages, but I haven't had much luck outside of those, either. I've been single for seventeen years, after the last divorce. Well, that's not quite true, I lived with a guy for ten years after that, but he never wanted us to become a real boyfriend and girlfriend, you know, so I finally had to end it. It's been rough."

For a woman with trust issues, she is pretty quick to trust me. I tell myself this is no different from the rest of my encounters on this trip. Being a reporter has taught me to be a good listener, and like Marc Bondarenko told me in Birmingham, you often create a temporary connection with a stranger when engaged in a creative exercise. I keep my eyes to the ground as we walk, noting how each square of sidewalk we are traversing through this industrial park is not quite square. The trapezoids permit the sidewalk to curve slightly left, then right. It reminds me of my own path on this trip, turns that take me away from the direction I had intended, but with each individual turn so subtle that I follow them without any real thought to the possible consequences of that deviation.

We reach her building and she guides me up a flight of stairs. I try to determine if the swishing of her rear in my face is as dramatic as I imagine it to be. When we enter her apartment she slips into a small kitchen, pours an iced tea, and hands it to me. The liquid hits my throat and I shiver. I had no idea that while filming Judith I had gotten so hot.

"I'm not yet ready to share with the world what I'm about to show you. But with my mother now gone, it's time for me to start." She takes a seat at a nearby dining table, then pulls another chair next to her. "Here," she says, patting the upholstered cushion atop the wooden chair.

Judith's smiling face reflects in the computer screen, ghostlike. For a moment I don't see Judith. Instead, I lock eyes with another writer, the woman who for years woke me up each morning and tucked me in each night. I see a writer who, while no longer speaking to me, has accompanied me this entire trip.

"So I've been writing a certain type of fiction for, I don't know, twenty-five years?" Judith says. "I guess almost thirty. But I never showed any of this writing to my mother, or even told her I was writing it. She wouldn't have approved. You know, I went to see her before she died. I was at her bedside, holding her hand—but I couldn't tell her. I let her go not knowing this about me. But she's dead now. I have no excuses to hide anymore."

She pulls up a simple web page, with a mauve background and the words "Lace Fortune: Seasons"in black script. She tells me Lace Fortune is her pen name. There are four boxes, each marked with a name of the season. She clicks on "Spring," the word written in green letters.

"Women want to be aroused as much as men—we need it, particularly when we live alone. But studies show—and they're right, by the way—that pictures of naked people just don't do it for us the way they do for you men. We prefer a story."

My mother's novels contain sex scenes that are quite explicit. She expected me to read every word of her books as she wrote them, which I saw not as a burden but rather an honor. Except for the sex. I did not find any pleasure in reading prose depicting intimate acts conceived in my mother's head. The discomfort I would feel when reaching one of those sections is with me now. I should leave, yet I am still here in this seat, inches from Judith, seeing once again how I am too often passive.

She asks me to read the story she has pulled up on the screen. The green font is hard to see so I lean in, requiring me to extend over Judith's lap. The story opens with a man on a park bench, sweating in the heat. I'm struck by the similarity to my situation minutes ago. A curvaceous woman sits beside him, sparking his instant arousal. I know this, because the prose describes his erection in great detail. The sexy stranger stands up as quickly as she sat down. He follows her, his throbbing prick pressing painfully against his zipped jeans. Soon they are near a river, where she shoves his back against a tree and reaches for his zipper. She provides him immediate relief from the jeans' tightness, and then a different kind of relief, first with her hands and then with her mouth. I feel a hardness pressing against my khaki slacks. The material isn't solid enough to hide my arousal. I refuse to look at Judith, not wanting to know if she's noticed.

Judith's writing invites the reader into the scene. It flows, but is too flowery for my taste. I also dislike the jarring use of words like "cock"and "prick."And then there was a disturbing moment where the point of view shifted from the man to the woman. I want to be the one

198

receiving oral sex, not giving it. I focus my mind on critique, as if I were Judith the editor, not Patrick the man far from his wife who is reading erotica within inches of its female author in the privacy of her apartment. The story is fiction, but the scene I'm in is real. It would only take a moment for Judith to find my zipper. The room is so silent I can hear rapid breathing, both mine and hers.

I have experienced few manic episodes in my life. If I do something inappropriate here, could I blame it on my condition? Part of what keeps my bipolar disorder in check is routine. My life the past three weeks or so has been anything but. I look over my left shoulder, away from Judith. Her bedroom door is open. There is a comforter on the floor and the bed's sheets are a tangled mess. If she had been planning to lure me here she would have made the bed. At some point during our interview I believe Judith opened herself to the unexpected, to once more choosing to trust a man.

That realization is what drives my next action. I stand up and step away from the table. I am going to leave now. Not because it would be wrong to cheat on my wife, although of course it would be. Not because Judith is far too similar to my mother, although she clearly is. But because I know that danger and tenderness do not easily combine. The tenderness in my marriage is possible because, through medicine and life choices, I have shielded myself from the enticements of danger. And this woman who has been largely alone for two decades, and now no longer has to fear her mother's judgment, is particularly vulnerable to danger. I will not be an instrument in causing her emotional harm.

I suspect the course of Judith's life has been dictated by vulnerability. Her wrong turns with men, her fear of showing her mother her true creative self, all must stem from that. I suspect that because I have seen the vulnerability that can stem from insecurity. In that sense, Judith is also very much like my mother. After a lifetime of trying, I still haven't learned how to heal my mother's wounds. I'm not about to try with Judith. So I compliment Judith on her writing. I tell her how grateful and touched I am that she trusted me with the words. I offer encouragement in her pursuits, as a writer and editor. And then I tell her I have to leave.

The awkwardness lies heavy as I walk out the door. She follows me, down the stairs, to my car. She tells me that if in my travels I meet any single, older men who live in the Denver area, I should suggest they look up a local erotica writer named Judith. I nod, slipping into the car. In my rear-view mirror I see her standing in the cul-de-sac of the parking lot, motionless, watching me drive away. I wish I had something to give Judith other than a short video promoting her editorial services, but she needs far more than I can give.

. . .

Cheyenne is even smaller than Alan O'Hashi described it. With no need to film an interview in this state, thanks to meeting Alan in Boulder, I am only here to look around and have a bite of lunch. No other tables are occupied in the train-station-turned-restaurant where I down a buffalo burger. Few vehicles are parked on the downtown streets—just a smattering of worn pickup trucks, all either Fords or Chevys—and I see no pedestrians. The only activity at all on this Friday before Labor Day weekend are a handful of individuals in matching white T-shirts setting up tents and banners for the town's annual Frontier Days, the festival celebrated in Jack Kerouac's *On the Road*. I've lived too long out East, I suppose, because I find this lack of population unsettling, almost post-apocalyptic.

Less than an hour later I pull my rental sedan into a truck stop outside of Laramie to refuel both my car and my caffeine level. The only non-truck I see is an early 70's chocolate-brown Trans Am up on blocks near the back of the complex. The credit-card swipers on the pumps all have yellow tape in an X shape over them, so I go into the store to pre-pay. Inside the customers all wear a uniform of sorts, baseball caps that advertise bait shops and hunting supply stores with logos printed on foam. The caps are as worn down as their owners. The young girl at the register fumbles with the credit card scanner, apologizing to me by saying most of the customers pay in cash.

Back on the road, rock formations rise only a few feet before falling off again. The GPS tells me my elevation is more than 6,000 feet, so I forgive the lack of geologic diversity, figuring I may be along a ridge line. The landscape is flat, not unlike eastern Nebraska, except instead of corn I see cottonwoods. Then I spot two manmade structures, one on either side of the highway. To the left is a windowless building advertising a topless live show, to the right a showroom for Murphy beds. I didn't know people still bought beds that you could hide vertically against a wall. Perhaps that's a term referring to bedding for eighteen-wheelers of which I'm unfamiliar. I imagine strip-club customers taking dancers under the freeway overpass to try out the store's merchandise. Then I attempt to purge my mind of half-naked women, still shaken from this morning.

My next distraction is a sign proclaiming I have reached the Continental Divide. I am as uninspired crossing it westbound as I was with my eastbound crossing more than two decades earlier in the New Mexico desert. Just as on that drive, the land before me is flat as it is behind. Scrub brush, half-dead from dehydration, creeps to the edge of the interstate fronting a lengthy stretch of barbed-wire. The sign tells me I am at an elevation of precisely 7,000 feet. I find the number disturbingly exact. It suggests a reality that is too neat to be real, as if crafted by a skilled fiction writer.

As I move west the rock outcroppings grow taller. Some now are several hundred feet tall, far bigger than the scarred cliff face abutting my Boulder motel this morning. Many of the formations line the highway while others lie off in the distance, breaking the otherwise flat horizon. Soon steep cliffs of brown and red rock surround me as I am stared at by a distant pair of black eyes. The pupils prove to be two tunnels bored through rock. I enter the westbound eye socket.

I arrive in Rock Springs a little after 7 pm, the place I've chosen to spend the night before pressing on to Salt Lake City tomorrow morning. There doesn't appear to be much to Rock Springs beyond a few motels and fast food restaurants. I find my motel, which is called the Outlaw Inn and boasts of a "saloon." The desk clerk, a heavyset woman in a leather vest and cowboy hat, tells me if I visit the saloon I'll have a rollicking good time. After dropping off my bags in my room I decide to see if she's right. I imagine walking through two swinging wooden doors to a scene with gunslingers playing poker, a bow-tied bartender pouring whiskey, and a brunette in a red corset and black garters descending the back stairs to greet me. Instead I find a

201

narrow room with a long bar lined with fake wood siding on the right wall and a few two-top tables squeezed against the left. An ancient color TV hangs from that wall, facing the bartender, not the customers. And there are only two customers, a man about my age in a suit, and a gray-bearded man in a plaid flannel shirt several seats to his right. I sit between them and order the most exotic beer they have on tap, a Coors Light.

The man in the suit is arguing with the bartender, an older woman with home-dyed blonde hair and an air of resignation. There's got to be some college football on, he says. Can't you go to the menu screen and look at the options? I don't know how to do that, she replies, and instead advances channel by channel. After several screens of talking heads, two football teams appear. There, the man says, but she keeps going. That was it, he says, but she shakes her head. Gotta go all the way around, she says, and her resignation becomes his.

It's the fault of our schools, the gray-bearded man says to me. I wonder what he means, if our teachers should be educating our nation's bartenders on how to operate television remotes. They don't teach kids what they need to know nowadays, he says. They just fill their heads with all sorts of nonsense. Stuff about how there isn't really a God, how we all came from monkeys. Hell, if I had kids I'd home-school 'em, make sure they learned what was what. I nod, counting in my mind the steps back to the door. I pound my beer.

The man in the suit gets up to leave. As he walks past he stops and leans over. "There's only one place in this shithole of a town worth visiting. The Wild Pony." And he leaves.

"The Wild Pony? I knew that guy was no good," says the gray-bearded man.

"What's The Wild Pony?"

"It's a strip club on the other side of I-80. Back hidden away on Rosemont Street, all cinderblock, no windows. What an embarrassment, that guy thinking all we have going for us here are young women dancing for dollar bills, lost because they weren't taught what's right, that God gave them those bodies, and they should be showing them only to their husbands."

I leave a twenty on the counter, not wishing to stick around for the change. I don't use the GPS, I just drive on instinct. It doesn't take me long to cross I-80 and find the cinderblock building on Rosemont Street.

I'm not new to strip clubs, although it has been years since I've entered one. I frequented one a few times in D.C. after I separated from my first wife. I enjoyed eyeing a variety of body types after ten years with one woman. Like listening to a radio station's playlist, I found if one dancer didn't do it for me, a few minutes' wait would bring another. I also liked that it only cost me a dollar to touch their bare flesh when I slid the tip into one of their garters, and only a few more dollars to place my hands all over their bodies if I paid for a lap dance. It was so simple, so streamlined. If you did X, you received Y. I never went beyond a lap dance, however, leaving the privacy of the champagne room to men with more money and less self-discipline. After a few visits the novelty wore off. I also began to wonder, as the father of a daughter, what had happened in these women's lives to lead them into that line of work. Such thinking tends to negate desire.

Inside the Wild Pony no one sits at the bar. The few customers are instead seated at small tables circling the stage. The man in the suit from the saloon is front and center. A tall blonde rides the pole, a straw cowboy hat her only item of clothing. I find a seat against the wall. A waitress brings me a watered-down beer even less palatable than the one at the saloon. I'm joined quickly by a dancer, older than the truck-stop register girl but younger than Judith. Deeply tanned skin emerges from a dress that starts halfway down her breasts and stops just at the bottom of her rear. It's as if she's bound in scarlet saran wrap. Her vaguely Asiatic eyes suggest both intrigue and fatigue.

"Mind if I join you?"

I know the way this works. If I say yes, I'll have to buy her a drink. It will be some kind of fruity concoction designed to create a false impression that she is consuming alcohol at the same rate as me. She will stay sober while I get drunk. She is paid not just to dance but to please the customers, and she can please me by being a conversation partner. I nod consent. The waitress reappears almost immediately, and I request she bring my new friend a drink.

"I'm Jasmine," she says, extending her hand.

"Patrick," I say, using my real name. I'm sure hers is fictional.

I watch one of Jasmine's co-workers on the stage and she appears to take no offense. In fact, as each dancer takes her turn on the pole—some more curvaceous than Jasmine but none as exotic—she rates each of them on a bitchiness scale.

"This seems like a pretty small town," I say. "I'm struck by the ratio of attractive women to the overall population."

"You sound like a scientist or something." She laughs, a full laugh. I like it. "None of us live here. The owner, Jack, ships us in. I'm from Denver. Scarlett," she says, pointing to the brunette on stage removing her top, "is from Salt Lake City. There's a motel just behind the building here, Jack puts us up for two weeks, three, six, whatever works for us. It's a sweet gig, free housing, although he doesn't pay us shit. It's all about the tips."

I catch her hint but don't respond to it. "Is there anything to do here when you're not working?"

"Sleep. And count your cash. I come up three or four times a year. When I get back to the club in Denver, my regulars are always glad to see me, and the tips are high that first week."

"How long have you been here?"

"Nearly three weeks. This is my last night before I head back."

I'm doing it again, I realize. I'm interviewing her, as if she were one of my video subjects. This road trip has been about telling the stories of others, but I too have stories to tell, too, and I feel I am creating a new one tonight. Before I can ask Jasmine another question she slips off of her stool and steps over. Spreading my legs, she slides her body up in between them, and then, with a hand behind my head, presses my face into her chest. Her beads of sweat are warm and intoxicating.

"Let's go dance. Only twenty dollars a song."

I'm tempted. She's provided me conversation and companionship. Perhaps I should let her earn a tip the way she's used to doing it. She points to an alcove across the room in which there are four padded chairs lacking armrests. Three of them are occupied by men, each with a dancer in various stages of undress gyrating on top of them.

Jasmine places her hand on the growing bulge in my jeans. "There's an empty seat," she says, "and it's the best one. The bouncer can't see us there. We can really have some fun." I see what she means. A bald, tattooed man in a too-tight black shirt stands not far from me next to the DJ. It appears the empty chair is around a corner and out of his view. Jasmine then leans in closer, her warm breath striking my ear. "And see that door right behind it? That leads to the motel. We can continue the party there."

So this isn't just a strip club. These are the ultimate working girls, shipped in to serve every need of the truckers and drifters and no-gooders who overnight in this godforsaken town. In *On the Road,* Jack Kerouac enjoyed a Frontier Days adventure in Wyoming. Now it could be my turn. I've been on this path ever since I drank all of that tequila back in Ann Arbor and lusted after the naughty-librarian bartender. Embracing my manic side would be so easy.

And that realization is what stops me.

"I won't do this," I say. I remove her hand from my jeans and slide off of the stool.

"Are you sure, sugar? I'm worth it."

"I've no doubt," I say. I'm lost, but not this lost. I pull two twenties from my wallet, place them on the table, and then head for the door. I drive on auto-pilot to the Outlaw Inn, its plastic sign backlit from unseen bulbs. My surroundings are otherwise sheeted in black, the town fast asleep. But my path appears fully illuminated before me. Four more motel nights alone and then back home to Laura. She married me despite my bipolar diagnosis, and her belief in me has kept me on a path of sanity. I take my daily medicine. I monitor those moments of temptation when racing thoughts tell me I am above the rules, not subject to the moral code I otherwise choose to obey, when bright lights lure me to embrace my inner outlaw. I park beneath the glowing sign knowing my adventure for this night is done.

SEPTEMBER 4: UTAH

I hate myself for rushing out of the Salt Lake City home of jazz singer and children's novelist Wendy Bradshaw. She was a welcoming host in her palatial white-adobe spread nestled under a striking Rocky Mountain range. She was generous with her life story, one that included beating cancer by embracing positive energy she believes was given to her in a dream by a Nez Perce ancestor. She invited me to spend the afternoon and evening with her and her daughter and grandchildren. Instead I am back in my car, alone. Perhaps my discomfort was from being in the presence of such wholesome women so soon after almost receiving a lap dance in a Wyoming strip club. But I believe it was also that it is proving more difficult to listen to tales of perseverance.

On my drive back to the motel I spot the spires of the Salt Lake Temple set against a stunning blue and orange sky. As a nonbeliever I don't think I'm welcome in that place of worship, but I drive by to see it from the outside and discover the grounds are open to the public. Moments later I walk through a tall gate like Saint Peter might monitor and find myself in a square filled with benches, fountains and tourists. It's a Mormon Magic Kingdom.

Then I hear it, voices soft and lyrical and, Wendy Bradshaw might even say, healing. Two young women dressed in matching black slacks, blue sweaters and American-flag name badges address a small crowd of elderly tourists. I imagine them working the pole together at The Wild Pony, then chastise myself, hoping my lechery is not visible on my face. But they might welcome knowing my mind went there, as it would be all the more rewarding for them were they to convert my wickedness into adoption of their true faith.

As I slip into the tour the woman holding the microphone flashes me a flawless smile. She guides us to a large fountain from which extends a granite column at least thirty feet high. At its apex is a sphere providing a perch for two golden seagulls. "You're probably wondering why we have a sculpture of seagulls when we're more than eight hundred miles from the ocean," she says. I learn that when the first Mormon settlers arrived here in Utah in 1848—the only place left the four thousand or so believers could find to live where no one was constantly trying to kill them—their first year's crops fell under attack from a scourge of crickets of Old Testament proportions. Then, out of a sky as clear as the one above us, salvation arrived in the form of cricket-devouring seagulls. "We call it the Miracle of the Gulls," the shorter one says through teeth even more stunning. It would have been far simpler for God not to have sent the crickets in the first place, but I still like the story.

Then we turn around to face the Temple itself. From this close its spires appear as if they reach Saint Peter at the gates of Heaven. The tall guide tells us that Brigham Young—the second Prophet of the Mormons after founder Joseph Smith was killed by an angry mob while jailed in Illinois—led the faithful here to the shore of the Great Salt Lake. He chose this very spot to build a temple to God. After about ten years of construction, they realized the sandstone wouldn't support such an ambitious structure, so they found hardier stone about twenty miles away. Each day whatever men could be spared from the fields would head to the quarry, carve out large chunks of rock, and drag them back over that vast distance in ox-drawn wagons. After a full two decades of construction they had managed to complete the first floor.

I try to place myself among them, growing crops amidst cricket infestations, hauling stones across an unforgiving desert, all the while having to ward off occasional raids from federal troops. They endured this because they believed God wished them to. Faith and hardship combined to form devotion. Our smiling guides have not known the hardships of their ancestors, nor have I. This morning on the phone I snapped at one of my employees, telling her I was sick of being pestered with questions about the details of the big event we are hosting on Capitol Hill in a couple of weeks. "I pay you a lot of money," I said, "to make smart decisions in my absence. I can't be bothered with D.C. drama right now." When I arrived for my interview this afternoon my mood matched the purple-blue mountain range behind her home. But Wendy's struggle, and the story of this temple, remind me of my good fortune.

SEPTEMBER 5: IDAHO

I don't believe it at first. I lean forward over the car's dash, as if being closer to the front windshield will allow me to see further. Then I check all of my mirrors, and turn to look over my right shoulder. I'm truly alone. For the first time on this trip I am the only vehicle visible in any direction. On this empty Idaho highway I am one with the asphalt and the scrub brush.

A siren breaks my reverie. In my driver's side mirror I spot a highway patrol car emerge from the gully between the westbound and eastbound lanes of I-84. I pull over and he stops behind me. Now nothing is in motion except a tumbleweed far ahead in the distance. This is my first speeding ticket of the trip, but I take it from the officer with grace. I'm tempted to tell him that going eighty-nine miles per hour endangered no one but myself. But there is no use in doing so, and besides, the speed limit here is seventy-five, which is fast enough. I'm eager now to get where I want to be, but that doesn't mean I need travel without restraint. Imposing a bit of sanity on my journey won't hinder my eventual arrival.

The officer returns his patrol car to its hiding place like a crouching tarantula while I resume my driving. More tumbleweeds appear, many more. The strong wind reminds me of my drive across Nebraska, but the parched landscape here produces not fields of golden crops but rather brown flora corpses, moving east in a steady migration. A large, spiky sphere resembling a skeletal snowman base whisks in front of my car and I swerve, narrowly missing it. Another arrives, then two. I bob and weave across the two lanes of highway, careful not to end up in the ditch that is deep enough to camouflage a highway patrol car. Soon the tumbleweeds prove too numerous and one strikes my car's grill with a combination of a thud and a pop. Twigs snap and whish into my windshield. I flinch.

But that was it. Thud. Pop. Whish. No harm done. It's fun, actually. Now, still alone on the road, I aim my two tons of steel directly at the zombies. More thuds and pops and whishes. I'm living a video game. Then the leader of this migrating brush pride approaches, spiky tendrils emerging from its base that are almost as wide as my car's front grill. I must take him out. I dig back deep into my brain to high school algebra and imagine the train that leaves for Pittsburgh and the other train that departs for Cleveland, and the varying speeds they must reach in order to pair up in Buffalo. I calculate the hypotenuse between me and my prey, imagining us meeting at the right angle of the triangle. A gust increases my foe's speed. I accelerate to meet it.

And I do. There is no thud this time. It is more of a boom, a rippling force of sound that chills and excites me. I am blinded momentarily by the spray of limbs that scatter across my windshield. When I can see again, two tendrils extend up from my grill, aimed out away from each other like a longhorn hood ornament. This is my trophy, the record of my kill. I didn't just take out the dried-up remains of a land in drought. I obliterated parts of myself. I leveled the man who surrendered his creativity to a questionable lobbying cause. I demolished the young adult paralyzed by fear of mental illness. And like a patient sniper, I took out that child who couldn't create without his mother's approval.

I feel light as Boise's skyline approaches. Cars and trucks replace the tumbleweeds, driven by people oblivious to my ecstasy. As the parched land bleeds into snow-topped mountains I see that Boise is less urban sprawl and more a frontier encampment. At a modest distance it resembles the village of the train set I received when my parents reunited. That first Christmas together I woke up to find under our tree a model train set complete with a tunneled-through mountain, a bridge, and a small village. The set's scale was miniature, much smaller than the one I had admired at the toy store, but I didn't complain. I was grateful to have my own artificial world into which my imagination could escape, even if that world was less than itself, underpowered, and going in circles.

After checking into a highway motel I head downtown seeking adventure, ideally one a bit tamer than my night in Rock Springs. I spin through the Boise State campus and take in their famous blue football field, which allows their blue-wearing receivers to camouflage themselves from defensive backs. I cruise by yet another capitol building, like in Wisconsin an undersized version of the one I've prowled for two decades in D.C. This model-scale building abuts a modest downtown featuring a variety of locally owned boutiques and, I am pleased to see, several inviting restaurants. I park in front of a Basque welcome center. I'm not sure if the Basques are welcoming me or if only Basques are welcome, so I keep walking.

I enter a lively establishment with high ceilings lined with exposed beams and pipes and take a seat at the bar. Some of the taps are for wine, which seems simultaneously pretentious and sad. The bar is occupied by two young women at one end and an older blonde man by himself at the other. I sit near him. I often eat dinner on the go, allowing more time to edit. This might be the last decent meal I get on this trip, so I glance quickly at the menu and order the most expensive item, a fourteen-ounce pepper steak as well as a malty tap beer. It's Sunday night of Labor Day weekend and the restaurant is filling up.

"Hope you don't have to work tomorrow," the man says to me as I place my order. He's a few years older than I but a bit shorter, with a weathered face and a form-fitting black V-neck T-shirt.

My honest answer would be yes, I do have to work tomorrow. But I don't want to spoil the mood. "Nope," I reply.

"Good to hear!" he says, and pounds the wooden bar with his fist. "Me, I work when I please. I'm a real estate mogul."

A young female bartender with auburn hair pulled back in a pony tail and braces along the top row of her teeth delivers my beer. As I take a sip my drinking companion introduces himself as Craig and hands me a business card with only his name and number on it. He tells me he's a Boise native who made a mint after founding a road construction business and selling it to an Irish conglomerate. He then shifted to real estate investing. Yes, the downturn in the housing market hurt, but he got out of some of his trickier properties just before it hit bottom and he's still investing. He boasts of a hacienda in Scottsdale, Arizona, and other properties in Oregon, but he spends most of his time here in Idaho, nestled in the nearby mountains in a home that overlooks the city.

He interrupts his narrative only when the bartender spins by. She's a blur, serving those of us at the bar but also the waiters and waitresses procuring drinks for the restaurant's patrons. "Angie, you look great tonight," he says. "I bought you a house in Scottsdale."

"I'd prefer Miami," she replies, flying away again.

Craig then tells me Angie's life story. She too grew up here, and graduated from Boise State two years ago. She got this job while still an undergraduate. She wants a different life, he says, but she hasn't figured out what. He also feels she also has lousy taste in men. There's a new one in the picture now, but he's waiting for that relationship to end, and he'll be ready to swoop in when it does. "I've been asking her out for years with no luck," he says. "That's gotta change at some point."

When he said he spends most of his time here, I thought he meant Boise, but perhaps it is here at this bar, longing for a woman less than half his age. She is attractive in the way that all women in their early twenties are, full of energy and possibility. Craig and I, by contrast, are like all men around the halfway point of our lives, full of history and lost opportunity.

During Craig's monologue my steak arrives and I down it without adding a word to the conversation. I then excuse myself to hit the restroom, knowing my companion will be in good hands with Angie. When I return I find him slipping a stuffed money clip into a back pocket. A stack of twenties rests on the bar. "That's all for you, Angie. Go out with me and I'll add a Ferrari."

Angie is pulling a tap with a Petit Noir bottle extending off of it. Red liquid pours into a stem glass. "I don't need a Ferrari, Craig. Just that house in Miami."

"I took care of your steak, friend," Craig says to me, then shouts in the direction of Angie. "What's the point of having money if you can't spend it on people you like?"

"I'm not comfortable with that," I say.

He stands and reaches up to put his arm around my shoulder. "You can make it up to me by buying us a round of drinks at the Matador. Who knows what pretty young ladies we'll meet there?"

I hold up my left hand to show my wedding ring. "I'm married."

"Then you'll make the perfect wing man. No competition! You just tell the ladies you're an old friend, and can't believe how much money I have, but it's so sad I have no one to spend it on. I'm all set for tonight, I got a hotel room down the street."

It seems wrong to go back to my motel to edit when it is Labor Day weekend and I'm finally surrounded by people. Boise is alive, so unlike Cheyenne or Rock Springs. So I shrug and follow Craig toward the exit. He stops after a few steps, however, to talk to the two women who were at the bar when I arrived. I've had my back to them the entire evening, listening to Craig. Craig pulls out his money clip and calls out to Angie to bring these two beautiful young ladies another round of whatever wine they're drinking. The black-haired woman peers over her sharp-pointed nose at some distant point past Craig, but her curvy blonde friend eyes the rolled-up bills and flashes him a dazzling white smile. Craig and the blonde alternate flirtations. I believe my job is to distract the friend. I say hello to her, and she turns her blank gaze to me. We stare at each other and say nothing. Then I look to the exit behind her, but there is no way to get to it in this cramped space along the bar without pressing by Craig.

I have no place in this drama. These individuals are all stuck, the mogul in his delusions, the bartender in her unfulfilled dreams, the blonde in her openness to being bought, the pointy-nosed woman in her defeatism. I tell the mogul I'm hitting the john again and he gives me no notice. I work my way to the bathroom and keep going, through the swinging metal doors into the kitchen. I enter as if I own the place, but my mannerisms matter not. A young woman in a hairnet continues to prep salads while a pimply teenage boy drops a basket of potato wedges into a deep fryer. I am finally noticed in the back alley when I startle an aproned teenage boy on a cigarette break. He almost stumbles off of the plastic crate he is using for a seat.

My car is only a short distance away. I run to it, hop in, start the engine, and drive. I keep going, far away from this bar. I welcome the forward motion.

SEPTEMBER 6: IDAHO

Before walking to the radio station's unmarked employee entrance, I stop to admire the tumbleweed road kill still embedded in my rental car's front grille. There is only one other vehicle in the parking lot on this Labor Day morning, a compact pickup truck. I'm working today, as I have every day for the last three weeks. Rochelle Smith is also working, volunteering to take her station's holiday shift so I can interview her at the station without interruption by co-workers. She's an acoustic singer/songwriter whose music is an intoxicating combination of structural complexity and spine-tingling pathos. I wanted to interview her the moment I heard her music online, but several days passed before she accepted my request.

Rochelle greets me in blue jeans and a faded black T-shirt. I thank her for agreeing to an interview, and doing it on a holiday.

She shrugs. "I like having the place to myself." The entire station is on auto-pilot, she informs me, robotic signals whisking along Boise's near-empty streets. Rochelle leads me down a narrow glass-lined hallway offering views of various recording and broadcast studios to what appears to be the smallest one of the bunch. "This is my favorite studio," she says. "Its coziness relaxes me." She says she has been nervous about this interview, that even though she talks on the air for a living and performs as a solo artist on stage, the prospect of talking about herself unnerves her. "It seems arrogant to think someone would want to hear what I have to say."

"I want to hear what you have to say," I reply. I decide not to ask her if we can film in a larger room, even though it will be difficult to set up the camera in here at a sufficient distance to capture more than her face. I place Rochelle at a large elevated control board featuring sliding switches in different colors. A guitar case rests behind me in a corner. As I position the camera I ask her why she finally agreed to be interviewed.

"I tend to ask the universe for guidance when it comes to

214

opportunities," she says. "I ask, and then I wait. What I heard was that something good would come of this."

"I'm glad the universe said yes."

She tilts her head slightly, then smiles. "I think I am too."

She clips the microphone to the V of her T-shirt next to a small tattoo of what appears to be a Chinese symbol. Instinctively I rub my right foot against my left ankle, where I have a tattoo that I purchased years ago after I sold most of my belongings and moved Marisa and Parker into a one-bedroom apartment. It's the ancient Japanese symbol for "simplicity," there to remind me to avoid complications in life. Well, that's what the tattoo artist says the symbol means, anyway. It could represent bacon or a sexual desire for goats. But a tattoo means what its owner chooses it to mean. My first tattoo, a compass rose on my left tricep, borrows my favorite symbol from antique maps as a reminder that I must not fear charting new paths in my life. I obtained that one shortly after my divorce. I embraced that lack of fear when leaving a steady job to launch a lobbying start-up, and have been rewarded in many ways, most notably financially. But I shouldn't let that comfort prevent me from following a new path if I wish.

I begin the interview by raving about Rochelle's music. "I love how ethereal it is."

"A lot of my music comes from dreams," she says. "And they're layered with harmonies, because I hear harmonies in my head all of the time. It's a curse, or a gift."

Rochelle recalls how as a child she'd seek escape from drama in her home by listening to music, distracting herself by picking out harmonies. "Growing up wasn't, well, it wasn't always fun."

Leah Martensen embraced religious music as a childhood escape. I am curious about Rochelle's past, if she too has a bipolar parent or some similar story to tell. But this interview almost didn't happen, so I'm hesitant to press her. I understand what she means about harmonies, however. In all of those years singing baritone in various groups I lived the challenge of being the forgotten part of a chord. The first tenor hits the top note, the bass the bottom, the second tenor the melody. The baritone sings whatever note is left over. He must learn to fit in. I think of what I've heard of Rochelle's music, and realize that one of the things that spoke to me about it is that sometimes she lifts that forgotten line and puts it front and center.

"Thankfully," Rochelle says, "people think it's a good thing when you're a musician and you hear things in your head. I'm blessed with a really good musical ear. I'm not good at other things. I can't remember people's names or faces, but I can tell when their B string is out of tune."

"That's a real gift."

"It can trip me up," she says, placing her left hand beside her on the control table. Her index finger finds its way to the groove atop a black lever. "Sometimes, after I've laid down the harmonies, I have to tell myself to get out of the way. I keep editing. I've destroyed a lot of my music because I couldn't just get it out of my head and leave it be."

I wince, seeing my daughter in Rochelle. Marisa carried self-doubt with her this past year, refusing to enter the contest she had done well in the year before because she was convinced all of her art was crap. The father in me wants to hug Rochelle, to tell her that she'll learn to trust herself creatively, the way so many of my interview subjects who are older than Marisa and Rochelle have done. Instead I find myself confessing to being a miserable failure at songwriting, despite a childhood as a musician. "I am a creative writer, though."

I hear the words so I know I said them, but I'm surprised. I blame the cramped confines of this studio for creating a false sense of intimacy and shift my focus back to Rochelle.

"If I were to ask you how you identify yourself, what would you say?"

"You're thinking I should say 'musician,' or 'songwriter,' or maybe 'deejay,'" she says. "I don't like labels. I guess I'd say I'm a person who likes music who happens to work in music for a living, but it's not who I am." She pauses, and turns slightly to the sound board, eyeing one of the needles. It's pointing to the right, with a strip of red beneath it. She slides a plastic lever down ever so slightly, and the needle moves left, to where the arc beneath it is white. "Actually, I quit playing music for three, no, more like five years."

Given how young she appears, five years is a significant length of time. She lifts her hand from the control panel and points to a guitar case I hadn't noticed before. "I couldn't touch it. I was so self-critical of what I was writing, I lost control of my inner critic. I thought, 'Who am I to think I can create something someone else would want to listen to? How dare I be so arrogant?'"

I think of what the Voice of Golden Eagle told me of his own creative dry spell. "You put your creativity in the closet."

"Oh, absolutely. I shut that closet. I locked that closet."

I now think of Colleen Doran, who told me in her farmhouse outside of Charlottesville, Virginia, that one day she woke up and couldn't draw anymore. She had hit the big time as a comic illustrator, the most successful woman in her industry. And yet she was as paralyzed as Rochelle. Colleen made her way back to an art-committed life by returning to school. "How did you get past that block?"

"It was a friend. I had known her for years, and I confessed I wasn't playing any more. She gave me a very loving chewing out, and said not everybody comes into this world with the gift of creating. She pretty much told me it was my duty to share that gift. I hated my job at the time, and she said if it was stifling me, I should find a different job."

"So you found your way to this radio station. Are folks here supportive of your music?"

"Oh, I don't mix work and music. A lot of people here don't even know I play. That's why I liked the idea of doing the interview today when the studio was empty, so I wouldn't have to explain why you were interviewing me."

"You broadcast music for a living and your co-workers don't know you're a musician?"

"I don't want to get my music on the radio because of my job. I'd rather have my music played because it's good."

Had I ever encountered the good fortune to work for a publisher when I was trying to be a novelist, I would have happily allowed my employer to publish it. "Your music is good, really good. It deserves to be played."

"I have to get there the way I think is right."

Rochelle's very essence is creative, yet I believe a part of her fears her creative core. "Okay," I say. "But you perform."

"Oh, I love performing," she says. "I had someone ask me before, 'Why do you perform? I don't understand what would inspire someone to get up and be in front of a group of people and be watched. Is it some kind of ego thing you didn't get as a child?'"

I'm troubled for Rochelle that the very first place her mind leaps when asked about performing live is a suggestion of narcissism.

"Maybe it is an ego thing, I don't know," Rochelle continues, her voice a bit less soft. "But the thing is, when I'm a deejay, I'm alone. I don't get to hear the reaction of my audience. I love it when people come up to me after a performance and tell me I touched them. We connect. And it's an excuse to feel comfortable meeting other people."

Her process is different, but her end result is the same as it has been for me as a journalist. Interviewing people gives me an excuse to connect with people I would never otherwise meet.

"So, have you been performing much lately?" I ask.

She looks back again at the console behind her, glancing over the indicators. None appear to be awry, at least from what I can see as a layman. She moves a red lever anyway. "Not solo. I've kind of fallen into a comfort zone of backing people up. I played bass in a girl rock band for a while, and it was a year before they even knew I played guitar. I guess I'm looking for that next project. I'm not sure what is coming, but I feel something is."

She's presumably asked the universe and is waiting for an answer. I think again of Steve Cox, the Voice of Golden Eagle. He said the universe had proclaimed to him that a wondrous new path would be coming soon, and that he'd be ready when it arrived. But what if you don't have the patience to wait? What if you've cleared your way through the tumbleweeds, the dried husks of your past, and are anxious to drive forward?

"Perhaps I'm ready to get back to my solo work," Rochelle says.

"Is that what the universe is telling you?"

"Maybe. At least I'm telling myself that."

"And you're telling me."

"I am."

"Thank you."

We sit in silence. I'm out of practice with give-and-take

conversations, but I realize it is probably my turn to reveal. "As a journalist," I say, "I've always found it easier to tell other people's stories. Like these videos."

"Exactly. It's hard to write about what I've experienced. But I've been through a lot, and friends will say, 'How come you're not writing music about that?'"

"Have you tried?"

She glances again at the control board. "I don't want to play the victim here. I don't. But I went through a really rough year. I had a very dear friend, who was also a musician, die of breast cancer. I'd go to her house every day, for months. I'd hang out with her, hoping she'd get better. And she kept getting worse, right down to the very end. I held her hand as she died. I felt the pulse leave her body."

Rochelle is almost inaudible, but I am deathly silent, so her voice grows omnipresent. I've never lost anyone truly close to me, but I think this is what the loss of a soulmate would look like.

"So you wrote a song about it."

Rochelle takes a deep breath, then nods. "It's 'Blue Water.' The version online doesn't have the opening I put on my demo CD. In that mix I actually open with her voice. I taped some conversations with her before she died, to have something to remember her by. This one passage turned out to be so precious I put it at the start of the song. You know, I could produce six CDs just out of those recordings of her, but I don't know if anyone would want to hear them. It would be pretty dark."

"Some of the best art is," I reply. "You said you're more comfortable telling other people's stories, and you told your friend's story. Do you think by doing so you also told a bit about yourself?"

"Absolutely."

Once again I think about the videos I'm producing, how they're morphing as I travel, from straight bios interlaced with gentle propaganda to intense interrogations into the creative life and its importance to one's own essence. I uploaded my video of Toledo singer/songwriter Leah Martensen this morning, and when I watched it online, it felt like I had just stood on the steps of Capitol Hill naked

219

and exposed. I was so present in that video, with every selection and every cut, even though neither my voice nor my face appeared. I wonder if my funders have noticed.

We sit in silence again. Finally I decide to ask my old standby. "What advice would you give to an aspiring artist?"

"It's really cool that you asked me that, because I actually have an answer. It's that one sentence I've been carrying in my head. Tell your story. Three words. You've got to tell your story. Don't be afraid of exposing yourself. Someone else has probably been through it, and putting it out there will help you get past it. If you're a songwriter, write music. If you're a poet, write a poem. If you're a painter, paint a picture. But tell your story."

"It sounds like you aspire to follow that advice yourself."

She smiles. "Yes, I do."

I remember her guitar case. "Would you play something for me?"

"I'd like that."

As she passes me to retrieve the instrument our shoulders touch ever so briefly. I'm reminded of the connection Marisa and I experienced in that motel room in Savannah. I find myself wanting to cheer for Rochelle's success the way I will be for my teenage daughter. I also recall Marisa wanting to celebrate me as a fellow artist. "I'm thinking of writing about this trip," I confess to Rochelle. "You know, telling the story of what it's meant to me."

"I can't imagine how you couldn't. Not if you're a creative writer."

She starts to play, a song I haven't heard. She doesn't sing. It's just the notes from the guitar, bouncing first in the instrument's sound box, then against the glass and acoustic tiles of the studio. Perhaps she's telling her story through the notes, in harmonies she's freed from her mind. I want this private concert to last all day. But when she finishes the song the guitar goes back into the case. She then hands me a demo CD. I place it carefully in my camera bag.

"I'm glad the universe gave you permission to meet with me," I say.

She nods slightly. "So am I."

. . .

With a long drive across Oregon in front of me, I decide to remove my tumbleweed trophies from the car's front grille to ensure proper air flow over the engine. A few light tugs is all that is needed. The branches form a small pile on the asphalt resembling a stack of kindling, suggesting I'm about to start a fire.

Soon after leaving Rochelle's radio station I rejoin I-84 in the direction of Oregon, the place of my birth. It's the state my mother and father grew up in, the state in which they fell in love, and the state they fled forever when I was two years old. It's the state that made my parents who they are but was hardly ever discussed. A sign tells me an exit for Bend, Oregon, is approaching. Bend is the largest city in central Oregon. If I took this exit, after Bend I could head due south to Klamath Falls, the small town where I was born.

I finally excavated my Oregon past six years ago. Before I asked Laura to marry me, she joined me on an exploration of this northwestern state known only to me through anecdotes revealed by my parents in moments of lowered guards. We chased ghosts in that high-desert town the locals call K-Falls, an isolated enclave of a few thousand farmers and lumberjacks. It's a town built on a lie, given there are no falls to be found. We bought a tourism guide to Oregon before the trip, and it said that to understand K-Falls, you should visit a bar and listen to the locals as they spin their "crazy schemes." The snarky author implied that the people there were stuck in their delusions. But my parents' scheme hadn't proved so crazy. They had married young and had a child young, as everyone in K-Falls did, but when I was a toddler they packed me into a Dodge Dart, drove to Phoenix, and never set foot in Klamath Falls again. Why Phoenix? Perhaps they were attracted to the city's mythical namesake, the bird who emerges whole and reborn from its own ashes.

Laura and I on that Oregon trip stayed for two nights north of Klamath Falls at the Crater Lake Lodge, the same place my parents had honeymooned exactly forty years earlier. Our June arrival found the high-altitude lake still in winter. Banks of snow taller than our car lined the lodge parking lot. The Rim Road around the lake was still closed, its presence only identifiable by tall shafts emerging from the snow that would guide the snowplows so they wouldn't careen over the 2,000-foot drop into the lake. The lake was hidden by dense fog that lingered all day as we killed the hours by the fake-wood gas-powered fireplace in the historic lodge, drinking brandy and hatching crazy schemes.

On our second and final day at Crater Lake we visited K-Falls and confirmed there wasn't much to explore. A run-down single-story shopping mall failed to lure us in with the temptation of a 4-H goat show. A museum to the local Indian culture did win a visit, but the modest space filled with little more than glass-enclosed displays of arrowheads disappointed. I felt a strong desire to leave, understanding my parents a bit more at that moment. We returned to Crater Lake. The fog had cleared and the ancient lake lay before us, still as blue glass. I felt a tug as I imagined my mother and father standing there, newly married, full of dreams their parents expected to be dashed. I wanted to shout out to my grandparents, all dead now, none known to me, and proclaim with pride that I am my parents' son.

Nothing disturbed the lake's surface that magical day. Water pure from a lack of contaminants glistened blue, forming a flat mirror that reflected the caldera walls and surrounding sky. Wizard Island—a cone rising out of the lake that represents the volcano's aspiring rebirth—appeared not like the wizard's hat for which it is named, but instead a floating diamond, coupled as it was with its mirrored doppelganger. I imagined this view must have calmed my parents, the passionate, emotionally tortured eighteen-year-old girl and the volatile, unmedicated twenty-one-year-old boy. Of course, that calm was built on a falsehood, a belief that what we see now is how things will remain. Wizard Rock is the lake's way of telling us that the day will come when this caldera will erupt again. We must always be ready for the explosion.

Passing the exit for Bend I turn on the radio and hear Rochelle Smith's voice. It's clearly her, but also not. The quiet, modest woman I was interviewing just a few minutes ago is now animated, almost perky. She nearly sings with pleasure as she describes an upcoming music concert her station is sponsoring, then slips into a seductive purr as she introduces the next song. This must be her radio personality, a bit of role play. I play a role every time I meet with a congressional staffer or an Administration official. I play a policy advocate paid to defend one extreme against the other, when my personal history inclines me to resist absolutes. Rochelle said her previous job stifled her creativity. I can't blame my funders for stifling my muse; I had already abandoned it when I first accepted their money. But what I do know is that their generosity has them believing they own my creativity. Any word I write must be for their cause.

I can't fault a writer for producing what others want, however. When I was just starting high school my father and I picked up my mother at Phoenix Sky-Harbor Airport as she returned from her first-ever writer conference. Giddy with excitement, she explained that publishers there had said they were desperate for new romance authors. That wasn't her reading genre of choice, but a year later she had consumed hundreds, and had written one as well. In no time at all she landed a publishing contract. That day at the airport her eyes had flickered the way they always did when she was hatching a crazy scheme, but once again she had managed to pull it off.

Rochelle's voice grows fainter as I lose the signal for her station. I turn off the radio and kill time by imagining walking away from this career I've found myself in. Like purchasing a new suit, I mentally try on every job that my interview subjects have held to make ends meet. None of them truly fit, but each one slides on easier than what I'm wearing now. My stomach twists as I imagine walking away from my generous salary, but I tell myself the pain is hunger. I ask the GPS to find the nearest fast food restaurant or convenience store, and am told that they are all behind me. I have entered an unpopulated stretch of high desert. No oasis awaits me.

I recall the loaf of banana bread that Tara Barney gave me in Sioux Falls. I have been snacking on it for the last several days, but a modest portion remains. I reach under the car seat and pull out this lifesaving gift. The bread is no longer moist, and after eating it I am thirsty. But so be it. I needed; the universe provided. That is how Rochelle might describe it, but I find myself differing with that take. When Tara gave me this loaf I placed it in the passenger cabin of the car for just this sort of emergency.

I'm chasing along the Oregon Trail now, pursuing the ghosts of William Clark and Meriwether Lewis. I wonder what Lewis' mental state was when he knew he was approaching the end of his journey. It's hard to know, because his journal falls silent. Were one to listen to the audio journal I'm keeping on this trip, they'd hear an honest account of a downward spiral in Michigan and Wyoming framing a brief lift in Nebraska. On that drive upriver along the Platte I felt spiritually lifted. My mind is soaring again as I descend parallel the Columbia on a fairly steep grade. A sign earlier said I was at an elevation of 3,400 feet, then another said 2,400 feet. Now one says 780 feet. As Portland grows nearer traffic thickens. It is the end of Labor Day weekend, and I'm surrounded by Subaru station wagons mounted with bicycles and canoes, adventurers returning from their mini-vacations. This trip has not been a vacation for me, but it is also coming to an end.

SEPTEMBER 7: WASHINGTON AND OREGON

Amy Buchheit's door is opened by a middle-aged man in a stained white tank top. A bit of breakfast is stuck in his untrimmed brown beard. "You're early," he says through gritted teeth.

I look at my watch, then hold up my wrist. "It's 9 a.m. on the dot."

"It's 8 a.m. Amy isn't ready. Come back in an hour."

As the fading maroon paint of the front door swings toward my face, I realize my error. I entered Pacific Time yesterday and didn't reset my watch. With an hour to kill here in Vancouver, Washington—a short hop across a steel-trussed bridge from Portland, Oregon—I drive to a park I saw on the way here. I find myself standing on the grounds of Fort Vancouver, a former trading post for Hudson's Bay Company. The entire complex of a half-dozen Lincoln-Log buildings and a two-story watch tower is surrounded by a weathered six-foot tall slat fence. The complex is a full-scale replica of the long-lost original, but I question how accurate the reproduction is, given the fence looks no different than the base model wood-slat fence enclosing my childhood home. Or perhaps I am now overly sensitive to measures of authenticity.

I have visited only a few tourist attractions on this trip. The Biltmore Estate. Graceland. The Hormel Spam Museum. The Mormon temple. I have driven past far more. I have crossed the country, but I haven't really seen it. Or maybe I have witnessed instead the creative face of America in the form of an array of artists living art-committed lives. When I conceived of this project, I imagined a journey like William Least Heat Moon. My trip has in some respects felt too fast, but my rate of travel hasn't differed much from his. In *Blue Highways* he chronicles thirteen thousand miles of driving in twelve weeks. I've now covered six thousand miles in about five weeks. Like him, I have found myself changed by my encounters with others, often against my will. I have engaged with creative individuals either in person or by video playback while living with their insights during long, quiet drives. Perhaps I have not sufficiently seen the America found in tourist literature, but I found the America I needed.

Back at Amy's front door I brace myself for a conflict with the bearded guy. Instead a smiling woman with pale, rosy skin greets me with an apology. "I overheard him before, I'm so sorry! He can be such an ass. No surprise I divorced him, right?"

She's wearing a T-shirt under a loose-fitting black cardigan. Her hair is untamed, dirty blonde curls bursting out in every direction with an air of whimsy and unpredictability. As she navigates me through a collection of half-packed boxes I learn she's hoping to move soon but is still stuck under the same roof as her ex-husband for financial reasons. It's proving difficult to find a place she can afford in the Portland area, but she didn't want to wait to pack.

Her studio occupies a bedroom at the end of a short hallway. Amy takes a seat in the corner of the room, a desk on one wall to her right, a credenza with a small easel on it to her left. On the wall is a framed degree, a Bachelor of Fine Arts. Two shelves run above the credenza lined with art textbooks. While I set up the camera Amy talks, her words quick and punctuated by full-body laughs.

"Thanks for having me," I say as I turn on the camera. "No worries here, we're just going to have a nice chat about art."

"I'll confess, I've been stressing about this all week. I've never been interviewed for anything before, and I'm not sure what to say."

"Everyone has a story, Amy, and I'm looking forward to hearing yours."

I recall seeing online that she has some photographs currently showing in an exhibition in Seattle, a series she took of old, well-worn toys. I was drawn to one that depicted a Barbie doll mounted precariously on a rusting three-wheeled tricycle with a severed horse's head mounted on its front. Barbie's platinum blonde hair is a matted mess. A rumpled wedding dress slides off of her shoulders and rides up her thighs. What I suspect was originally a veil is now secured around her head as a blindfold. The tricycle sits on loose gravel in what appears to be a municipal dump. When I tell her I was both impressed and disturbed by the photographs she laughs, then tells me she originally took those them to be models for a series of paintings.

"Are they childhood toys?"I ask.

"Not from my childhood," she says, another laugh rolling through her. "I never collected anything in my life, actually, because I moved so much when I was younger. I bought those toys in local thrift shops, like Goodwill. I look for the beat-up ones, toys with some personality."She says she is an Air Force brat, which led to a lot of moves, and then with still more moves when her parents divorced. She's moved twenty-eight times in her first twenty-seven years. "I never had the time or the opportunity to have more than a couple of toys at a time, and as an adult I started buying used toys to fill that void."

In the five years after the failure of my first marriage I moved four times, the first three to find ever-cheaper rent, the fourth because Laura and I became engaged. Marisa and Parker, of course, experienced those moves with me. My children survived the Simplification, when we relocated from the three-story rental house to a one-bedroom apartment. I let them keep as many of their toys and stuffed animals as we could accommodate, but I could see the pain in their eyes as we created piles of what we would take with us and what we would sell or give away.

Amy points to a half-finished painting on a large easel to my right. "I'm still working on the paintings that go with the photographs. The series grew out of my college thesis project. One of the things I learned in school is that if you have a theme, you can use as many mediums as you want."

"So you just recently went back to school."

She nods. "A local commuter school. Before that I was miserable because I couldn't find work I was passionate about. Finally I said, 'Okay, I'm going to go back to school part-time.' And then I got laid off, drank half a bottle of wine, and said, 'Okay, this is a sign.' I signed up for school full time and said 'I'm going to become an artist.'"

"How did you choose to study art?"

Amy laughs again. It's a relaxed laugh, however. She's forgetting the camera. "There wasn't any doubt. I was eighteen months old when I did my first drawing. By the time I was three I was telling people that I would be an artist. Now I'm forty-two and a recent college graduate, but I've always been an artist."She takes a sip of water. "My parents called my art a hobby. They'd say, 'What are you going to do for a living?' I heard that so much, over and over. I know now that's not unusual, though. Many, many artists hear that growing up."

She's right. Many do. But I didn't. Not everyone has a mother who supports herself with her art.

"I ended up going into the military," she says. "I moved around some more, then left and did all of those odd jobs. But I have no regrets about my life choices. They've led me to where I am now, talking art with you."

Amy says she recently sold a painting she had finished ten years earlier, teaching her that economic returns may not be immediate, but they can come. She's plugged in with the local art community, seeking support and encouragement, and has completed an artist professional development program. She's painting murals for local homeowners. In other words, she's doing all the right things. "I know how hard this will be, trying to be a professional artist," she says, as if reading my mind. "There's this perception of artists as slackers, hippies, marijuana smokers, whatever. But for most of the artists I know who are professionals, it's just the opposite. You work really hard. You have to. You may have a part-time job, or even if you're successful you're still running a business. I had someone say, 'Oh, you're a professional artist. I wish I could sit around and paint all day,' and I laughed and said, 'So do I, that would be great!'"

It would. I'd love to sit around and write all day, but I know that is not a believable future. My interview subjects have taught me that there are always aspects of one's life that press against you, deterring you from being alone with your muse.

Noon approaches, and I politely wrap things up. I will enter my final interview this afternoon on a high. Amy's determination to move forward is infectious, cleansing me of lingering malaise left by those trapped Boise bar patrons. On my way to Amy's front door I chart a path back through the maze of half-packed boxes. Amy knows that at some point she will again be on the move, but she has chosen not to wait to pack until that destination is determined. I leave Amy's home, and leave Washington. The Oregon welcome sign greeting me today is tiny, suspended from a steel girder spanning across the top of the short suspension bridge crossing the Columbia River. I suspect a lot of people miss it. But my eyes are open now.

Unlike my first encounter with Amy's house, the front door is open when I arrive at Erin Ergenbright's Northeast Portland single-story duplex. No screen blocks my access, so I approach along the porch past a ten-speed bicycle resting against forest-green siding and reach in to knock on the wooden door. As such, I take in the home's interior before I meet its resident. Amy's home was boxes and bare walls. Erin's speaks to nesting. Everything one would expect in a longtime place of residence can be found, including a set of framed black-and-white family photos artfully displayed on an eggshell white wall. None of the furniture appears to have been purchased to coordinate specifically with any other piece, yet somehow it all harmonizes together as one.

"Come in!" an unseen voice calls.

A thin woman dressed as if she has just returned from a dance recital greets me. She's sporting a form-fitting spandex top revealing toned arms. Like Amy, Erin has chosen black for this interview. Her hair color matches, and is chopped short. Along with the photos on the walls, hair appears carefully crafted to simulate random placement.

"You have a lovely home. It's quite an eclectic collection of really interesting furnishings."

"I don't like to buy anything new," she says. "I live by the mantra that it is possible, especially in Portland, to have a lovely living space simply by trading, and with garage sales and Goodwill."

Amy said she bought the toys she photographed at Goodwill. Each of those toys had a story to tell, but Amy hadn't been part of that story's original formation. Every item in this home came to Erin with a story, but like Amy she's now adding to the pieces' legacies. What I know of Erin is that she is a published author and essayist who teaches creative writing at a local college. I booked the interview weeks ago, but only received final confirmation of our meeting yesterday. I had been leaving her voice-mail messages the last few days, wanting to make sure my final interview was still on. She finally called back last night, explaining she had taken a solo trip deep into the Oregon woods, intentionally leaving her cell phone in Portland. She's back on the grid now.

"A fair amount of what you see here are family heirlooms or gifts from loved ones," Erin says as I set up the camera. "I hold on to everything, every sort of meaningful artifact I've ever received from someone."She says she has shoeboxes full of old letters and postcards. Her time in the woods made clear to her that all of these treasured objects connect intimately with her creative writing.

"How so?"

"Well, I love collaging. I don't know if you can call yourself a collagist, but I've always loved drawing and painting and collecting things, being sensitive to color and shape, and sometimes I think it's just because I love cutting out paper, I love the shapes and working with them, I love rubber cement, I love materials of all sorts, and I kept feeling like there was something wrong with that, and I should be writing about more serious things, like what I teach. But I'm starting to realize that collaging has everything to do with what I'm writing, that it very much has to do with a non-linear narrative style that is the way much of women's literature has tended to be told, a little bit more circular than linear."

Erin goes on, explaining how her first book, *The Ex-Boyfriend Cookbook*, was in fact a work of collage, combining prose and visual elements as she wove together stories of broken hearts with tasty recipes. She goes on, and then on some more. Erin seems incapable of finishing a sentence, but she has so much energy I am hesitant to interrupt.

"It can be tough to describe my writing. You say, 'I'm a writer,' and people say, 'Oh, what do you write?' and for some reason that's the question that just makes me want to kill myself, like, 'Oh, I don't know, I write about people,' and I guess they're expecting me to say, 'Oh, I write romance novels.' They're expecting a sort of genre, and I've never wanted to do that."

They're expecting someone like my mother, whose writing is in fact pretty describable, like any work meant to be mass-marketed. I hear the dismissive tone in Erin's voice when she says "romance novels," and I know my mother hears it in her head each and every day. I've learned on this trip that while insecurity has been a paralyzing agent for me, it is my mother's driving force. It has carried her to a tremendously high level of commercial success. Any scaled rung on the bestseller charts increases her self-doubt. It magnifies her unspoken—but now transparent to me—doubt in the credibility of her own talent. It is illogical, but it is her truth, and I am powerless to change her self-perception. It is not easy for me to admit that.

My mother is a published author, like Erin, but also has something in common with Amy Buchheit, my morning interview. Both left college soon after starting it, and then married. And both pursued artistic dreams. My mother enrolled in an English program at a local university just after my father left us. I would help her study, quizzing her on literary quotes. She excelled as a student, acing courses and wowing professors. Yet she left school a few credits shy of graduation. Perhaps she felt that liberated her to pursue not the literary style of writing her professors were promoting, but the commercial direction with which she was more comfortable.

Erin, I learn, followed a path not available to Amy or my mother. She had no barriers to staying in college, where she studied art and writing. Then she earned a Masters in Fine Arts from the Iowa Writers' Workshop, the gold standard in creative writing programs. The book she wrote in that program was published by one of New York's largest publishing houses.

"I've been spending a lot of time lately going back through things from my childhood," Erin says, "indulging, looking for things to inform my writing. I thought I would enjoy looking back, but it hasn't always been the most fun."She mentions a Joan Didion essay on the importance of keeping a notebook. "That essay talks about being able to look back, and to remember always who you were then, and staying on nodding terms with your former selves. I love that idea and I love how as much as we want to try to change, we can look back, but I think for a long time for a lot of personal reasons, I didn't feel that I had the right to write what I was observing in my own life."

I haven't read the Didion essay she mentions, but I can relate to Erin's resistance to writing about her life. Journalism has been that escape for me, being paid to write about others. But I understand now what Ernest Whaley was trying to tell me about songwriting, that what informs one's writing is the life one has lived. I know Joan Didion worked as a journalist, and also wrote a Pulitzer-Prize-winning memoir. That would seem to make her a good role model for Erin, and for me.

"It sounds like you're looking to write a memoir," I ask.

"Oh, I'm not trying to limit where this is going with labels. I don't know what to call it yet. But I'm bringing the collage aspect of it, these heirlooms from my youth, into the project, and that brings me in as well, and my past. I guess right now I'm giving myself permission to explore, and to write, about those things I wouldn't have before."

"Permission," I say. "I like that word."

"I've been thinking a lot about my dad in that regard," Erin says. "He's a professional photographer. I remember how we would go on family trips, and if the light was right for a good photograph he would stop the car. Sometimes we'd be stopped for three hours. My dad had a right to do that, but I think I've gotten away from that a little bit, that way of thinking." She explains how, instead of giving herself the time to write, she has allowed other's needs to consume her time. Teaching. Volunteer work. Social commitments. Like the poor souls in that Boise bar, she's been stuck. Unlike them, she is self-aware.

"So you're telling your students to write, but you're not writing."

"Exactly!" Erin leans forward, her hands on her knees, almost out of frame of the camera. "I tell them to dedicate themselves to their craft, but I don't always do that. And sometimes I think I'm almost giving them my creativity."

"I feel that way about my job."

She nods. "That you're giving them all of your creativity, and don't have any left for yourself."

I nod, giving myself permission to admit this to her.

"I think it's good to know what feeds your creativity," Erin says, "what fills that well, and what drains it. You need to find ways to fill it up, and then you need to make use of it for your own art. Sometimes you know everything you need to do."

"I like that. 'You know everything you need to do.' It would make a good bumper sticker."

She smiles. "So it would. And along those lines, I'm going through these items from my childhood, and I'm sorting them and arranging them, and I'm seeing they're all about this journey, about figuring out what's important to me and how to be creative. And I have a hard time being creative when there's so much to do, when I'm too busy, because it takes me a long time to get to this creative place. But I want to be there. After this trip I'm feeling the flow again, the flow of creativity, and I feel everything I've done the last nine years is now taking shape."

"I'm so happy for you," I say, and I am. "But I'm also worried, because there are going to be those same things pulling on you again. You're back from your trip to the woods."

"Right, right," she says, patting her knees. "So I've been thinking about that. I've had this happen a bunch of times before, the inspiration comes and then I drift, so I'm aware of this, aware of the challenge."

"I'm going to make a deal with you," I say. "If, three months from now, you're finding yourself in a rut, give me a call. I'll stick this recording next to the phone and you can hear yourself."

"That would be great! But I think I get it now. I just need to start retreating a little bit from the world." She says she's just starting a new semester, so she's going to insist her students approach her after class or in office hours, not by email. She adds that her boyfriend moved away a few months ago, and the resulting demise of that relationship still hurts, but she realizes now that he brought a lot of drama into her life that she is now free from.

"My collaging is helping me remember that when I was young, I spent a lot of time alone, reading, journaling. I find my creativity when I'm isolated, cut off from things. I'll come back to my friends, to my life, but they're going to have to let me be alone for a while. I've come to be okay with being alone. I turn forty in eighteen months, and I've decided it's okay I didn't do that thing you're supposed to do, get married, have kids. I like my life, and I have the freedom to withdraw and be with my creativity."

Amy, Erin and I are all very close in age. The three of us have taken very different paths, but we've all ended up in the same place, trying to find ways to honor our muse. Erin needs to withdraw from social contact in order to create. I think my mother is the same. She was three years younger than I when she quit her sales job and locked herself in a spare bedroom day and night with an IBM Selectric typewriter and a dream of being a published author. She would tap away in that room, and my father would work late to keep our household finances afloat. It was then, at the age of fourteen, that I learned how to cook. There was no guarantee my mother would emerge to make dinner. I understood that she needed to do this, just like Erin understood that her father needed to stop the car when the light was right. That didn't mean I was always successful in masking my resentment. I'm sure now that she sensed it, and resented my resentment. The light was right for my mother, and she needed to write.

Erin plans to withdraw from friends and family. When my mother did that she achieved her dream and became published. And she has continued to write each and every book that way. But the idea of cutting herself off from others wasn't new. She had done it long before, with her parents and her sisters and everyone else she had known growing up. Isolation is as important as insecurity to my mother, I realize now. She associates isolation with those times in her life when she's succeeded. I need to share this insight with Marisa, who is still in great pain a year after my mother cut ties with us. I don't know if this insight will help my daughter, but it helps me. If my mother needs isolation in order to create, then it has nothing to do with Marisa, or with me. As Erin might say, my mother knows everything she needs to do.

"This interview has come at a good time for me," Erin says. "You're making me say out loud the vision that has come to me in my mind. Sharing it with you puts it on the record, if you will. You know, there have been so many times in my life where I've seen the right person or found the right book, when I've received the right message, exactly when I needed it."

"Well, at those moments you were open to receiving it."

Erin nods emphatically. "Yes, yes. It's about being open."

"Then let me go on the record with you as well," I say. "I too am going to live an art-committed life. Starting today."

Erin leans forward, almost in a pounce. "Be sure to play this

recording back to yourself in three months," she says.
"I promise."

SEPTEMBER 7: GOING HOME

There is only one more item on my agenda, to fly home tomorrow to my waiting wife and children. I have been absurdly busy these last few weeks and have accomplished a great deal. I should feel relieved, or proud, or victorious. But I feel empty, not in the sense of being drained but rather like an empty page. I am near the western edge of the North American continent, but I feel as if the Earth is flat and I'm about to sail off into darkness.

I left Erin's home without any additional appointments. That absence of mind has brought me here, sitting in my car at a park near downtown Portland on the shore of the Willamette River. The blue sky I saw yesterday in Boise has remained hidden today under a blanket of clouds. I watch the water lazily flow to the Columbia River, from which it will enter the Pacific Ocean.

Lewis and Clark may have stood right here. Did they realize how close they were to the end of their journey, only seventy-five miles from traversing a continent? If so, I have reached the same point as them with a mechanical advantage. In my defense, however, my route was far longer, full of zigs and zags, cutting back on itself. My path has in no way been direct, but it has gotten me here.

When William Clark finally did finally spy what he believed to be the Pacific Ocean, he wrote in his journal "Ocian in view! O! The joy!"Beyond his misspelling of "ocean," Clark also was in error. They would not see the actual ocean until later, once they passed the sandbars that divide the Columbia River basin from the sea. Lewis was far more regular in maintaining his journal, but he offers us no record of his thoughts on completing their journey. In fact, their arrival fell within a period in which he kept no notes at all, despite the fact that once reaching the western edge of the continent the party had little more to do than locate where they would camp for the winter. I suspect his melancholy took hold as the end of their voyage arrived. He had spent two years focused on one singular mission. Now it was complete, and he had to wonder what challenge lay next.

The river is calm and steady. And, I realize, so am I. Perhaps I should get out of the car and go sit on the river's grassy bank, which could become my Walden Pond. But while I mean no offense to Thoreau, I believe I have achieved tranquility here in the passenger cabin of this internal combustion vehicle. This chamber of solitude has been my incubator. It has tolerated constant ramblings into my voice recorder as I sought to capture not just what I was seeing but what I was becoming. I reach over to the camera bag and shove my hand inside, digging around for the recorder. Instead I encounter a thin piece of plastic. It's the demo CD Rochelle Smith gave me yesterday as I was leaving her radio station. A few moments later Rochelle's ethereal voice and acoustic guitar fill my sanctuary. The music's moodiness melds with the overcast sky.

My conversation with Erin confirmed for me that I must leave my job. Tomorrow morning, before I get on the plane, I will send an email to my board requesting a meeting. I must be true to my funders, who have given me so many opportunities, including this trip. So I will stay on as long as they need me to while helping to recruit a successor. But first and foremost, I must in leaving that job be true to my wife and children. I know from past conversations that Laura will support this decision, but I have obligations as a husband and father. Like the artists I've interviewed, I will perform whatever labor is necessary to avoid financial setback. I don't need the pride that comes from a prestigious job with a fancy title; I will derive my professional satisfaction from my creative writing. Of course I must have an ethical comfort level with whatever new work I take on, which in Washington means I'll be earning far less than I am now. But I will no longer be paying such a high emotional price for my income.

Once again I am learning from my mother. She earns a good living from her writing, but that was not always the case. My father took on extra work when she quit her job to write full-time, but our household income still declined precipitously. I was just starting high school, and my mother purchased my back-to-school wardrobe at stores where they sell what are called "remainders," outfits with flawed stitching or botched dyes rejected by traditional retailers. Marisa began her high school career mere weeks after her role model and muse, her grandmother, cut her out of her life. I don't believe my teenage predicament was as traumatic, but you couldn't have convinced me of that at the time. I was angry at my mother for what I deemed an act of selfishness. But she knew the light was good. I know now that my mother had a right to chase her dream of becoming a published novelist, and I believe my family will understand that I need to pursue an art-committed life. I know Marisa longs for me to.

It has been more than a year now since that night in Knoxville, and nine months since my mother and I last spoke on the phone. The first time she cut me out of her life, the resulting isolation lasted three years. This one may last far longer. The complicating factor in a reunion with my mother this time is that I have repeatedly impressed upon my children the importance of authenticity. Amy Buchheit went back to school for a fine-arts degree, but there is no academic program that teaches us how to be parents. I learned the same way I learned when I shifted from reporting to advocacy, by imitating what I had seen that I liked and avoiding actions I had observed and disliked. I very much disliked living in a home where one loved one would hurt another and then both would pretend it never happened. We all make mistakes, I tell my children, even your father—especially your father—but we must own those mistakes. Marisa is waiting for her grandmother to own her mistake, but that will never happen. It was clear in that phone call that she has already reinvented the story of that night in Knoxville. How can you apologize when your mind paints you as the victim? To be in my mother's life means playing by her rules, and the first rule is that you accept reality as she defines it.

My mother will not change, and it is not fair of me to expect her to. Her reality formed from the life she's led. When she isolated herself from her family by moving to Arizona, her liberation meant she could finally make her own decisions. When she cut herself off from the world of salaried work shifts, she began writing commercially successful books. And now, by isolating herself from the complications of familial connection with her son and her grandchildren, she presumably has cleared her mind of distraction sufficiently to produce even more bestsellers. I will help Marisa and Parker understand that her absence from our lives is not a personal rejection of them. I will aim to do so more effectively than my child psychiatrist did with me so long ago, when he bribed me to say my parents' divorce was not my fault by offering me free plays on his Pachinko machine. I will also remind my children that I love them, and assure them that my own return to creative writing will not have me focusing solely on my muse. Erin's father would stop and study the light for several hours, but he would then get back in the family car and resume the vacation.

But can I embrace that balance? How can I trust that I won't descend into a solitary embrace of manic creativity? I'm consciously avoiding my mother's life decisions, but can I liberate myself from my father's biological legacy? How can I be sure that my bipolar disorder will not manifest itself in ways harmful to my family once I allow myself to be creative? Can I accept the fact there are no clear answers to these questions?

I see no geese here in this park, but Ernest Whaley and I were greeted by three of them on the bank of the Lampley River in New Hampshire. The sky that day was bright and clear. The geese, known to Ernest as The Girls, honked requests for food. But instead Ernest and I fed ourselves with a passionate discussion of creativity. Ernest called me a creative peer. I questioned his assessment that day, but he was the more insightful one. I was practicing creativity with my films. I now see that I never completely abandoned the practice of creative activity, only the conscious pursuit of an art-committed life. And I have practiced creativity without descent into uncontrollable madness. I have, throughout my adult life, coupled personal discipline with creative expression.

I will no longer be filming videos for my employer. I still have several to edit, including both of the ones I filmed today. But what will be my next creative project? What will I do for myself, to mark my return to an art-committed life? I reach into the camera bag again, to

239

find the recorder so I can share my thoughts aloud. But then I stop. I am not ready to speak this aspiration, to form the words on my lips and hear them with my ears. But I know what my next project will be. I will write the story of this journey. I will do what I swore I would not at the beginning of this trip. I will tell my story, and I will tell it true.

A woman's spoken words fill the car. It's coming from Rochelle's CD, but it is not Rochelle's voice. I remember Rochelle telling me that she had placed a recording of her close friend who was dying from cancer at the start of her song "Blue Water." I skip back to the beginning of the track and let the voice from the world beyond flow over me.

I imagined myself diving into the ocean, and not floating, but sinking down and assimilating, being able to breathe water. Which is, you know, kind of a mermaid thing, I guess, but mermaids are so prissy. I don't want to imagine I'm a mermaid. But the act of transcending this form, I mean, it's something that has fascinated people for hundreds of years. And it's inevitable that the dream is going to fade, or the state is going to change. So dive on in. I mean, dive in, in everything dive in. And don't be afraid of drowning, because you can breathe water.

An explosion rocks the sky, followed by sheets of rain. The dark clouds that have threatened all day now execute their mission. Within moments the downpour is so thick I can't see through the windshield. The river vanishes, hidden by a curtain of angry water. But my Walden Pond protects me from the assault. If I were a fiction writer, I would redraft this scene. The sky above would be as clear as it was that day in New Hampshire. Portland's famous clouds would part to let in shimmering beams of sunlight. I would be sitting not in this car but along the bank of that river. A short distance from me a woman would be painting the gentle current on an easel-held canvas. A pair of Mallard ducks would rise up from the river and take flight, echoes of the first romance ever captured in prose by my mother, the short story she wrote as a child after she was told ducks mated for life.

I can see that scene in my mind. It's intoxicating. But it isn't true to this story. The rain is fitting. It is Portland being authentic to herself. The windshield in front of me reveals nothing but sheets of pulsing liquid. But I don't need to see beyond the rain. I don't need to see some other artist at work. I see everything I need to see, and I know everything I need to do.

AUTHOR'S ACKNOWLEDGEMENTS

It must be evident to you, the reader, that this book would not have been possible without the generosity of the many artists I interviewed on my cross-country road trip. It is my deepest regret that I could not give each and every one of them the full amount of focus they deserved in this work. Their authenticity and commitment remains an inspiration to me.

There are three other characters in this work of nonfiction who also played an indispensible role: my wife Laura, my son Parker, and my daughter Marisa. I am writing this acknowledgment four years after I began the trip. Over that span these loved ones have lost hundreds of hours with their husband or father as they allowed me to indulge my renewed passion for living an art-committed life. I will do what I can to make it up to them.

The first draft of this memoir was written while pursuing a Master of Fine Arts in Writing degree in the low-residency program offered by the Vermont College of Fine Arts; researching MFA programs and enrolling in VCFA were among the first steps I took upon returning to an art-committed life. I was constantly inspired by my talented and supportive fellow students, including in no particular order Nancy Levine, Sue Hall, Kathy Pauli, Martha Petersen, Laura Warrell, Georganna Millman, Deanne Gertner, Haley Hendershot, Barbara Cummings, Julie Farkas, Kelley Rossier, Sarah Braud, Pamela Cooper, Melissa Cronin, Laura Diener, Anne Ney, Cheryl Wright-Watkins, Angela Sparandera, Sophfronia Scott, Sion Dayson, Whitney Groves, Donald Quist, and my "residency buddy"Jonathan White. But I must extend ample credit to my semester and workshop advisors, namely Kurt Caswell, Larry Sutin, Sascha Feinstein, Connie May Fowler, Patrick Madden, David Jauss, and Sue William Silverman. Their positive influence can be found on every page and in every sentence.

I remain grateful for the encouragement and guidance of writers I've befriended in the Washington, D.C., area, such as Sara Taber, Zahara Heckscher, Kathryn Veal, Callie Feyen, Barbora Bridle, Danielle Meitiv, Cara Gabriel, Shelley Walden, Andrea Solarz, Lauree Ostrofsky, and Sue Eisenfeld. I must also salute my fellow acolytes in the study of creativity, including David Goldstein, Jayme Cellitioci, Michelle James, Melanie Sklarz, and Carrie Brummer. And although there were many times I doubted this book would ever be finished, let alone published, I was often buoyed by supportive and inspirational individuals including Stefanie Schmidt, Irving Lachow, John Mason, Jessica McCann, Porter Anderson, Carole Jane Treggett, PJ Reece, Stan Stewart, Charlotte Rains Dixon, Milli Thornton, Cynthia Robertson, Melissa Crytzer-Fry, Julia Munroe Martin, Kate Arms-Roberts, Carolyn Flynn, Roz Morris, ML Hart, Donna Marie, Jessica Baverstock, Jolina Petersheim, Terre Britton, Anjali Enjeti, Annie Neugebauer, Elizabeth S. Craig, Terri Kent-Enborg, K.M. Weiland, Sue Mitchell, Sheila Lamb, Orna Ross, Shari Lopatin, and Dario DiBattista.

Any reader of this memoir will know I am forever indebted to my parents for raising me in a creative household in which they modeled the importance of honoring your muse. I also gained from my childhood a fierce commitment to authenticity and truthfulness, which I saw modeled in the artists I interviewed and which I applied to the writing of this book. So it is fair to say this book never would have been written without the role my parents played in making me who I am.

Finally let me thank Reagan Rothe and the creative team at Black Rose Writing for believing in this book, and, just as importantly, believing in me.

Purchase other Black Rose Writing titles at www.blackrosewriting.com/books and use promo code PRINT to receive a 20% discount.